# Singing Lizards

A Mystery-Adventure set in Africa

by

Evadeen Brickwood

EVADEEN BRICKWOOD

"Singing Lizards"

This book was first published in paperback by
Evadeen Brickwood at CreateSpace

Paperback Copyright © 2015 by Evadeen Brickwood
E-Book Copyright © 2014 by Evadeen Brickwood

Find this book in digital format also at:
Kindle Store, Smashwords and Tolino

All rights reserved.

No part of this publication may be reproduced, stored in a retrieval system or transmitted in any form or by any means, electronic, mechanical, photocopying, recording or otherwise without the written permission of the publisher.

The moral rights of the author have been asserted.

This is a work of fiction. Names, characters, places, brands, media and incidents are either the product of the author's imagination or are used fictitiously. The author acknowledges the trademarked status and trademark owners of various products referred to in this work of fiction, which have been used without permission. The publication/use of the trademarks is not authorized, associated with or sponsored by the trademark owners.

First edition 2015 by Evadeen Brickwood on CreateSpace
Second edition 2016 by Evadeen Brickwood in South Africa
Third edition 2019 by Evadeen Brickwood in South Africa
Fourth edition 2020 by Evadeen Brickwood

CreateSpace ISBN: 978-1-502-732668
NLSA ISBN: 978-0-9946916-0-6

Cover Design: Yvonne Less, www.art4artists.com.au
Bildquellen: 'Depositphotos.com' licensed
Book Layout: Birgit Böttner
Marketing: Alphalogic International

This mystery adventure tells the story of 22-year-old Bridget Reinhold who is not exactly the adventurous type, but when her sister Claire disappears in Southern Africa, nothing can hold her in England. Bridget launches herself into the search in Botswana and encounters obstacle after obstacle. She learns the basics of the native language and culture and soon moves to the capital city of Gaborone. Soon, her mission is plunged into turmoil as everything seems to be going wrong. Just coincidence or is there something more sinister at work?

## For Barbara

Other Titles by Evadeen Brickwood

**In the youth series:**

"Children of the Moon" ("Remember the Future 1")

in the German Edition:

"Kinder des Mondes" ("Erinnerung an die Zukunft 1")

"The Speaking Stone of Caradoc" ("Remember the Future 2")

"The Secret of the Bird God" ("Remember the Future 3")

**The novels:**

"Singende Eidechsen" (German edition of this novel)

"A Half Moon Adventure" (An Adventure Mystery)

"Abenteuer Halbmond" (German edition)

"The Rhino Whisperer" (A Crime Mystery)

"Der Nashorn Flüsterer" (German edition)

"Charlie Proudfoot Murder Mysteries" (series)

# Acknowledgements

A big thank you to my family for putting up with the long hours I spent writing behind closed doors, all my test readers for their honest comments; especially Peter Böttner and Phyllis Hyde for their enthusiasm, editing, constructive proof-reading and unwavering support. My gratitude also goes to all my editors and test readers, to Andreas Eschbach for his advice on e-publishing and to Cobus and Bernard Griesel for filming the interviews and their help with all technical issues.

"There is nothing like returning to a place that remains unchanged to find the ways in which you yourself have altered."

*Nelson Mandela*

# CHAPTER 1

Why did I have to think about Botswana now? It had taken only a brief look at my steaming Johannesburg garden through the big window in the study.

The tall avocado tree and pink protea bushes were still glistening from the summer rainstorm the night before...

I tried to concentrate on the work before me: the translation of an urgent divorce decree. *In the case between Joachim Meissner - plaintiff - and Nhlanhla...*

The phone rang. 'Hello.' I answered.

'Can I speak to Bokkie please?'

'Umm, there is no Bokkie here.'

'But this is Bokkie's number.'

'I'm afraid not. You must have dialled the wrong number.'

'Oh – sorry.'

'No prob — ' The man had already hung up.

I had known a Bokkie in Botswana once... an unpleasant character. There it was again: the thought of Botswana creeping up on me.

I didn't even know that this remote African country Botswana existed, before my sister Claire decided to work there. To be honest, I found the mere thought of Africa somewhat unnerving.

Southern Africa, with its vast areas of dry and thirsty desert seemed especially intimidating. Claire didn't mind all that. In fact, it was exactly what she wanted. And then she went missing in Africa - on 16 July 1988.

M i s s i n g - such an ugly word. Oh, how much I had

missed Claire! I must have been temporarily insane. Why else would I have just upped and left England so suddenly for Africa? It had taken all my courage, but I needed to find Claire, needed to see for myself what had happened.

At first, I'd found the silence there unsettling. I was still reverberating with a western rhythm, an inner buzzing, driving me on and on…to find her, to do more… it took me a while to learn how to listen to the silence, giving in to it…

The phone rang. *Why do people always call when you really don't feel like talking?*

'Hello?'

'Can I speak with Bokkie?'

'Wrong number.'

This time it was I, who hung up. I sat down at my desk by the window and looked out into the garden. Just outside the window, a yellow weaver bird was busy stripping a palm leaf to build his nest on the tip of a bouncing branch. I let my thoughts wander.

It had taken her new employer two weeks to inform us. Two long weeks! They thought she might have taken a few extra days on her short trip to the Okavango Delta. Apparently it was quite normal to be late in Africa.

Back then, I didn't know that time passes more slowly in a country like Botswana. A couple of days here and there – what's the big deal? 'African time' they called it. More time passed until the police in Botswana got involved. Then Scotland Yard.

Would it have made any difference - the time?

Remembering the year before Botswana was bittersweet. We always called each other *Foompy*. Even at the age of 22. I suppose that's one of those strange things twins do when they are in their own secret world.

I am Bridget, the older one of us, by two whole minutes. We both have the same blue-green eyes, but Claire is blonde and petite (Mom's 'mini-me') and I am the taller brunette, who takes after Dad's side of the family. My face is rounder and I have an English rose-and-cream complexion. We were walking opposites really and Claire was way ahead of me.

She always smiled and was popular. I was serious and shy. Boys flocked around her and Claire took it in her stride, because she usually had a steady boyfriend anyway. I was more of a wall flower, had my small circle of girlfriends and lukewarm short-lived relationships. She wanted to travel. California, Denmark and Peru. We had just been to Peru with our friend Liz. For an entire three weeks! I was done with travelling for a while after that, but Claire wanted more.

I was content with my life in England and knew every nook and cranny of our small town, away from the hustle and bustle of big city life.

I loved everything about Cambridge. Its moss-covered roofs and the medieval feel of the town. The carols by candlelight at King's College and the punters in their boats under the bridges. Why would I want to live anywhere else? The world was a big and scary place. Filled with things I didn't understand.

I had my work as a freelance translator and Claire was a technical draughtswoman. We were doing well and that was good enough for me. But after the trip to Peru, my sister had serious plans to leave Cambridge; on a 2-year contract with an international engineering firm in Gaborone, Botswana. Botswana was on the Southern tip of Africa!

There would be an ocean and a huge continent between us. I couldn't even imagine it. And anyway — what about me?

It had all been Pierre Boucher's fault! If it hadn't been for his glowing stories about Southern Africa, she would never have wanted to go and live there.

Claire had met Pierre Boucher years ago at college in London. He and his Tswana girlfriend had gotten married and settled in Botswana. Just recently, Claire had met up with them again in London. That's when Pierre told her about their big house in Francistown with a swimming pool, a maid and a gardener and all the trimmings. Not to mention the incredible landscapes and the peaceful solitude around them.

All of a sudden, Claire had to see this fabulous country, wanted to enjoy the easy-going lifestyle and the freedom, the endless savannahs, the wildlife, the huge sky...

She had gone all the way and applied with an agency for a job in Botswana — and was accepted at once.

A dream come true for Claire - a nightmare for me.

Nothing worked, not complaining, not being reproachful, not pronouncing threats. Nothing could sway Claire's decision. Then I tried bravely to support her. As much as I suffered and as much as we argued, I didn't stand for anybody else criticizing my sister. Most people knew that.

David obviously didn't. My boyfriend David and I actually quarrelled about it in our favourite pub on Norfolk Street. We practically never discussed feelings, but my nerves were in a raw state and truth be told, things weren't so brilliant between us anymore.

He didn't approve of my sister dragging me halfway across the world. 'What's wrong with the Midlands or good old Cornwall?' He had wanted to know just the other day; as if life was that simple.

We were savouring our usual pasta while comparing cricket teams, when he hit me with his observation.

"Your sister's odd. Why does she want to live in Africa of all places? I could never live in Africa! Idiotic." *What?* I nearly choked on my Tagliatelle Alfredo.

"Oh really, and why is that so idiotic?" I glowered.

He took a swig from his beer bottle. Grolsch was his favourite beverage.

"Everybody knows that. It's not safe there and Africans get drunk a lot and all that..."

David saw my expression and groped for an explanation

to make his point. It didn't occur to him that he himself was on his second beer in half an hour.

"...and they start a war at the drop of a hat. There is so much dangerous jungle and it's dirty and way too hot... and so uncivilized," he quickly concluded his brilliant argument. When he saw my face, he took another fortifying swig from the beer bottle and grew quiet.

A group of students had just walked in, looking for a free table. A couple of girls stared as if to say 'get up and go, it's our turn now'. This irritated me even more.

"So, everybody knows that about Africa! Really? Since when are you so prejudiced? We are talking Botswana, that's by South Africa, you know, not on Mars. Miles away from Angola and Eritrea. There's no war there and no dangerous jungle." At least as far as I was aware of it.

"I knew that," David stammered. "But still...South Africa isn't exactly safe either. With apartheid and all that."

Bull's eye! In the year 1988, South Africa was still in the middle of its struggle for freedom. I also thought it was too dangerous, but Claire couldn't care less.

"You know what, David? I think you are odd!" I flew at him to cover up my fear. "Flip! Claire's just following her dream and she is lucky enough to have a boyfriend, who wants to go with her. I wonder if you would do the same for me. Probably not!"

That wasn't fair, but I was cross with David and I was cross with Claire. Why did she have to go to such a dangerous country in the first place?

David had just blabbered away without thinking, insensitive as ever. Anyway, what did *he* know about other countries? England was his world and he didn't know anything about the feelings broiling inside of me. But as far as I was concerned, Claire had forced me to think beyond England, even about Africa. Like it or not.

And she would be in good hands. Claire's boyfriend of eighteen months was called Tony Stratton. A nice guy, actually. A teacher of economics and maths, who had found himself a job at a private school in Gaborone straight away. Would she have gone without him? Definitely.

David didn't know what to make of my sudden outbreak. He nervously scanned the pub and kept pushing back his thick brown hair. I could guess that he was embarrassed by the scene I made. Were people staring at us? Were his friends coming already?

"Wow, I didn't see that one coming!" David laughed and acted as if I had made a joke. "Oh come on Bridge, what's wrong with that? I like living in England. Africa is too…too different. A holiday maybe, although that's pushing it a bit. I prefer Mallorca. But moving to Africa — That I just can't understand." He shook himself. That was just too much. I couldn't take another word!

"You can't let it go now, can you? Oh, you just don't understand anything at all," I cried. I found my purse and paid for the Tagliatelle Alfredo. "I must go now."

"What, why?"

I felt the fleeting urge to shake David. The truth was full of raw emotion and how was I supposed to express that without rattling him even more?

Instead of telling the truth, I made up some excuse about a head ache. I needed to walk home by myself, needed to walk it off. The thought of the comfortable home in Tenison Avenue made me walk faster. My favourite place of all. Just big enough for our family of four, Mom, Dad, Claire and me.

In summer, red holly hocks and blue forget-me-nots framed the soft green lawn at the back of the house. Here we came together to talk and relax on white garden chairs, having tea, while Hinny, our wily grey cat, watched us from the top floor balcony.

I turned into Sturton Street, then into Tenison Avenue. Even in the dark, the warmth of our house pulled me closer. My anger blew itself out quickly, but thoughts that I had so successfully evaded, popped into my head. I was forced to face things for what they were.

Claire was leaving me behind and it hurt. Badly. My twin moved to Africa and I was stuck in a rut with David. Movies on Wednesdays, pub dinners on Thursdays, sport on Fridays. Same old, same old, while Claire launched into the unknown. I hadn't really thought of it that way before. Claire was the spice of my life.

Was I being selfish? I decided that I would soon visit Claire in Botswana, and stepped out more forcefully. *Perhaps I should have a good chat with her*, I thought as I opened the front door. But Claire was not at home.

The next few days, Dad answered the phone. I was too chicken to speak to David and we wouldn't speak about feelings anyway. Then David stopped calling. The breakup was quick and painless. My feelings about Claire, on the other hand, were so much more painful, Not something I could share them with him.

"Don't leave me here all alone," I begged her. "I don't want you to go." Oh, I knew how pathetic I sounded.

"That's not fair, Foompy. And anyways... you are not alone." She spoke to me as if I were a child. "There's Mom and Dad and David...and Zaheeda, Liz and Diane...and you do like it here, don't you?"

*Not without you I don't, not without you!* I didn't dare say it. Claire sat in the wicker chair leaning her head against the wall. The dappled shade outside the window was throwing patterns on the David Bowie poster behind her. I hadn't told Claire about *my* breakup with my David yet. It didn't really matter right now.

"What if something happens to you?" I grumbled and rolled over on the quilted bed cover, lying on my tummy, chin in both hands.

"What's supposed to happen to me? I'll live in a company house with lots of colleagues around. Probably won't ever have time to myself. And then there is Tony, of course. He'll look after me," Claire tried to calm me, while she drew doodles on an empty envelope.

She seemed already far away. *Probably somewhere with Tony*. The thought made me feel jealous for half a second. They had mentioned marriage, but as far as I could tell there was no clanging of wedding bells just yet.

"Won't you miss me at all, then?" I sulked.

"Of course I will! You'll come and visit me in Gaborone as soon as you can, right?" Claire tried to sound excited for me. "Then we go and explore the Kalahari together."

"Yes sure, fine," I said casually, more to annoy her than anything else.

"Oh don't be so cross, Foompy." She made a funny face and I had to laugh.

But Claire had been wrong! A few weeks later, my world had turned on itself. Something *did* happen to her — Claire had disappeared!

When the news broke, I was numb with sadness and worry about her. Nothing made sense anymore. It couldn't be true, just couldn't! I crept upstairs into Claire's room, threw myself on her bed and buried my face in the pillow. Then I screamed until I didn't have a voice left to scream. And then came the tears.

I shouldn't have let her go, I kept thinking, I should have stopped her somehow. The needle-sharp thought poked out any kind of logic. As if I had the power to stop my stubborn sister from doing anything. What was I supposed to do now?

The news exploded in our town. Newspapers were full of articles about Claire and her mysterious disappearance. Was it murder or perhaps an abduction?

Opinions chased each other. What did you expect? Africa was obviously a dangerous place. I felt nauseous every time I saw the headlines and stopped buying newspapers. A week later, sports news had mercifully replaced Claire's story on the first page.

Her old red Mazda was found abandoned in a field somewhere close to Mochudi. The name Mochudi meant nothing to me then, because I had no idea what Botswana looked like. The police interrogated the locals, but they hadn't seen or heard anything. Of course not! The fingerprints were apparently inconclusive because children had been playing in the car.

Even a British MI 5 Special Unit, doing some training in Botswana at the time, had allegedly found nothing useful to speak of. So, we were to assume the worst!

Claire had travelled to the Okavango Delta on her own. Tony was busy marking exam papers and couldn't come with. How should *he* have known what would happen? But I blamed him anyway. At least in the beginning, for a minute or so.

She had been planning to visit Pierre and Karabo in Francistown and on her way back, she would take a detour to the Tuli Block, a remote national park. She had a booking at a lodge to see the elephants, but had never arrived there.

We waited for Tony's phone call, but Tony didn't call. Maybe he didn't have our number. I sent him a letter. I waited for his answer... and waited. I guess I began to contemplate right there right then that I should take things into my own hands. I couldn't bear all this waiting anymore.

The 'International Missing Persons Bureau' got involved. My father asked the authorities, if he shouldn't help them by going to Botswana. The answer was a resounding 'No'.

Everything humanly possible was being done already. Family presence would only hamper the investigation. Unbelievable! I was furious. Why didn't they do their job properly, then?

You couldn't tell me that there was no trace of Claire to be found anywhere with all this investigating going on. And to tell us that we should assume the worst and otherwise just sit around and wait!

Then the nightmares started. Blurred images of Claire behind a misty veil. She laughed and said something I couldn't understand... then she faded back into the mist. I wanted to call out to her, grab her and failed. I woke up with tears running down my face into the pillow every time.

But there was also hope. She had to be alive, but was I the only one who could feel it? And just where exactly was she?

I didn't tell anybody about my dreams. The atmosphere at home was becoming unbearable and our house in Tenison Avenue had lost its warmth for me. Mom cried all the time and Grandpa had come up from London a few days ago to console her. I didn't tell anybody about my dreams.

The atmosphere at home was becoming unbearable and our house in Tenison Avenue had lost its warmth for me. Mom cried all the time and Grandpa had come up from London a few days ago to console her. Dad usually withdrew into his study and ruminated. I wasn't at all sure that their marriage would survive the pain of their loss.

Dad... the handsome, brooding engineer from Germany who had followed my mother to England, after they'd met in their twenties on a train in France. Moving to England to marry the most beautiful girl in the world. It was probably the most courageous thing he'd ever done in his life. It must have been awfully romantic.

Dad... the handsome, brooding engineer from Germany who had followed my mother to England, after they'd met in their twenties on a train in France. Moving to England to marry the most beautiful girl in the world was probably the most courageous thing he'd ever done in his life. It must have been awfully romantic.

Mom now lectured history of art and Dad had retired before 'the thing' with Claire happened. Their life had been picture book perfect until now. I, for my part, felt just powerless. After a while my mood had changed. There

were no more tears. I felt angry now. Angry at everyone. To me it felt as if they had given up. The lot of them! Didn't they know that Claire was still alive? I saw Dad in the kitchen the next day and I tried to talk to him.
"We have to do something," I began carefully.
"Do something? What?"
"Perhaps you should just go over there..."
"To Botswana? And what am I supposed to do there? Mom needs me here and the police are already doing their job. And they don't want me to get involved... in Africa," Dad flared up, only to apologise seconds later. "Sorry darling, I didn't mean to be so gruff, but my nerves..."
I could have yelled at him: *the police are doing their job? Really?! Fix it, Dad, why don't you fix it?* But I didn't. I couldn't say another word because it hurt too much to speak about Claire.
Mom took tranquillizers and wanted to speak only with her therapist about the whole matter. I had the inexplicable feeling that she held me somehow responsible. The idea of going to Botswana and take matters into my own hands began to take shape.
When the dust had eventually settled and news about Claire's vanishing had disappeared for good, my friend Diane organized a meeting with my friends for tea. Our doe-eyed friend Zaheeda was at her sister's wedding in Manchester that day, so it was only the three of us. After a while I wondered whether they would ever understand why I needed to go to Africa to find Claire.
"Oh Bridge, what do you want to do there - in *Botswana*?" Liz pronounced the word as if it was a disgusting insect. "I knew something was going to happen when Claire moved there." Her pointy nose trembled.
"Oh bloody hell, Liz, how can you say something like that in front of Bridget?" scolded Diane with unusual vehemence. "You didn't know that. Nobody could have known what would happen and Claire knows the ways of

the world."

We stared at her. Diane was the soft and gentle one in our group.

But Liz didn't let up. "I guess so, but that didn't help her now did it? Why couldn't Claire have moved to Italy or Spain instead? Or even to America? At least she would have been in a civilized country." She didn't mince her words and I knew she meant well in her own way.

"Sometimes I can't help but think that it was fate. I mean that Claire went to Botswana and that I must go there and find her."

I knew it didn't make much sense but I was still searching for a logical explanation for what had happened.

"Oh Bridge, of course you would think that..." Diane said soothingly. They looked at me as if I was about to fall completely off the rocker.

"Oh stop staring at me like that! Claire needs me and that's a fact. She's still out there somewhere and she is all right. I can feel it."

"Sure you can, love..." Liz said and quickly changed the subject. "What going on with David, Bridge? Haven't seen you two together for a while."

"Because we broke up, I think."

"You think?" cried Liz aghast. She had played matchmaker for us after all.

I just shrugged my shoulders. "We had a fight beginning of May and haven't spoken since. So I guess, we're no longer an item."

"Really?!" Liz couldn't believe her ears.

"Yes, really."

"Well, that didn't last very long. Was it the whole of two months?" Liz hinted at my usually rather brief relationships.

"Three months - almost. He doesn't know that I'm going to Botswana... unless somebody told him."

"You haven't told him!"

"No, what for?"

"Do you want to talk about it – about David, I mean?" Diane looked sad on my behalf.

"Not really, but I guess I should give him a ring later. To clear things up before I leave."

"I think it's a good idea…" Diane said softly. "More tea anyone?"

*

That afternoon, David and I had a heart-to-heart at 'Jesus Green' to talk things through. The park was full of people soaking up the sun. I told him about Claire's disappearance and he gave me a brief *I-told-you-so* look.

"So I don't count anymore then?" He threw a flat pebble into the lake. "You don't talk to me anymore and now you just go away."

"David, please understand. It's not about you."

"I thought we could give it another go." The pebble skipped a few times across the water surface before it disappeared.

"David, please understand. It's not about you."

"I thought we could give it another go."

"What for?" Didn't he notice how lukewarm things had become? Skip, skip, skip. Another pebble travelled across the water and sank.

"Don't I deserve another chance?"

"David, I think we're wasting our time with each other."

"Gee, thanks a lot." He squeezed his eyes together and watched another pebble skip.

"I didn't mean it that way," I apologized.

"Sure you did."

We squabbled for a while in this pointless, repetitive way so many couples squabble. In the end we at least agreed to disagree and there was nothing more to be said.

It must have been before the launch at Heffer's Book Shop when Tony's rather short letter arrived. Oh, why didn't we have e-mails back then?

He blamed himself for letting Claire go by herself, for thinking that she would be safe. I had skipped past *that* point long ago. He asked me to give him a call at the hotel in Palapye, the village where he had found another teaching job.

How did one pronounce that? P a l a p y e .

Tony didn't have a phone at home and had booked a time slot for 7:00 p.m. on Friday. One had to pre-book a phone call! Apparently, nobody in Palapye had their own telephone. We were in luck that the letter had arrived before Friday, then. I couldn't wait to speak to him. Tony would surely understand.

We spoke on Friday as planned and afterwards I went to Heffer's Book Shop to attend the launch of the novel 'Talk to the Wind' by Frederick Humphrey. My parents were already there. Frederick Humphrey was a famous novelist — and he was my Grandpa.

The blurb on the back cover promised: 'A tantalizing crime thriller set in the colonial Kenya of the 1920s. Fear holds sway among the decadent expatriate society of Nairobi...'

The blurb on the cover was usually all I read of Grandpa's books. What if I didn't like the book and he asked my opinion? I simply couldn't hurt his feelings, but each book launch was a nice little party.

Grandpa smiled in the picture. He had classical features and a full head of grey hair. Rather good-looking for 72 and right now he was sitting inside the store and signed books.

"I'm going to find Claire in Botswana," I announced to my parents at last.

We all held a glass with white wine, as we stood outside on the sidewalk to get some fresh air. Music and laughter reached us from inside the shop.

"You are what?" My father was flabbergasted. I noticed how grey his hair was getting. "Have you gone daft?"

"I'm going to Botswana," I repeated stubbornly and endured the pained stares. I had no choice but to get it out in the open.

"No you're not." Dad's German accent always became a bit stronger when he was upset. A lonely truck rattled past us over the cobblestones. Fred's Office Furniture.

Oh no, Mom had tears in her eyes again. "You can't just leave us now," she pleaded, shaking so hard that she spilled some of her white wine.

"I'm so sorry Mom. I don't want to hurt you, but Claire is out there alone. I need to find her and I can't do it from here," I said firmly. "I cannot wait any longer. I just have to do something!"

My heart sank at the mere thought of going away, but my parents didn't have to know that. I could see Grandpa through the large shop window, chatting to adoring fans.

"Why not let the police handle it? They told us that we would be in the way... and what if something happens to you as well?" My father demanded to know.

I had asked Claire pretty much the same thing and Claire had to calm me down. Now it was my turn to calm my parents down. Another car rattled past the bookshop. The noise was grinding on my nerves.

"Nothing is going to happen to me, I promise," I insisted stubbornly. "I've already spoken to her boyfriend Tony and he said that I can stay with him at this place in Palapye for a while." Palapye. Paalápeea. The foreign word prickled on my tongue.

"When did you speak to him?"

"Just before I came. We'll manage to find Claire together." Tony hadn't exactly said that; just that he would help me wherever he could, whatever that meant. His surprise at my plan had carried across the shaky phone line, when I proceeded to invite myself. But right now, I couldn't talk to my parents about any doubts I might have. I needed their blessing.

"Oh child..." Mom's eyes took on a pinkish hue but she bravely managed to hold back the tears. And it was my fault. I felt a dangerous tickle in my throat and had to cough a little. I hated breaking her heart even more, now that she seemed to be on the mend.

"I don't like that idea at all." Dad's face looked crestfallen. "Not at all."

"I'm not doing this to hurt you," I repeated," but Claire is my other half and I just can't wait anymore. I have to go there. To Africa." I declared this in desperation, close to losing my courage. We didn't speak for a few painful moments. Grandpa saw me through the shop window and waved, smiling broadly and I waved back.

"If this is what you have to do child…" Mom sobbed and wiped away a tear, then she looked at my father. "Mike…" He stared crossly at a carved wooden gate across the street and I closed my eyes.

"We cannot keep you here, Bridget," he began and I stared at him, "if you must go… but you will report back regularly and…" Dad took a deep breath and gave me a list of rules that grew longer during the next couple of days, although he knew that I would ignore most of them. I was 22 after all. My parents were still free spirits after all! I knew right then that they would be okay.

Mom reluctantly promised to pass messages on to my most important clients. That I would be working overseas for a while and to please contact Diane Langer so long. It was decided that I should travel to London with Grandpa. The night before I left, I overheard my parents and Grandpa talk outside in the passage.

"What about the civil war in South Africa?" My father demanded to know and I held my breath.

"Please lower your voice, Mike," Mom said alarmed. "She might hear you."

"I can get in touch with the High Commission in Gaborone, if you want. They'll keep an eye on her, to be sure."

That was Grandpa. I knew that he still had certain connections from his time in Africa.

"It's in the news all the time. Bombs are going off in shops and nightclubs and Botswana is right next door. What if Bridget is caught in a running gun battle?"

"Oh Mike, we talked to Claire about that and it didn't make any difference," Mom sniffled.

"Look, the last bomb blast in Gaborone was two years ago and I've never heard of running gun battles. The military is on the alert," Grandpa declared. "In any case, things are changing fast in South Africa. You'll worry yourself silly with all this talk about bombs."

There was a brief silence, then I heard sobbing noises. "My babies!"

"There, there Sarah, it'll be all right. You never know, Bridget might just find our Claire and bring her back home." Had my Dad really said that?

"You never know," Grandpa agreed.

I heard shuffling sounds when all three of them went into the lounge.

Tears rolled down my cheeks as I folded the last t-shirt. I blew my nose and contemplated my trusted duffel bag that had followed me around Machu Picchu and Los Angeles and was popping at the seams. I felt guilty for just leaving like that but Claire was in trouble and that's all I needed to know. I couldn't let myself think of all the dangers or I'd become scared.

The following day, I kissed my parents goodbye and went with Grandpa to London. I left my comfortable Cambridge life behind to find my twin sister. The following day, I kissed my parents goodbye and went with Grandpa to London. I left my comfortable Cambridge life behind to find my twin sister. The formalities in London would take at least a couple of weeks. I had to apply for visas, get vaccinated at the Institute for Tropical Diseases and go shopping. Two weeks to pluck up my courage. Two weeks – all of a sudden it didn't sound like a lot of time.

Soon, I sat in the stylish flat Grandpa owned at number 327 Arlington Road in Camden. I stared at the list of prescribed vaccinations. My heart sank. Cholera, typhoid, yellow fever, immunoglobulin... what on earth was immunoglobulin? According to the pamphlet, it had something to do with hepatitis. Surely it was necessary, but were all these other injections on the list necessary? I hated needles. Would I drop dead at once if I didn't have all of them right now? I decided that I had no choice; it was part of the travel requirements like a passport and visas.

Outside, the wind changed its direction and a gentle rain drummed against the windows. Down in the towel-sized back garden, the spiky leaves of slender cordyline palms waved forth and back. It was puzzling that the London climate was mild enough for exotic palm trees.

Suddenly, the enormity of my plan hit me - what if I failed? What then? Why did it have to be such an unhealthy country that required a battery of vaccinations? *No need to panic – breathe in, breathe out...*

I leaned back against the leather couch and eyed accusingly the painting on the opposite wall. It was an African landscape in - a broad golden frame of all things. The painting was beautiful with its baobab trees against an azure sky and a herd of elephants in the distance. In the bottom left corner, a leopard was stalking grazing gazelles.

"Does that mean that I must really get those awful injections?" I asked the painting. The African landscape didn't answer. On closer inspection, the elephants seemed to be moving a fraction and on the left, the leopard had appeared fully from the undergrowth. Was it moving closer towards the gazelles?

"You know what, picture? Let's just get it over and done with. Enough with the self-pity." *Bridget you're going bonkers,* I scolded myself, *pull yourself together already, you are talking to a picture!*

The last time Claire and I had been in London together, we went to see David Bowie in concert. My heart ached at the thought of Claire and I. By the end of the concert, she was dancing with other people on the stage, but as usual, I was too shy to do something like that. We had been so excited to ride on the tube and shopped up a storm in Oxford Road with its rows of little boutiques.

I took out Claire's letters. There were five of them. She had written one letter every week on thin, blue airmail paper. They were the last link between us. Claire had written about the landscape, the weather, her colleagues, her job and how excited she was to be visiting the Okavango Delta, even if it was just for a few days.

I tried to imagine Africa. It had to be full of vibrant colours, teeming markets and laughing people. Drumbeat and dancing in the streets. Restaurants where tantalizing dishes made from coconuts and freshly-caught fish were served in odd-shaped calabash dishes.

Hot humid air, pith helmets, lions and elephants, waterfalls and... Tarzan swinging on a liana. I know it was a stupid cliché, but that's how I imagined Africa. Back then, I knew nothing about witchdoctors, tokoloshes and the realm of ancestors...

I found almost all episodes of a South African TV series in the dingy video shop around the corner. The series was about Shaka Zulu, the great and cruel warrior chief of the Zulu people in the 19th century. Not exactly modern, but it would do for starters. Soon I could sing along to the opening tune. "Bayete, kosi, bayete, kosi...we are growing, growing high and higher..."

I don't know if this Shaka Zulu had anything to do with it, but I began to notice all the 'africanness' around me. The clothes and baskets in shop windows; drumbeat coming from a downtown flat.

Did dark-skinned people in the street or on the tube smile at me more often? Perhaps they sensed that I was going to visit their mysterious continent soon. Perhaps, they were just friendly 4$^{th}$ generation Brits from Hackney with a droll Cockney accent.

Claire would have made fun of me. Claire... During those two weeks in London, I still waited for news from

Botswana. Perhaps, I wouldn't have to go to Africa, after all. I also dreamed that Claire had been found in some village in the Tuli Block and was now sitting in a nice lady's farm kitchen, sipping hot cocoa. You won't believe what happened to me, Foompy,' she said on the phone with a smile in her voice. 'I must tell you all about it, Foompy.' I could actually hear a chuckle in her voice.

I was in a constant state of nervous tension and wound up like a tightened spring. No wonder then that I started speaking to paintings.

When it was time to get my vaccinations, I took the C2 bus to Great Portland Street and then the tube to the Institute for Tropical Diseases in Bloomsbury. It was half a world trip in itself. The needles were just as horrid as I had imagined and I suffered for a few days with a fever and a swollen arm. But at least all that distracted me from my sadness for a while.

I hadn't seen much of Grandpa since we arrived. He was busy with book talks and such. Then one evening, a few days before my flight, he felt the urge to cook.

When I came home from the video shop, a simple meal stood on the polished beech-wood table. Classical music played in the background. Claire de Lune by Claude Debussy. I was touched.

"Hi Grandpa!" I called.

"Hi poppet, feeling hungry?"

"Sure, that looks good."

He came in from the kitchen. "Sit down and help yourself. Here is also some salad." He put a large bowl on the table.

"Did you also get vaccinated when you went to live in Kenya, Grandpa?" I asked, while sucking green pesto spaghetti through my teeth. Grandpa had lived overseas a lot when he was a fledgling journalist. I guess Claire had inherited her adventurous streak from him.

"To be honest, I don't remember. But I'm sure I had to

get some injection or other over the years. How is your arm doing?" He pointed to my left upper arm. It was still a bit swollen, but the redness was gone.

"Getting better. Tablets seem to be working, because the fever is down." I rolled more of the green spaghetti onto the fancy silver fork.

"Did you speak to your mother today?" Grandpa asked me.

"Yes, this morning. She wants me to reconsider the whole trip," I sighed deeply.

"I see, but you have made up your mind about it?" Was there an undertone? If Grandpa didn't want me to go to Botswana, he should just say so. Not that it made any difference.

"Of course, I have! I would never get so many injections and then not go to Africa," I replied. "Mom said they'll come to see me off next weekend. Well, to say goodbye and all that. She has to be back in Cambridge by Monday morning." My flight was on Tuesday.

"Pity. But I'm glad they are coming, even if they can't see you off."

"Mhm," I uttered in consent and swallowed the spaghetti. There would be a lot of tears for sure. "I must just phone about the visas tomorrow morning."

"Splendid. Then you're all set."

"Grandpa, what is it like – in Africa? Is it as dangerous as people say?" I asked impulsively. "Somebody even said to me the other day that I must be mad to go into a country like Botswana."

"Who says things like that?" Grandpa looked up in surprise.

"Some businessman I met at the Institute of Tropical Diseases. We sat next to each other in the waiting room. He said they only have witchdoctors there, no proper doctors, but he couldn't tell me what exactly witchdoctors are."

"People should mind their own damn business," Grandpa growled. "Of course they do have hospitals and proper doctors. Don't be silly. He's probably never been anywhere near Botswana."

"No, I guess not. He said he always flies to South America."

"To many Europeans, Africa is nothing more than one big blob of jungle. Just a single country and not a continent with many different cultures. 'African' covers just about everything from appearance to food and clothes... But Africa is just as diverse as Europe. Kenya is completely different from Togo or Sudan or Botswana. Even Zimbabwe and Namibia are different, although they are right next door to Botswana."

Guilty as charged! I was one of those ignorant Europeans, but I was too ashamed to admit it. So, Zimbabwe and Namibia were next-door neighbours to Botswana?

Maybe I should pay the library a visit tomorrow. Watching episodes of 'Shaka Zulu' was obviously not enough preparation for my trip.

On the weekend, my parents arrived in London in a last-ditch attempt to persuade me not leave for Africa.

"Love, what happens if you need help and have nobody to turn to?" Dad argued. We were standing inside Victoria Station, waiting for the bus to Cambridge. "Or you could get sick."

"I've had all the injections a human being can endure. Germs that know what's good for them won't come anywhere near me!"

"Oh Bridget, you have changed so much," Mom lamented.

"Of course I've changed. Claire is out there all by herself. How can I not change? I have to find her."

"Well, you can still change your mind…"

"No Mom, there is no way I'll change my mind. This is something I really, really have to do and - I won't be on another planet, you know. You can get hold me there, and I'll keep you posted. Tony says one can pre-book phone calls at the Botsalo Hotel in Palapye and you can also leave messages there. I've written the number underneath the postal address. He's already booked a call for Friday evening at 8 o'clock. That's 6 o'clock here in England. Wait,

I'll write it down for you."

I took the piece of paper with all the addresses and phone numbers, including the ones of the British High Commission in Gaborone and scribbled 'BOTSALO Hotel in Palapye phone 6:00 Friday night' on it.

"I'm sorry we can't see you off at the airport on Tuesday, Bridget. You know, Mom is teaching again and…"

"I know."

"Phone us the minute you land, so that we don't have to worry. Oh dear, Botswana is so far away! You do know what happened with that airplane last week, don't you?"

I knew. Reports of the crash had been splashed all over the media. 169 lives lost. It would have been difficult to miss.

"Thanks Dad, that's very encouraging. But don't worry, I'll do my best to make sure I arrive safely in Gaborone."

"Oh Bridget…" Mom clutched me and cried a little more.

I felt like crying again just watching her like that. My heart ached, seeing my parents like this. When would I see them again? I couldn't allow myself to think like that. Not now. I pulled myself together and hugged my parents goodbye, then they boarded the Cambridge bus.

Two days later, I said goodbye to Grandpa as well.

"Take good care of yourself, love, and we'll see you soon."

"Not to worry, Grandpa. I'm sure I'll be back in no time with Claire in tow," I promised, but would I be able to keep my promise? He waved until I had disappeared behind the luggage check.

We landed in Gaborone's small Sir Seretse Khama Airport on 15 September 1988. I stepped off the 30-seater plane with wobbly knees after flying for nearly 14 hours, a stop-over in Kinshasa and bumpy transfer from Johannesburg's Jan Smuts Airport to Gaborone.

On that day, I became one of the Lekgoas in Botswana. Lekgoas were expatriates who stay in the country only a short while. A few years pass in the blink of an eye of the mighty

Kalahari Desert and I had so much to learn.

That the passage of time is slower here; that the Tswanas take everything in their stride, which can be sometimes maddeningly slow. That they commune with their ancestors and find it strange that we don't – and that not all witchdoctors mean well.

Perhaps things would have been easier, if my own ancestors had become involved somehow. Perhaps. But perhaps everything had to unfold just the way it did.

The shrilling of the phone made me jump. This time, I didn't answer. I wanted to be alone with my thoughts and my life in Botswana.

Working was no longer an option. When the ringing stopped, I made myself a cup of tea in the kitchen, put the receiver next to the phone and settled into the comfy armchair by the window.

# CHAPTER 2

Tony had agreed to meet me at the airport. He could hardly refuse to help me, but it was also awkward. We didn't know each other well and Claire was our only link. Would we understand each other? These things went around in my mind when we took off from Jan Smuts Airport.

The small passenger plane had hit a few turbulences while negotiating the space over a vast expanse of bush land. All that to the soundtrack of Simon and Garfunkel playing on my walkman.

The constant ups and downs left my stomach hanging a few inches above my head every time we hit turbulence.

Lucky for us, the stewardess had only served a snack of dried biltong meat, a Bushman specialty we were told, and salted peanuts. Nevertheless, I eyed the paper bag neatly tucked into the net in front of me. Would I have to use it? But my stomach behaved.

When the plane landed safely in what seemed to be the middle of the savannah, everybody clapped with relief. The smell of wilderness and a wave of hot air hit me as I walked the short distance across the tarmac to the quaint airport building. There was so much blue sky, so much savannah. The air glimmered above the landing strip, drenched in harsh sunlight. For a second I had to squeeze my eyes closed.

This was it.

This was Africa! The place that Claire had longed for.

How different everything felt. I had left behind England, dressed in the rainy colours of early autumn and stepped into an African spring day: bright, hot and dirty green. September was early spring in Botswana! I had nearly forgotten that the seasons were reversed in the southern hemisphere. I slowly took in the earthy smell.

Picking up my luggage and having my passport checked didn't take very long. Just long enough for me to admire the modern interior of the airport building.

Was it my imagination or did the airport personnel look happier than their London counterparts? Their movements seemed less hurried and I didn't remember seeing anyone smiling at Heathrow.

The queue moved past one of the cleaning ladies taking a rest, leaning against a stone container with some tropical plant. She greeted me with a broad, happy smile and so did the next one, who mopped the floor around our short queue.

When it was my turn at the passport check, the uniformed African official said, "Welcome to Botswana, Miss Reinhold. Enjoy your stay..." as he handed back my travel document.

This was so not like the oily-grinning officials in the movies, wearing ill-fitting uniforms, with the power to throw an innocent traveller into jail just for looking at them the wrong way.

"Thank you." I smiled back and walked on.

There was a line of trolleys waiting for us. I heaved my bags on a trolley and marched toward the exit, a number of well-dressed businessmen right in front of me.

I saw a double-chinned Indian lady in a bright-green sari and dripping with sparkling jewellery herd her four children deftly toward the sliding doors. Doting family members welcomed them and took luggage and children off her hands.

A young man came bounding towards the glass door. It was Tony, tall and handsome in washed-out jeans and a casual shirt. His dark, unruly hair was longer than I remembered and his bright eyes contrasted starkly with his tanned face. Gold-rimmed glasses gave Tony an air of learned sophistication, despite the three-day stubble on his chin and cheeks.

Sadness washed over me. It had been seven weeks since Claire's disappearance and Tony was the only real link. For a brief moment we clung to each other. It was somehow okay to greet him like an old friend, talk to him as if we had been close forever.

"Hi there sis," Tony finally said and cleared his throat.

"Hi Tony," I sniffled and peeled myself away.

He turned to more pragmatic matters. "Come, let me push that for you. How was your flight?" We moved.

"Long. We stopped over in Kinshasa for a couple of hours. Thank goodness I had my walkman with me." I tried to speak in a normal voice.

"Yep, music can be a lifesaver on a long trip. The car is this way." I just followed Tony and the clattering trolley down the near-empty parking lot.

"When we landed in South Africa, I saw so many houses with swimming pools. We waited in Johannesburg for over an hour in the transit area. That was quite boring." I tried to sound carefree.

I opened the zip of my backpack and pushed the walkman inside, parting with my travel companion for the first time since London. But now I had Tony to talk to.

"Yes well, it's a different lifestyle here," he said and stopped behind a dirty, blue Toyota Corolla, fumbling for his car keys.

"You mean people in Botswana also have swimming pools in their gardens?"

"Well of course. Not in a village like Palapye, but there are plenty in Gaborone and Francistown."

I was duly impressed. Imagine, having your own swimming pool!

Tony tossed my bags into the boot of the Toyota and abandoned the trolley. He opened the car door for me and I gratefully plunked myself on the passenger seat.

After a few turns around the parking lot, we pulled into a long, straight road through the savannah. The earth was very red and dotted with pale green shrubs. I was tired, but far too excited to sleep.

"Everything is so dusty here. And look at all this red colour," I said.

"Oh, that's because of all the iron oxide in the soil and it hasn't rained yet. It doesn't rain here in winter," Tony pointed out. "Nature explodes when the rains come in late spring, or so I'm told. Should be anytime now." That was curious. It rained a lot in England, especially in winter.

"And here I thought nature had already exploded."

"Ha, just wait and see. Close your window or the air conditioning won't kick in."

I cranked up the handle. "Are we going through Gaborone?"

"No, Bridget, we'll drive straight to Palapye." Tony turned left into what had to be the main road, judging by the three dusty cars that passed us. We travelled east now.

"Oh, why is that?" I had been looking forward to seeing Gaborone, where Claire had lived for all those weeks we had been separated.

"We have to get to Palapye before dark. We can go to Gabs soon. On the weekend, perhaps," Tony said, turned his head and hooted.

Palapye. It was the name of the rural village where Tony now worked at a vocational training centre - close to the Tuli Block - and closer to Claire. At least it was my hope. The Tuli Block, a remote nature reserve, where the Zimbabwean and South African borders met with Botswana's.

Claire had been so excited to see the elephants there. Staying in Gaborone without her must have become a pain for Tony. Then there must have been all those questions. Questions he had no answers for. At least not yet.

Tony had brought something to eat and drink, because we would be on the road for some time. I opened the brown paper bag with sandwiches and cans of coke.

"So you're trying to avoid the traffic then?" I asked, taking a sip of foaming coke.

"No, Gabs isn't that big. There won't be much traffic around this time."

"I see. So, why can't we drive after dark?" I munched on a cheese and ham sandwich, mildly interested and suddenly feeling very tired.

"Because of the cattle and goats. They tend to lumber into the road at night and sleep on the warm tar. Nights can be quite cool around here," Tony said.

"Really, cattle and goats?"

"Yep, can be dangerous in the dark, if you travel more than 5 miles per hour," Tony said patiently. I considered the cattle and goats for a moment.

"It's only early afternoon. Does it take that long to get to Palapye?"

"No, a couple of hours now, but nightfall is much earlier here. We are closer to the equator, you know." Really?

"Hmm, I see. What about lions and zebras? Do they also run into the road?" I took a swig from my coke to wash down the crumbs.

"Not around here they don't," he laughed. "You'll find wildlife further up north in the Okavango Delta, in the Tuli Block and so on. This here is more farm country."

"I see."

Too much information to take in on my first African day.

Some of the coke spilled onto my jeans, when Tony slowed down for some women with bulging blankets wrapped around them, balancing large bundles on their heads. I wiped myself with a paper tissue that Tony handed me and studied the landscape while there was daylight.

All I saw was reddish sand, bushes and grey gravel on either side of the tarred road. Now and again a dilapidated thatched house. The hills in the distance looked inviting. Dreamy somehow.

I wasn't used to seeing Africa properly yet or I would have noticed the villages, animals and heaps of Shake-Shake cartons next to the road. Shake-Shake was Botswana's most popular beverage: thick, sour sorghum beer. More food than drink.

Then I began to see wooden poles and wires whizzing past. And fences.

"Why are there are so many fences all along the road?" I asked and yawned.

"That's to keep the farm animals away from the road," Tony said. I was confused.

"Didn't you say they run into the road anyway?"

"The cowherds don't always keep the gates closed, so it's better to be on the safe side," he said. "Friend of mine got into trouble a couple of weeks ago. He hit a cow and had to pay an arm and a leg for it. His car was scrap as well, but he only had a scratch on his forehead."

"Oh, that's ... awful."

"Yes, it is," Tony agreed and swerved around a pothole.

I couldn't help wondering how an accident like that would have made the headlines in Cambridge. 'Young Teacher Hits Cow in Road with Golf GTI. Car and Cow Both Deceased. Farmer Demands Spot Fine from Injured Driver.'

"We are passing through Mochudi. Over there by the hill is a small clinic run by a German doctor, Dr. Ritter."

Mochudi. I flinched. This was the place where Claire's car had been found abandoned in a field. Would Tony stop to show me the spot? But he didn't.

As we headed further east, Tony pointed to a hill with a white building to the right. Dr. Ritter had been in the country with his wife and five children for over ten years. His small but well-equipped hospital was preferable to bigger ones in the cities.

"You looked for Claire in that clinic, of course." I already knew the answer.

"Of course, all the hospitals were searched." Tony's

gaze was fixed on the road, which was a good thing really, considering the cows and goats and all that.

I took Claire's first letter out the backpack. A well-read piece of paper. There were photos in the airmail envelope. One showed my sister in Peru, leaning against a ruined wall. Another one was at home in our kitchen. I was on the third photograph with my arm around her, together with Mom and Dad.

Looking at my parents brought on a pang of guilt and homesickness. Was it right to just leave like that, leaving them to worry about me too?

It was done, I decided. I was in Africa now and there was no turning back. I squeezed the backpack down in front of the seat and put my bare feet up on the dusty dashboard, hoping that Tony didn't mind. Then I re-read the letter for the umpteenth time:

*'Gaborone, 11 June 1988*

*Hi Foompy,*
*Arrived in Gabs, as the locals call the capital. It's so small even compared to good old Cambridge. I have seen only two traffic lights so far ... It's really cold at night, because, can you believe it, it's winter here. One moment I'm in balmy England in June and now it's winter. Only at night, though.*

*It's hot and dry during the day. Who knew that winter could be like that? It was so cold last night that I crept into my sleeping bag. Must buy a proper thick duvet and blankets tomorrow, if I can find a shop. Tony's lucky he doesn't get cold easily. He's been here for almost a month, so he should know the shops in Gaborone.*

*I swear I saw ice-covered puddles this morning. The gardener, who looks after the company house garden (and it's a huge house), watered the lawn yesterday and... '*

The letter went on about the features of house and garden and how sweet Tony had been. He had greeted

Claire with a bunch of flowers at the airport and after delivering her luggage to the company house, they had gone to the office to meet her new colleagues.

Those colleagues were something else. Comical, almost. I had to smile again as I read on. There was this obnoxious fellow draughtsman from Chicago, who liked to wink suggestively at her.

'...*Maybe he has a nervous tick...*' Claire wrote, but I already knew from her subsequent letters that he didn't.

Rather, a case of thinking that the sun shone out of his backside, leaving females mesmerized. Chad Sullivan fancied himself a ladies' man. Apparently, women ran for the hills when they heard his pick-up lines.

'...*Then there is Liesl, the dull, blonde girlfriend of a young engineer called Desmond Kahl. She spends the whole day in a back office with her boyfriend, but doesn't seem to work. I'm sure she dresses like her mother.*

*Wolfgang Klein, head of the design team and my direct boss, is firm and fair with his staff. He's a tall, good-looking man in his mid-fifties and very smart. The design team consists of Wolfgang's right hand, an engineer called Werner Pfeiffer, his spunky PA Emily van Heerden, Kgomotso Min the Tswana bookkeeper, whose stepfather's a Chinese banker and Thomas Taylor, a senior engineer, who looks like a wild Scotsman with a flaming red beard. A clutch of less interesting people complete the team...*'

Claire got on easily with people, but she didn't like the corpulent office manager, Mr. Feindlich. I knew that his name meant 'hostile' in German. Telling.

'...*Mr. Feindlich took me to a French (!) restaurant called The Bougainvillea yesterday. He filled me in on my colleagues over lunch. The man had nothing good to say about Emily. Thinks she's a slut* — *imagine. How can a manager be so crude? And I didn't have the impression at all.*

*In fact, I rather like Emily and Kgomotso. You know I always go by my instinct.'* (I knew) 'Does this man think I don't have a brain to make my own mind up?'

I sighed. Would I meet any of these people while I was in the country?

*'...Mr. Feindlich likes Desmond and his girlfriend a lot. Liesl seems to be some relation of his. She's quite young and chubby, but looks a lot older in a cute pug-faced sort of way. I'm sure she dresses like her mother. Feindlich wanted me to go shopping with her. Oh dear! Came up with some excuse. He's going to hate me, if he finds out that I'll go shopping with Emily and Kgomotso instead...'*

So there was a clue. Did this Mr. Feindlich really hate Claire? Perhaps not. Don't read clues into everything, I reprimanded myself. I had scrutinized the letters over and over, but couldn't find anything enlightening. They had little more than sentimental value in my quest to find Claire.

*'...Emily is intelligent and headstrong. 23 and quite pretty with her light-brown hair. She's a South African from Johannesburg and goes home to visit her family at least once a month. Kgomotso is Emily's best friend. The two girls are stark opposites in the looks department, but they have the same liquid movements and friendly personalities. I've been to the smaller company house in Tsholofelo. They share it with two other people. Tsholofelo is a nice suburb. Emily loves to wear sunglasses and has at least five pairs. She's not aware of it, but men are quite attracted to her. Mr. Feindlich is aware of it...'*

Claire didn't write much about Kgomotso in her first letter, but I gathered that the three of them had become pals. I tried to picture a company house with Claire in it.

"Bridget, hey!"

"Umm, yes?" I must have dozed off for a while. A street sign read 'Mahalapye'.

"Wake up."

There were soldiers in the road. We were stopped at an army roadblock.

"What's going on Tony? Is there something wrong?" I was alarmed. Bombs, street battles...

"No, nothing wrong. Sorry I forgot to tell you. Soldiers often search cars for weapons and things to do with the military. Leave it to me. Just smile."

I rubbed my eyes. Tony was ordered to open his boot and I smiled.

The soldiers looked very young with their machine guns slung over one shoulder and seemed nervous. Were they trigger-happy? The harsh tone and the guns made me nervous too. I had never been so close to a real weapon before. We had to produce our passports and were waved on after a couple of minutes.

"That was scary," I said and started breathing again.

"Better get used to it. They have roadblocks in the cities as well."

"What happens if they actually find something?"

"Well, that rarely happens. A British salesman, who travelled with an old camouflage jacket from his army days, was interrogated for a few hours. Poor chap was still rattled, when he told us his story at the Botsalo Hotel."

Botsalo Hotel. That's where I had phoned Tony a couple of weeks ago.

"Very comforting," I mumbled. How could people get used to something like that?

"Just don't carry anything army green in your car and be friendly," Tony said.

*Okay, nothing army green*, I thought sleepily. The sun now wavered over the hilltops and a fine mist rose over the fields, but it was still early afternoon.

I ate another sandwich and offered Tony the one with

salami. He took one bite and then stared at the road again. Did he expect a cow to come charging out from behind a hut any moment now?

"Tony, tell me something about Palapye." We had just passed a road sign with the name of our destination on it, just below the name 'Francistown'.

Tony took a deep breath as if he was waking up from a dream.

"Well, there isn't much to tell. Don't be surprised if you don't see the houses at first." He took another bite from the salami sandwich he had deposited on the dashboard.

"Most of the kraals are hidden by motsetsi hedges and dried branches."

"Motsi what?" I didn't understand.

"Motsetsi. Tall evergreen plants. Then there is a new tar road all the way up to the new training centre. That's where I work. It's the only road in the village. The alternative is to drive or walk through deep sand past the kraals. We are staying in the complex up by the training centre. There is a high school. And the Botsalo Hotel, of course."

Tony took another bite and finished the sandwich. He chewed, wiping his hand on a tissue.

"The complex is behind the training centre. The houses are all fenced in. Very monotonous, like a garden colony in the sand," he said.

"I can help you plant a garden," I offered spontaneously.

Some green around the house would be nice and comforting like our back garden in Cambridge.

"Mhm," Tony said.

"These green hedges seem a good idea," I said, but the conversation was over.

We drove on and eventually, a dusty green road sign with 'Palapye' on it pointed right. Tony turned between an ancient-looking petrol station and a curio shop. The fast-sinking afternoon sun lent a golden sheen to the surroundings.

"And this is Palapye," Tony announced.

This was supposed to be a village? Tony had been right, I didn't see any houses. Just trees, hedges and dried wood to the left of the black new tar.

"Impressive!" I lied in jest and we both laughed.

There was surely plenty of nothing here. Not at all the vibrant, buzzing African village I had imagined back in England.

My vision was still adjusted to high-rise brick buildings in London, small spaces, the busy roads and traffic lights, billboards, shopping precincts, trains and buses. Lots of people. At home, nature was neatly packaged into manicured parks and fields outside of town.

"Not long now. By the way, that's the local shopping mall." Tony pointed to a short row of very dirty single-story buildings with a broad walkway upfront.

He swerved around a few goats and a cheerful group of boys in ragged shorts. They edged into the road while pushing toy cars with long steering wheels all made of wire, waving at our car. Tony hooted and I waved back at them. They laughed and made faces at us.

Then the Corolla hummed up the long, black tar road to the vocational training centre, leaving the village behind.

I couldn't help thinking that Claire had never even seen what I was seeing now. It felt odd somehow. I never wanted to live in Africa in the first place!

Soon we drove through the boom in front of the vocational training centre, and we still hadn't spoken a word about Claire.

# CHAPTER 3

What had I gotten myself into? I could tell that Tony was heartbroken and confused and all that. But it was just impossible to speak to him about Claire. The tender moment at the airport had passed. And he didn't seem in a hurry at all to start with our investigation. Why was it so difficult for him?

Tony had to feel the same urgency to find out more. Why else was he still here? But I couldn't get him to speak about my sister, never mind making some sort of a plan.

Maybe Tony was under some kind of spell. *Don't fall off the rocker*, Bridget, I called myself to order. Things would fall into place. They just had to.

I did my best; tried to be understanding and give him time. But I didn't have time. I had come all this way from England for the sole purpose of helping him with the search.

Just that he didn't show any interest in searching. Here I was in a remote African village, virtually without support, ready to get started. And all I got were awkward silences.

I didn't know Tony very well. Perhaps he'd throw me out, if I argued with him. And I hated confrontations anyway. But no way would I give up. So I had no choice, but to make the best of the situation.

I had to acclimatize. Literally. The dust and the heat were getting to me and now - to top it all - the rains had started. The rain cooled the temperatures during the day, but never for long. And my ability to think clearly suffered considerably in this heat.

Mom promptly phoned on Friday and I was so glad to

hear her crackly voice. At least *she* wanted to help me.

'Perhaps Claire has crossed the border into another country.'

'I'm not so sure about that, Mom,' I said cautiously.

'It's worth following up on, though. The police should check their records.'

'Yes, Mom, I'll look into it.' How could I explain to my mother how easy it was to cross the green border without leaving a trace?

'Good.' She sounded pleased.

'Mom?'

'Yes?'

'I love you, Mom.' I choked back homesick tears.

'I love you too, Bridget.' I heard my Mom swallow hard.

'Tell Dad I love him. Speak to you soon.'

I pulled myself together. It was awkward to become all emotional in a hotel lobby. People were listening.

'Bye, be safe my child,' Mom said slowly and waited, as if she didn't want to let me go.

'Bye, Mom.' I hung up and was alone again amid all those bustling hotel guests.

The Botsalo Country Hotel boasted a large restaurant, a bar in the lobby and two pool tables. And on the counter resided the priceless telephone. On a Friday night, the Botsalo was the meeting place of the area.

Tony's teacher friend, Neo Moletsane, came from a nearby town called Serowe. Neo was single and the two of them often spent the evenings at the Botsalo Hotel. The new school term hadn't started yet and there wasn't much to do. So I tagged along.

Neo Moletsane was a well-educated young man. He taught the bricklayers at the vocational training centre, while Tony was head of economics. He was a bit on the stocky side and always wore clean cotton shirts, never a t-shirt and never jeans. Tony told me that Neo was trust-worthy and knew why I had come to Botswana. That was a start.

The two of them played pool, had a meal, drank a lot of

beer and chatted to the other patrons. I sat and read in one of the comfortable tub chairs in the lobby.

Hotel guests stayed at the rooms that were arranged around the swimming pool at the back and travelling salesmen often had stories to tell from other parts of the country. Nothing of use to me, but I listened politely.

For the sake of keeping up appearances, Tony introduced me generally as his visiting girlfriend from the UK. We had discussed that it would be better not to draw attention to the actual reason of my presence. I wondered how long it would take before the truth came out in this small community.

There were local girls at the hotel, often for two reasons: to meet a boyfriend or to find a boyfriend. Neo had said that with a sad expression. Most were from the village and lived in houses sponsored by their expat boyfriends.

On the main road halfway between Gaborone and Francistown, this was a convenient place for travellers to stop over. It took some getting used to the rough manners of men around here.

Other women were employed by the training centre and felt comfortable enough around the Lekgoas. And then there were a few expatriate women like myself. Generally their area of interest revolved around gossip and G&Ts. I stuck with reading my books and the Government Gazette.

We often headed home along sandy back roads in the dark. I understood by now, why driving at night made people so nervous. One day, Tony had to come to a halt in front of two cows, resting in the warm sand.

After much hooting and yelling, the beasts heaved themselves out of their soft bedding and plodded away mooing reproachfully. On another occasion, the car skidded against a mud-covered rock and spun off into the spongy field. It took two wooden planks and a lot of elbow grease to get it back on the dirt road.

"If I hear the question 'so when are you getting married?' one more time, I'll scream!" I complained to

Tony as we headed back to the complex one night.

Tony drove slowly through the wet grey sand, deeply carved from small rivers that had formed during the last rainstorm. The headlights revealed random rocks and pebbles sticking out of the sand. One had to be hellishly careful.

"I know everybody wants to stick their noses into everybody else's business," said Tony. "They will have something else to gossip about, soon. Right now we are the bee's knees when it comes to topics."

Two mining prospectors had invited us to have dinner with them at the restaurant after a gin and tonic in the lobby. We were reluctant to accept, but they seemed starved for conversation, so we caved in. There were worse things than being invited for dinner.

The 'Kingklip Thermidor', the hotel's specialty, had been fresh and tasty and the prospectors had ordered some wine.

"Remember when you went to the loo? The one guy actually told me to leave you and come with him to Orapa. Said he was making a lot of money at the diamond mine. Wanted to take good care of me," I chuckled. "You should have seen his face when I told him off."

Tony was quiet. Was he listening to me?

"When did that happen?" he asked in a worried tone.

"Well, when you went to the loo. He just took a chance, I guess."

"I bet, he won't offer himself again in a hurry."

"I wasn't really cruel to him. Just explained that money can't buy love and that I would never leave you," I said. "My sermon had him close to tears."

"He probably remembered his wife and children in South Africa. And what a dog he is," Tony said with contempt.

The car creaked along the sandy path. We reached a familiar fork in the road with a piece of trampled-down fence straight ahead.

"Yes, it was definitely worth a little white lie," I giggled.

It had been one of the lighter moments. There were still

these uncomfortable silences between us.

I just couldn't understand Tony. For one thing, I wasn't used to the slow pace and lack of urgency in general. I also felt that Tony had exaggerated his zeal to find out the truth about Claire. Or perhaps, I had misunderstood him. Perhaps I just wanted to think that he was as eager to solve the mystery of Claire's disappearance.

But if that was the case, what was he still doing here in Palapye? Why had he invited me?

I convinced him somehow to come to the local police station with me. The grimy building sat lazily across the railroad tracks next to the grimy post office. Mail was delivered to the post office in a rickety van on a Thursday or Friday and had to be collected. So it was convenient to pop into the police station.

"Good day officer. We are here to inquire about this case..."

Tony pushed a piece of paper across the counter. The attending charge officer looked at the paper and disappeared into a back room. He came back with an older policeman, who blew us off with no further ado.

"Sorry sir, but we are still investigating."

I persisted with questions, which were met with an enduring indifference. It was like bouncing off an invisible wall. It was discouraging, but I put it down to things happening very, very slowly in Botswana. I had learned that much.

Then I paid the police station a visit once in a while by myself. Something had to happen sometime. Just how was I supposed to explain the situation to my family and friends back in Cambridge?

I chickened out and wrote about how wonderful Palapye was, how the sunsets glowed between the hills behind the complex. Pure magic. That Tony was helping me find out more about Claire's disappearance, that the police was being helpful...in other words, I lied through my back teeth.

The sunsets were rather spectacular, but Tony wasn't

being helpful. And especially not the police. What to do?

I would go to Gaborone and speak to the police there — and then to witnesses in Bobonong and Mochudi. Yes, that's what I would do. In the meantime, I had to find my feet in this strange place.

In the last weeks of the holidays, the vocational training centre was slowly coming back to life. Very slowly.

Except for ground staff and a handful of expatriate teachers, the complex was still deserted. As much as I sometimes wanted to get away from the crowd in England, I now craved the company of a few sensible friends I could talk to. Oh Liz, Diane and Zaheeda, forgive me if I ever took you for granted!

Those were the dinosaur days before communication became easy. No e-mail or mobile telephones. And something like Skype only existed in science fiction movies. In order not to lose my mind, I began to plant flowers and herbs and weeds that looked like flowers in Tony's garden.

Tony thought it best to leave the project up to me. I spent day after day digging up the sandy soil. Then putting down foul-smelling manure, Tony had ordered by the truckload and digging everything over again. Bulky motsetsi cut-offs from the village lay in great heaps next to the driveway. The ground staff thought it hilarious, how I worked away. For me it was therapeutic.

Neo had assured me that the Motsetsi plants would take root quickly. All I had to do was stick them into the ground along the fence and water often.

So that's what I did.

A little rock garden was next. A rocky ride over sticks and stones to a dried-up riverbed had yielded a collection of smooth rocks. And it didn't stop there. Neo mentioned that one could create a vegetable garden with different-sized car tyres.

"Stacked on top of each other and filled with compost, they make a 'wakah'. It needs little water and maintenance.

You can have lettuce and herbs at your fingertips," he said.

A three-story wakah tower was built in no time. The constant rain soon helped tiny green leaves to break through the soil. A hardy acacia tree completed the garden.

My hands were dirty and my nails ragged, but I was proud of my achievement.

All that must have been a breath-taking sight for Ethel Poppelmeyer to behold. Ethel was the prim and proper wife of the new school principal. A balding man, whose paunch just fit into his light blue safari suit. They were Tony's direct neighbours.

We hadn't been formally introduced yet, but I knew that she lived next-door. She often watched me from behind cream lace-curtains that had travelled with her from England. I suppose there was not much else to watch.

Apparently she thought that Tony and I were living in sin. At least that's what I'd heard at the Botsalo Hotel. In the English town of Cobblestead, where she was from, such conduct would surely not have been tolerated. I found that amusing.

I went inside to wash after a day's work, still bits of garden stuck to me. The water ran sparse and brown again. Great. It took me a while to scrub myself clean.

I readied myself to take a cool drink out to the porch, when I noticed Ethel inspecting the empty pre-fab houses on the other side of the road. It had to be Ethel, because there weren't too many middle-aged women with neatly permed hair around. She came over to inspect the new motsetsi hedge. Come on Bridget, take the first step in the spirit of good neighbourhood, I said to myself.

After all, she took such great interest in my garden work.

"Hello Ethel, I'm Bridget, nice to meet you," I greeted her, while sauntering down the driveway. Everybody around here used first names to address each other, so I thought nothing of it.

A startled Ethel pushed herself off the fence as if it was electrified. Her eyes under the bushy blonde eyebrows observed me suspiciously. She made a feeble attempt to shake my hand, then changed her mind and began to nervously stroke one of the young Motsetsi plants. She hadn't realized that I was still at home. *You're letting up, Ethel,* I thought with some satisfaction.

"How do you do?" she replied stiffly and set her face in a self-important expression. " We should address each other by our surnames. I'm the principal's wife, you know."

"Right then." Everybody knew, of course, that she was the principal's wife.

"A certain level of decorum must be observed at all times, especially in such foreign lands. In this wilderness. I shall address you as Miss Reinhold and do kindly address me as Mrs. Poppelmeyer."

She lectured me without the trace of a smile on her thin lips. I wondered whether Ethel understood that it helped to be nice to people, if she didn't plan to die of loneliness in the wilderness.

"Of course, beg my pardon. We shall observe propriety then, Mrs. Poppelmeyer." I said in an ironic tone, which seemed entirely lost on her.

"Yes," she mused. "Perhaps I'll be able to greet you as Mrs. Stratton soon?"

Wow, I hadn't seen that one coming.

"I doubt that very much. Tony and I have no plans to get married."

"Oh how regrettable, Miss Reinhold," Ethel said icily. "Then I'm afraid we shan't have a great deal to talk about, Miss Reinhold." Her nose went up a little higher.

She seemed to like the sound of my surname, since she kept repeating it so often.

"That's indeed regrettable Mrs. Poppelmeyer. I'm sure you have good reason for that."

"I certainly have." She let go of the poor motsetsi plant at last and nervously stroked her embroidered apron instead.

"Well it was nice meeting you all the same."

I could have said a great deal more, but kept smiling for Tony's sake.

"Good day Miss Reinhold. If you will excuse me, I have very important matters to attend to."

With that she turned around, nearly collided with a stray dog and marched back into the principal's house. The drawn lace curtains moved a little. I just shook my head and went on to have my juice on the porch.

I couldn't help thinking, with a touch of pity, that Ethel might have lost her marbles in the African heat. On the other hand, the Poppelmeyers had been on a similar assignment in South America, according to Tony. If that wasn't just as exotic as Africa!

Tony laughed the whole thing off.

"Her nose is permanently out of joint," he said. "Ethel Poppelmeyer is a very lonely woman. All of her maids run away after a few days. She seems to think that she's the lady of the manor around here, surrounded by lowly serfs."

"Just that there is no manor here. And no lowly serfs."

"Exactly."

"Maybe she's just in the wrong place, you know. Some people don't easily adjust," I offered.

"Probably more 'wrong century'," Tony grinned.

Palapye was not exactly the lively place I had pictured in my mind.

No teeming marketplaces, no riotous music and dancing and no smiling fishwives in colourful garb. The locals could be rather shy until sorghum beer got the better of them.

And not one single African warrior in sight, who remotely resembled Shaka Zulu in the video-series. And nobody wore such creative, African attire I had seen on film.

There was just a lot of red earth, grey sand, dusty plants and searing heat. Only very few people to speak to, but far too much time to think.

Mrs. Poppelmeyer did me the honour of another brief

visit about a week later. For lack of another listener, she complained to me bitterly about her gardener, who had torn a pair of work pants. He had not returned after she took 10 Pula quite rightly off his monthly pay.

Never mind that the poor chap only earned about 50 Pula a month and needed to feed his family. 10 Pula was a fortune to some in 1988. About 1 Pound Sterling if I remember correctly. A fortune for a simple gardener.

"When my husband and I lived in Bolivia, where he was of course the principal of a very large college, servants were so much easier to handle. My husband would just say 'Hey chico, come here and do that' and the servant would obey. But these blacks are so difficult —," she grumbled.

I kept my peace and went back to my garden work, giving Ethel some excuse that Tony expected me to finish the planting by the end of the day.

Ethel didn't speak to me again. I just heard rumours later that she had returned to Cobblestead for good, leaving her oh so hard-working husband to his own devices in the African wilderness.

Another neighbour had come back from England. Alfred Jones lived next-door. He was the woodwork instructor and one of a kind. His heavily pregnant wife had stayed behind in Cardiff.

Alfred was quite a character, burly with a mop of unkempt grey hair and a big wiry beard hiding most of his face. He wrote to his wife Judith every day. Usually in the afternoon before downing a few beers on his porch. He often gave me a lift to the police station when he posted the letters. Alfred Jones also sometimes competed with me for telephone time at the Botsalo Hotel.

Now and again, Tony invited him over for a chat to help ease his loneliness. It was a sight to behold, when our neighbour got onto his footstool and climbed clumsily over the fence with a candle in his hand. Power cuts were frequent.

On one such occasion, he had even grabbed my hand in

the darkness and held it tight — drunk of course. He didn't remember afterwards, but Tony had requested that Alfred should bring a candle with him.

The beginning of the term drew closer and the wives of two Tswana teachers were setting up home in the complex. They were busy with meal preparation for their extended families all day long.

Mieliepap, the staple food, was cooked in three-legged black pots in the garden. The stiff mash was made from crushed white maize and the wooden stomping sounds never ceased. Surely driving Ethel Poppelmeyer around the bend.

The pap was often eaten with marogo, wild spinach. The women also had to run after their brood of children and wash everybody's clothing. Or they supervised young girls doing these chores for them.

Unfortunately, there was an insurmountable language barrier between us.

My Setswana was non-existent, which put paid to a meaningful conversation. At least Mrs. Matija, a matron with five young children, managed to say Hello in English, while giggling and staring at her feet.

"Good morning, Mrs. Matija, how are you? Oh, is this your youngest? Hello."

"Good morning, Miss Reynole." That was usually it.

Her husband was one of the heads of department at the training centre. A position he assumed with dignity and a sense of tradition.

By now, I'd had to make peace with the fact that I would be staying longer than expected and I realised that I had to learn how to speak Setswana.

Tsanana, our maid, came up from the village every day to clean for both Alfred and Tony. She was the only female I could have a meaningful conversation with. Tsanana had been to school and — lucky for me — spoke some English.

She cleaned the house and taught me the bare basics of Setswana: "Dumela mma - Good day 'm'am."; "Dumela ra -

Good day sir."; "Le kai? How are you?"; "Re teng - I'm fine."; "Ke utlwa Setswana gologonje - I understand a little Setswana."

I had to repeat the phrases parrot-fashion. But she never grew impatient if the words didn't roll easily off my tongue. Oh, all those harsh 'g' sounds. And then those little intricacies, such as pronouncing 'ph' as 'p' and 'sh' like 's' and that a 'he' often became inexplicably a 'she'.

Finally I could say a simple greeting in Setswana: "Dumela". Not enough for a conversation yet, but a good start. In the afternoon the rain drummed onto the tin roof and we had to shout at each other.

"Tsanana, why don't people look at me when I speak to them?" I asked. This curious habit of Tswanas staring at their toes had puzzled me for a while.

"No madam, she look at feet, because she respect!" Tsanana explained.

This was of course against the very principle of respect in western communication. Tsanana still called me madam. African hierarchy rules were rather strict. She looked at me in wide-eyed horror when I told her to call me Bridget.

'Oh madam, I cannot call Mma Bridget. Must have respect," she told me.

She also refused to eat with me in the same room never mind at the same table. Instead, she preferred to sit on the kitchen floor. The floor was admittedly very clean, but I still didn't understand. Tsanana insisted that it simply was her custom. She had to show respect. As her employers, we were like her elders. That's all there was to it. If anyone found out that she didn't respect us, she'd be in trouble. I gave in reluctantly.

Communication with England was dragging. Apart from the phone calls, letters were my only lifeline to the outside world.

Despite a considerable delay, they kept me up to date with news from Cambridge.

That's how I found out from Zaheeda that David had a

new girlfriend. I knew Pippa and that she was nowhere near as stroppy as yours truly.

Good, David had found his match. No jealousy, not even a twinge of pain. Just a little homesickness. What I missed sorely by now were pubs and cinemas. And to my great shame I had to admit that I missed British television.

But the more I got into tune with my African surroundings, the less I thought about pub grub and the next episode of Coronation Street.

I wrote back diligently. About the birdsong in the mornings, Tony's garden and the stony smell of the savannah. About Mrs. Poppelmeyer and how noisily Tswanas spoke to each other in the streets.

They wanted to know my as yet unsuccessful search for Claire. Just how was I supposed to explain the insurmountable obstacles piling up in front of me?

How naïve I had been. One couldn't just take a bus or train. In Palapye was simply no infrastructure to speak of.

Bobonong was apparently close by. I wanted to go there. And from there to the Tuli Block. But, even if I had a car, taking the tedious trip through rain and mud on my own was likely to be crowned by failure.

There were virtually no street signs, but many side roads. Tony's Toyota was in the repair shop and I couldn't even drive to the Botsalo to phone the Tuli Block game lodge. Tony didn't have the time or inclination to accompany me there in a cramped minibus.

And what if the car broke down? One couldn't ask direction with 'Dumela mma'.

Not even Claire had to drive through muddy roads and she had been on her way to the reservation. I was scared. The risk that I could lose my way was just too great. Again I had to wait.

Much to my parents' relief, I reported that there were no gun battles or bomb blasts anywhere. The only guns I knew about hung over the shoulders of soldiers at roadblocks.

I missed Claire the most! She would have had some idea what to do. She would not have waited. I was already being as brave as I dared to be.

A small valley marked the boundary behind the housing complex. Because of all the high fences, one had to leave the complex and pick a narrow path back to a good spot in order to get an unobstructed view. I often day-dreamed that somewhere behind the hills, I would find Claire one day. Soon.

In the meantime we needed food and I had to walk to the shops. The long road from the training centre to the 'mall' was newly tarred, but took a wide berth around the village. Not a speck of shade from the blistering sun and the oily tar got stuck to shoes.

It was better to take the shortcut between trees and motsetsi-kraals, even if it meant wading through deep grey sand. A trip I wouldn't recommend barefoot. The sand was too hot and there were sharp objects hiding in it.

To my disappointment, Palapye did not have a traditional market place. The only thing that resembled a village hub was the short row of brick houses we called the mall. The Botsalo Hotel was far away, on the other side of the many kraals.

The only two shops were a greengrocer, where one could purchase mainly cabbage, spinach and squash and a little corner market that offered the mere basics. Bread, Crosse and Blackwell mayonnaise and long-life milk.

Next door was the local shebeen. A sort of pub, where one could eat a bite. Tswanas went to shebeens mostly for the sorghum beer.

Neo Moletsane had invited us proudly to try the local specialty of pap and fatty boiled meat with tomato relish.

We sat down at one of the wobbly tables covered in brightly patterned oil cloth. The food he ordered was served on tatty plastic plates with beetroot salad and none too clean knives and forks.

I was no fan of fatty meat and stuck to the pap and beetroot.

I had to try hard not to spit out the unusual-tasting sorghum beer. Neo noticed how I was struggling and ordered a coke.

My shopping trip to the mall ended pleasantly when Alfred, who was on his lunch break, gave me a ride back to the complex.

When the car was in running-order again, Tony took me to Serowe and Selebi Phikwe to stock up. There were real supermarkets! With fridges and one could buy fresh milk and produce.

"Finally," I moaned. "I'm tired of tinned food."

"That's why we need cooler boxes. In the heat, lettuce can boil to mush in no time. Like cooked spinach."

"Crummy. And instead of yoghurt we end up with cheese cake."

"Exactly. Although that wouldn't be so bad."

"Claire loves cheesecake."

"Mhm."

That was all he said. Nice try, Bridget. How long would he carry on like this?

Tony wasn't in a bad mood or anything , so after the shopping, we went to the Museum of Tswana Culture. The gate to the modest building was locked, despite a sign declaring that the museum would be open on a Saturday.

Tony asked a few passers-by, who spoke broken English and told us that the director of the museum lived around the corner. They offered to fetch him and soon he came running.

"I didn't expect any tourists at this time of year," the director apologized.

I began to like the flexibility of rules. In Britain, if a museum was closed, it was closed. End of story.

"Just look at that Tony, what is it?"

I was fascinated by the small wooden animal statues made by the Khoi San. A small wooden board with flattened nails that could be played with one's thumbs lay on a pedestal.

"That's a bushman piano," explained the director, "all

hand-carved by Bushmen from the Kalahari Desert."

Bushmen. I had read about bushmen.

Still out of breath, the man took his position behind the counter and charged us two Pulas entrance fee per head. A group of Americans had also found their way to the museum and queued behind us.

"Awesome man. They have a museum in the middle of the desert, hey Bob?"

"Yeah, wonder if this statue's for sale. I still need a birthday present for Meg."

After viewing the exhibition of huts, cooking vessels made from clay and grass, the museum director told us everything there was to know about Tswana beer making. The Americans oohed and aahed and took lots of photographs.

"Beer - that's my kinda thing, hey Bob?"

Next, we stopped for lunch at a cheerfully painted restaurant on Serowe's dusty thoroughfare. The place was run by a sweaty Scotsman and his fat Tswana wife. We had a simple meal of hearty stew and samp, a mash of whole white maize kernels.

Surprisingly tasty.

We sat by a large window with the best view of Serowe. The view consisted of a great number of houses painted in shades of pink and green. Donkey carts plodded along at snail's pace between hooting motor cars.

Babies were strapped to their mothers' backs in bath towels. The women dawdled along the road in the middle of the traffic chaos. Serowe wasn't the bustling African market place I had imagined, either. What was Bobonong like, I wondered, and the Tuli Block? I shouldn't get distracted too much from my mission in Botswana.

But I did get distracted.

Tony and I were invited to barbecues, which were called braais around here. Our hosts were mostly South African contractors, who worked at the mine in Selebi Phikwe. An American teacher, who lived in a hippie-style house in the hills, far from the main road was our most unusual host.

Of course, everybody thought that I was Tony's girlfriend and we were teased mercilessly about not being hitched yet.

Women were either wives or fiancées in this close-knit society. Not twin sisters of missing girlfriends. We kept quiet and smiled.

People in Southern Africa — black or other-skinned — were rather hospitable. They were also rather religious. In a Christian sense.

On weekends, Tswanas could be seen wearing long robes and church 'uniforms'. They congregated underneath large trees, singing, drumming.

Purple was for Catholics and white and green for apostolic church members. Groups of women in bright red garb would often meet at bus stops, but I never found out to which church they belonged. Some of the white women wore white doilies on their heads on their way to church. Astonishing.

The season was moving into early summer and I soon learned the importance of wearing sun block and a hat during the day. My arms had turned an angry red after hiking to a deserted settlement, once built in the hills west of Palapye for the McAlpine Company.

I could feel that my face and neck didn't look much better and it took a good few days, before my skin started to peel. A painful lesson.

As time dragged on, I wondered if it was wise to be so secretive about my identity. Perhaps someone had information about Claire's case and would have told me. But it was too late to change my story now. There had to be another way.

I should be making contact with Gaborone. The central police headquarters and the British High Commission. Just that communication with Gaborone was still difficult.

Mr. Poppelmeyer categorically refused to make the

telephone at the training centre available for private calls. I had managed to phone the British High Commission once from the Botsalo Hotel, but had to give up after five minutes of holding to the tune of Greensleeves.

Adding to my woes, I couldn't discuss salient details at the hotel without risking undue attention. What could I do but wait for Tony to take me to Gaborone.

I didn't have long to wait.

The following weekend, Tony decided to take a day trip to Gaborone. At last!

Gabs could have passed for a small country town in Britain. But it had the regal appearance and bearing of a capital. The flow of traffic was unhurried. The roads were dusty but properly tarred. There was the occasional traffic light and even a few roundabouts.

We took a tour around town and I saw spacious houses with lush palm gardens. Bougainvillea bushes in shades of pink, purple and red spilled over walls and climbed into majestic blue-flowering jacaranda trees. I was enthralled by the beauty of Gaborone. Plants I had only ever seen in British indoor flowerpots grew hugely in the open air.

In the centre of town was the shopping mile, also ingeniously called 'The European Mall'. Not at all like our mall in Palapye.

This mall stretched from a monument in the east all the way to the government buildings in the west. There were banks, a book store and a supermarket, a cinema, a couple of clothing shops, a hardware store and a curio shop. Consulates and offices completed the picture.

In other words: civilization! The British High Commission was just across the road and although there were other smaller malls in Gaborone, city life was happening right here.

*Claire has walked along these streets*, I thought woefully. She must have bought warm bedding in one of those shops.

In the middle of the mall, the multi-storied President Hotel graciously oversaw the pedestrian precinct. Broad stairs led the way to a popular restaurant on a large, shady terrace. The bustling mall came close to the African market I had imagined.

The book store was well stocked and I cheaply purchased a couple of Jane Austen classics. There was even a copy of Grandpa's earlier work 'El Jadida' in the historical fiction section. I bought the copy.

On the way out, I bumped into a portly gentleman in a light blue safari suit. Although it had been my fault, he apologized to me. How polite. "Ah sorry, no matata," he said. Roughly translated, it means 'no problem'. The word sorry was useful and versatile.

My trolley bumped by mistake into an ample behind inside Corner's Supermarket and the answer to my stammered apologies was 'Ah sorry, madam, no matata.'

To greet people in the street was an important part of Tswana etiquette. Even in the capital, nobody could just walk past without being polite. So, I respectfully greeted two elderly ladies, who gave me curious looks in the supermarket's fruit and vegetable section. The opening signal!

"Dumelang, bo-mma."

"Dumela, mma." The matrons nodded smiling approval and walked past.

I would have liked to meet with Claire's former colleagues or go to the British High Commission. But it was a weekend. Tony's priority was to shop for necessities. Before we left, we had lunch at the Gaborone Sun Hotel some ways off the mall. Then we had to get back to Palapye.

I couldn't believe my eyes, when cows were herded through the city streets right in front of traffic. Tony said, they were probably on their way to the big abattoir in Lobatse.

"Where did you and Claire stay here in Gabs?" I asked Tony randomly." Where about is this company house?"

"Oh somewhere over there —" he waved his hand without

looking.

"I would like to see it. Can't we quickly drive past?" Perhaps I thought I would pick up Claire's scent there or that I would have an epiphany.

"Rather not now. Next time maybe," he mumbled.

I knew that Tony was still avoiding other expatriates. My sister's disappearance had caused a small scandal in those circles. And anyway, he avoided everything to do with Claire.

"What am I supposed to do?" I wailed as we waited in traffic. "I'm getting absolutely nowhere with my search for Claire."

"Well, you could come to Gabs on your own and stay for a few days with Uli Winckler and his family," Tony suggested. We saw the backside of the last cow disappear behind some trees and drove on.

"Uli is a senior guy at the Automotive College and his wife Rita is just terrific. I'm sure they won't mind if you stay with them. You can catch a lift with one of the mining guys next week and I'll fetch you on the weekend. If Poppelmeyer doesn't need me, that is."

That sounded almost as if Tony tried to get rid of me.

"What, and risk another marriage proposal?"

"Yes —" Tony had to laugh.

"What about you, then, don't you want to come with me?" We had to stop a red light.

"I, I can't...not...not yet," he suddenly stuttered.

"What if I find out something important about Claire?" I probed. We had to talk about her, so why not now?

"I have to work and just can't deal with it right now, okay?"

*There we go again,* I thought and stopped probing. I didn't want to fight and what was I supposed to do without Tony's support?

"We have to talk about this sometime, Tony." We drove onto the main road again.

"I know. But not just now." Why ever not? Oh, he could drive me nuts sometimes!

"Okay, then I will go by myself," I pushed. "What about Monday?" Why wait any longer?

"I'll give them a call on Monday," Tony promised.

But then nothing came of it. On Monday, the English teacher still had not returned back from her village in the Okavango Delta. She had no phone.

Tony was head of department. he couldn't wait any longer and begged me to take over her classes. The last term of the year was vitally important and exams had to be prepared.

"We urgently need a substitute," he said.

"What if this teacher has also disappeared?" I said. Who knew what could happen out there in the bush?

"I doubt that. More likely that she had to go to a funeral or a wedding. Maybe she simply changed her mind and doesn't want to work here anymore. Time works differently in Botswana, you know."

"I've noticed that. But what about the exams, doesn't she care about the students?"

Tony just shrugged his shoulders. "Who knows what she's thinking. Nothing seems to compare to a good old funeral around here. Chances are she'll be back before the exams."

"But Tony, I've never taught anybody anything - ever," I groaned.

"Doesn't matter. You have a degree in linguistics. That counts as a qualification around here."

"I don't know —"

"Please help me out, please," he begged.

What was I supposed to do? I couldn't let Tony down. Oh well, no matata.

My visit to the Wincklers in Gaborone had to be put on hold for a while. Instead, classes needed to be prepared and I prayed that I wouldn't make a complete fool of myself.

A few nights before my debut lesson, I woke up scratching all over. I felt for my alarm clock. 1:34 am. Ouch! I jumped out of bed and switched the bedside lamp on.

An army of red ants was trekking right down the centre of the mattress and onto the floor. And they were all over me!

I pulled my pajamas off me and wiped my arms and legs in a panic. The nasty little fire ants were biting relentlessly.

I bravely ripped the sheets and covers off, piled them into the bathtub and let water run over the linen. Ants hated water.

Then I took a shower. Oh, what was wrong with the water? Why didn't it run quicker? I watched the last of the red-brown critters disappear down the gurgling drain amid the soapy foam.

My skin was still itchy, but at least I could put on another pyjama. Where was the insect spray? The bright yellow bottle of 'Instant Death' was on top of the fridge, where Tony also kept the spirals that were burned at night to keep the mosquitoes at bay.

I grabbed the spray and ran back into the room.

Although I hated anything to do with poison - this was an emergency. I pushed the bed away from the wall and sure enough, the ants came crawling through a hole just above the skirting board.

Tony's sleepy face appeared in the door. The commotion had been enough to wake even a sound sleeper like him. Great, he could help me get rid of the ants!

"What you doing?" he asked and yawned broadly.

"Red ants!" I sounded hysterical. "In my bed, everywhere."

I could still feel the burning bites of the little devils all over me.

Tony yawned. "Oh no, sorry 'bout that. Spray's on fridge." He turned around and tottered back into his room to go back to sleep.

"Thanks," I said as he closed his door. "For nothing."

I copiously sprayed the skirting with 'Instant Death' and felt like dropping dead myself from the smell alone. I opened the window and moved into the guest room.

Luckily, it had been only fire ants and not a large hunting spider or worse, a scorpion or snake. My standards of what was normal were shifting by the day.

During my near insect-free existence in Cambridge, I would have had a heart attack at the mere sight of a tiny spider on the bathroom wall.

I soon forgot about the ants and snakes and scorpions and fell asleep.

Only to wake up to another African morning with birdsong, the crowing of roosters and incessant donkey braying. This morning would turn into a scorching day, so I jumped out of bed to make the best of a few cool hours before midday.

Before long, Tony's word processor droned away, printing out worksheet after worksheet.

There were still piles of documents to go through and the first day of term drew closer by the minute.

# CHAPTER 4

Suddenly, everything was about school. Aptitude tests, study plans, time sheets. I had no idea what I was doing. I just did what Tony said I should do. He was the teacher and knew the drill after all.

Africa began to grow on me. I no longer missed the trappings of modern living quite so painfully. It had become quite normal to wear shorts and t-shirts instead of smart clothes. And make-up was more of an after-thought.

I had the feeling that I was getting closer to my goal. At least I had seen Gaborone and could sleep over there at a family called Winckler, if necessary. And my Setswana made progress. Life was peachy.

Nothing could have been further from the truth.

One afternoon I returned to the house from a trip to the shops. A young man was sitting on the doorstep, waiting. When he saw me walking up the driveway, he jumped up.

It was unusual for a stranger to come into the housing complex, unless they were family or friends of employees. He was tall and well-mannered, dressed in a clean white golf shirt and jeans. Perhaps he was a cousin of Neo's.

"Dumela ra, le kai?" I greeted him in the proper manner.

"Dumela mma. Re teng, re teng. Wena o tsoga?" The young man answered and showered me with a speech in Setswana that left me dumbfounded. I just shook my head and tried to speak English with him.

"Are you looking for a job?" I asked.

"Job, job?" he shrugged his shoulders, confused. Oh dear.

"Did Neo send you? Our neighbours need a gardener,

not us. Perhaps you should introduce yourself —" I was about to send him over to Mrs. Poppelmeyer, but he didn't understand. Obviously he had come for some other reason.

"You must be Tsanana's boyfriend, then. Let's see, if she is still in the house," I said and took out my keys.

"Ga ke na —" The young man shook his head and walked away from the door.

"Tsanana, Tsanana! Can you come here please?" I called. There was no reply.

"She must have left already." I turned around, but the man was nowhere to be seen.

*Now that's odd,* I thought and walked back to the gate, catching a glimpse of a white golf shirt by the main entrance to the complex. Then he was gone.

Somebody on the other side of the road disappeared quickly behind one of the empty houses. Odd.

Tsanana worked for Alfred the next day, so we had a brief chat over the fence.

"Oh madam, the young man, she come yesterday and I ask what do you want. He say she want to see madam. Mma Bridget. I say not here, come later. I leave and he sit down here." Tsanana pointed to the doorstep.

"Yes, that's where I found him when I came home, but we didn't understand each other and he left."

"I not know, madam." Tsanana shrugged her shoulders.

Neither Tony nor Neo had an explanation, so I tried to forget about the encounter and got on with my lesson preparations. I grasped only much later how important a chat with this young man could have been or why he had run for the hills.

This language barrier was such a nuisance. Tsanana taught me already as much as possible. How she managed to do this, while she washed and cleaned, is still a mystery to me.

One day I asked her about the shouting conversations between locals I had witnessed in the street and was flattened by her answer.

"No madam, they not fight!" she laughed heartily. "No, people talk normal shouting. Better than quiet voice. Then people will think speak secret about them."

Who would have thought of that? Yelling was used to dispel suspicions of gossip!

She also told me about the Kgosi, who was the chief of a tribe. One of his many tasks was to sit in judgement every so often and mete out punishment, if rules were violated. If problems arose between a married couple, the families got involved and even the Kgosi. This might entail the whipping with a stick on the back of an abusive husband in the kgotla, the village gathering place. I had been to a kgotla meeting before, but only to honour the new principal of the training centre.

Court days seemed to be an internal Tswana matter. Honestly, I don't know what I would have done, if punishment of wayward husbands had been on the programme.

Marriage was a complicated matter. Lengthy negotiations between the clans were necessary, before men were allowed to pay lobola for a wife. The dowry usually included cattle, appliances and some money. A man had to provide and prove his mettle as a protector. Women with children were desirable, because they had proven their fertility. Tsanana had two young sons.

"Why are you not married, then?" I asked her.

"No man must hit and treat me bad. I want be free." Tsanana snapped her fingers to make a point. Who knew that our clever maid had a feminist streak in her?

Tsanana was proud that she worked for teachers. Teachers were highly regarded morutis. Strangely, a moruti could be a 'teacher' and also a 'priest'.

I understood that she felt honoured to educate me, the moruti, as I was about to share my knowledge of the English language with the students at the training centre. I wondered whether the teaching profession was met with similar respect in

England.

One morning Tsanana came in with a nasty cut on her finger and I asked her if she had seen a doctor about it.

"No, madam," she laughed cheerfully. "I go to witchdoctor. To sangoma."

I hadn't heard of witchdoctors before Tsanana mentioned them, but assumed that they were shamans of some sort. I wasn't too far off the mark. Witchdoctors were rather more important in African society than a doctor in Europe. Next to the Kgosi, the witchdoctor was the most important person in the village.

"What does a witchdoctor do?" I inquired.

"Oh many things. Sangoma heal with muti medicine and helps with tokoloshe..."

"With what? Toklosh?"

"No, madam, t o k o l o s h e," Tsanana pronounced the word slowly.

"What is that?"

"Tokoloshe is small people."

Did she mean dwarves as in pygmies? "Small people?"

"Yes, and ghost people." She struggled to explain.

"Ghosts?"

That sounded thrilling. Spirits maybe, African magic.

"Yes, bad ghost. Naughty."

"Oh. Why bad, are they dangerous?"

"They naughty. She come in the night and scratch children on back and hurts cattle with the head." She described a bony ridge from the forehead to the nape of the neck. It sounded more like some fantastic creature like the bogey man.

"Bed is on bricks, so they cannot come. They small." Tsanana's face was serious. My goodness! I had to think about that for a moment.

"How does a witchdoctor help?" I asked her.

"He throw bones and gives muti medicine and do spell."

Right, maybe that's what I needed. A sangoma, who could use a spell to help me find Claire. Throwing bones sounded grisly though and I wondered what it meant. I didn't know at the time how badly I needed a sangoma.

A couple of days later, Tsanana's finger was purple, not from the infection or ready to fall off, but because of the antiseptic Gentian Violet.

"Ah Tsanana, the witchdoctor gave you Lekgoa medicine?" I asked her.

"No madam. Sangoma muti not work. I go to clinic."

No matter how hard I tried to understand this culture, there was always something else I didn't comprehend.

My attempts at speaking Setswana, earned me even broader smiles at the police station, but didn't seem to speed things up one bit.

How was I supposed to gather any information in Bobonong and Mochudi at this rate? My talent for languages let me down badly. I needed a new plan.

And then it was the first day of school.

Who knew that teaching could be enjoyable? There were 31students in my class. They were all aspiring secretaries. And as attentive as any teacher could wish for.

After my baptism of fire, when I still worried whether there was food stuck between my teeth or a button open on my blouse, I settled down into a pleasant routine.

The aptitude test revealed that many of the young ladies had only a limited knowledge of the English language.

The eldest student had even been an English teacher in a village near Francistown, but she couldn't exactly speak the language. That didn't stop her from trying. I knew that despite my shortcomings, I had to make an effort myself.

I stumbled over such unpronounceable names like Ogaisitse, Tshidiso, Galisano, Gasinone, Daitapelo and Keitatole and practiced them with Neo's help. Although I had absolutely no clue when it came to teaching techniques, I soon got the hang of it. Tsanana's lessons also proved to be useful. When my students looked at their feet while speaking to me, I understood why.

Tony helped where he could and Mr. Matija gave me the well-meaning tip to 'cane them if they don't listen'. A stick or ruler that came crashing down on desks and sometimes on the students seemed to be an indispensable teaching instrument.

Not in *my* classroom.

The girls studied well and could even be comical at times.

I often put on pink lipstick and one day the entire class had pink lips. All of them. If you wanted to become a successful person like your teacher, you had to copy her lipstick, a sure-fire tool for success. I tried not to laugh and ignored the pink lips. The lipstick phase didn't last very long. Students were not allowed to wear make-up and another teacher made them wash their faces.

Despite my impatience at being stuck in Palapye, I took my new role very seriously. The regular English teacher didn't come back, but I couldn't just run away.

Ironically, I earned only 100 Pula a month. A measly sum even by local standards. A maid often earned more money than that, but I was only a temporary substitute after all.

Mrs. Poppelmeyer seemed to have something to do with it. Everybody knew that principal Poppelmeyer did nothing without first consulting his wife. I didn't mind and just carried on without complaining. No matata.

Only one student by the name of Susan began to give me grief. She was sixteen and rather bossy. Susan would get up in the middle of a lesson to close the windows, or she walked out of the classroom or back-chatted the inexperienced new Lekgoa teacher.

Her behaviour became so irritating that I spoke to her mother Tshidi, who was a cleaner at the school. Tshidi listened with a horrified expression.

"Oh madam, sorry, she is very naughty," she said and promised to talk some sense into her daughter.

Susan didn't come to class on Monday or Tuesday. Then I heard from Mr. Matija that she had run away to

Gaborone, where her father was a policeman. What I didn't know then was that talking sense into a child, who didn't respect an elder, might involve corporal punishment.

Susan had been summoned by the elders of her clan, who sacrificed a lot for the youngster's education. When she became cocky, the elders had given her a good hiding. Susan was retrieved from her father's house a week later.

I felt guilty and decided to be more lenient with the girl when she came back to school. I needn't have worried. Susan was no longer disrespectful and as docile as a lamb from there on. Oh dear, that's not what I'd had in mind.

Suddenly there were only weeks left until the year-end exams and I hadn't made any progress with the police whatsoever. Were they being deliberately uncooperative or just lethargic?

As much as I enjoyed teaching by now, I couldn't wait to get to Gaborone.

Summer had arrived. Not the lovely mellow English summer. No, summertime in Botswana was of a different sort altogether. A fierce sun beat down on us, taking turns with fierce thunderstorms that battered the parched land into renewed growth. Only to make way for more scorching heat. Would I ever get used to this heat?

Insect life exploded and mosquitoes, cockroaches and spiders were ever-present. I began to understand the importance of the little fly net umbrellas that were placed over the food. And why insect spray was indispensable.

The cooler mornings were buzzing with a flurry of activity, but everybody tried to take more breaks as the day wore on. I got used to it. Also, having to speak over the constant whizzing of ceiling fans in the classroom. But I had my limits.

A hot afternoon was bearable, sitting in a comfortable chair on Tony's shady porch. With a jug of some ice-cold juice right next to me. And unless there was a power failure, a fan was trained directly at my face.

From the porch, the view was rows of staff houses, enclosed like chicken cages. In the distance, behind the spanking new training centre above the tree, were the misty hills tops. Tony's chicken cage was now lined with a green motsetsi hedge.

I sometimes mustered the energy to read letters or page through ancient English magazines. It was too hot to listen to music and even for feeling sad.

I no longer tried to talk to Tony about Claire. It was just too hot. And I no longer asked myself what he was still doing here, so close to Claire. I just wanted to get through this heat.

Zaheeda writes about her extended family and some football player she likes. Diane complains about my impossible clients. Everybody wants their translations yesterday. Or was it the other way around?

During the weeks before the exams, most classes ceased.

At last, I could look forward to another trip to Gaborone. With its malls and cool hotel bars. Tony and I had to leave early on a weekday morning to avoid the midday sun. I had a vague plan.

I'd start with the British High Commission. Then the central police headquarters. Grandpa had already announced my impending visit at the High Commission.

Tony went to the bank and ran some errands, while I was busy in meetings. This time we wanted to hook up later at the President Hotel.

So off to the High Commission I went. To my disappointment, I came away with nothing except polite chit chat and sincere affirmations of how sorry everyone was about my sister's disappearance. Thanks for nothing. What did I expect?

The hot air hit me when I stepped into the street. It was just a short walk to the central police station, but I was drenched by the time I arrived.

Surely somebody here was able to clarify the circumstances. These were the police headquarters. Like

Scotland Yard. I would deal with experienced detectives and not with country yokels.

Indeed, detective Sidney Sibeko came across as a seasoned policeman in his forties, who just wanted to get on with his job.

A few pleasantries and praise for the fact that I had greeted him in Setswana later, he handed me the folder on the case. A wad of typed pages, stapled together repeatedly.

This must be the report I had been waiting to see! Handwritten notes were scattered between machine-typed lines. They were largely illegible.

But the main report mentioned a dent in the front of the car with goat hair stuck to it. Claire must have hit an animal, a goat. Nobody had mentioned a thing to me about Claire hitting a goat. Until now.

I read about the lack of conclusive fingerprints. That was not exactly news. Then I asked questions.

And at last I received answers. Just not the ones I wanted to hear. Tony had been a suspect at first. That was a routine thing. There was neither motive nor opportunity, so that was dropped again.

His apparent lack of interest and my subsequent arrival had also not gone unnoticed. But since I kept asking questions at the police station in Palapye, no further steps had been taken. And here I thought the police in Palapye were uninterested. Instead, our seemingly passive, rural police had sent reports through to Gaborone all along!

The good detective wasn't exactly enthusiastic about my theory that someone could have helped my injured sister.

"We have no evidence for that or as to her whereabouts at this stage," detective Sibeko said in impeccable English.

"But perhaps she is unconscious and somebody found her. Perhaps in a remote place in the Tuli Block."

"I believe that this would be near impossible, Miss Reinhold. There are many ... dangers out in the bush."

His remark choked me off. An icy shiver moved down my back. Images of feeding lions and hyenas flashed past my inner eye. Stop it at once, I scolded myself, focus!

"Is it possible then that she somehow left the country?" I asked, trying to sound composed.

"That sounds daring, but as I mentioned, there is no evi…"

"…dence as to her whereabouts, I know." I finished the sentence for him. He cleared his throat.

"Apart from this, we have already examined the possibility. It is however difficult to determine in the border area. And even if we assume that your sister survived such an accident and lost her way in the direction of the border. She would hardly manage on her own."

"My sister did survive the accident, I just know it!"

I couldn't allow him to take this from me. The only thing that kept me sane.

"We are still treating her as a missing person," he said.

"Good."

"We have also questioned the people in Mochudi and nobody recalls seeing a white woman or how the car was brought to the field."

"What if these people are lying? How is the car supposed to have ended up there?" I asked.

"And what would the motive be? We cannot pinpoint yet how the car got there or be sure of anything at this stage."

Right, there was a problem with the motive.

Detective Sidney Sibeko sighed. He wanted to help. "We will keep you informed of any new developments. Don't give up hope, Miss Reinhold."

"I won't."

I closed the report, looked at the cover page and hesitated. The heading read Stratton/Reinhold – Claire, Reported missing: 16 July 1988. Stratton?

"I'm sorry detective Sibeko, but there must be a mistake. My sister's surname is Reinhold. Stratton is her boyfriend's surname."

He checked in the file and shook his head. "No, Miss Reinhold, that's no mistake. Date of Birth: 27/03/1966;

Place of Birth: Cambridge, United Kingdom; Marital Status: married, 2 June 1988 in London; Name of Spouse: Anthony Lewis Stratton." He held the document under my nose and showed me the entry I had failed to decipher.

I must have turned really pale.

"Are you feeling alright, Miss Reinhold?" he asked and sat me down again. "Would you like some water?"

"No, thank you. I'm just taken…by surprise. I didn't know she was married."

"I'm sorry. Didn't your brother-in-law tell you?"

"No, he didn't." *Why didn't you, Tony?* I thought exhausted. *Why on earth can't you talk to me?*

Detective Sibeko gave me a few moments to find my bearings. Then he didn't lose much time in dismissing me. "If there is nothing else, Miss Reinhold…"

There was an indifferent undertone in his voice. He wanted to get back to his regular work.

"Yes, yes of course. Thank you for your time, detective."

I rose and handed the document back. He shook my limp hand and I walked numbly out, between bustling officers and the clatter of typewriters.

"You look so pale, sis. What did the police detective say to you?" Tony seemed at least interested.

I just gave him the basics, that there were no clues yet, about the accident and so on, leaving out the bit about the lions and hyenas. I needed to get my head around the fact that Tony and Claire were actually married and that he hadn't told me a thing during all this time I'd shared his house.

Unbelievable that not even Claire had been honest with me. My own twin sister. Here I was in a country I never intended to visit before she moved there. Had given up my old life to find her. And she had not even told me that she was getting married. Had it just slipped her mind? It was difficult not to feel betrayed and it was enough to nudge me into action at last.

I had the entire trip back to Palapye to get used to the

news. In the evening I spoke to my mother from the phone in the lobby at the Botsalo Hotel and had my nerves under control again. I couldn't share with her that Claire and Tony were married. Not yet. So my parents only found out much later.

'Are you sure?' my Mom asked. 'An accident?'

'Yes, that's what the detective said. And in the report was something about goat hair in a dent on the front fender.'

'Oh my word! Was there…any blood?' she forced the question out.

'No, no blood. Only some of the goat's with the hair. And the fingerprints are inconclusive. Just enough evidence that she had hit this goat somewhere.'

'But, what does the police say, how does this change the situation?' My mother's relief was audible.

'How? It changes everything. She might still be out there in the bush. Hurt. On her own or with some strangers. And the police still can't figure out where she is!'

'Bridget, just listen to me, dear. Don't do anything rash! If Claire was hurt, how did she drive the car to this town…' Mom searched for the name.

'Mochudi,' I said.

'This town Mochudi in the middle of a field. That is not too far from Gaborone, is it? How long do you think did it take for someone to find her?'

'You're right, it doesn't make sense. But still, there isn't much in Mochudi. Just a very small place. And the detective told me that nobody saw her. Perhaps she was kidnapped somewhere!'

I looked around, worried that the receptionist or one of the hotel guests might have heard. Nobody was in earshot.

I lowered my voice. 'But that's impossible!'

'Well, there is a possibility. I heard on the news that girls are kidnapped and sold to men in the Middle East. They have just arrested a ring of human traffickers in

London. Perhaps girls are also kidnapped in your part of the world.'

'Bit of a long shot, Mom. I can't see that happening around here in the bush. And where do I even start trying to find out about that?'

'I could speak to your grandfather, maybe he has an idea...'

The conversation ended by me promising to look into the kidnap theory. All the time I had wanted to share the news that Claire was married.

Tony and Neo had waited in the bar for me and we decided to have dinner at the restaurant.

"What's wrong with you today? Too much sun on the brain?" Neo tried to tease me.

"Leave her alone, Neo. It was a long day and Bridget isn't feeling well."

"Sorry to hear it. Nothing serious I hope –"

The two of them carried on chatting about this and that, mostly work, and they seemed to be making plans for the weekend. When I was alone with Tony at last, I could hold back no longer.

"Tony..."

I hurled everything at him. That I didn't understand him. That I didn't understand Claire. He looked at me guiltily and confessed at once.

"I've been expecting this," he said.

"Why didn't you tell me? Why didn't Claire tell me?"

"We were planning a proper wedding with the family, after the two-year contract."

My face had to register some of the anger I felt.

"But not to say anything. Not even to me!"

"We got married on the sly in London to make it easier with the applications and visas. It was just in court and very unromantic." Tony seemed relieved that the cat was out of the bag.

"I don't understand."

"Claire didn't want to complicate things. She thought

you'd tell your parents and they would have told mine... fun and games," he said.

It was the first time I had heard him say Claire's name.

"My own sister doesn't know either if it makes you feel any better," Tony said.

"No it doesn't," I said. "But that means, you are actually my... brother-in-law." Saying it out loud made it more real - we were family.

"I guess so."

Tony's eyes watered. Perhaps there was hope after all.

"Why didn't you say anything all this time I've been here?" I asked.

"I don't know, it wasn't important anymore."

"Not important anymore? We want to find her, or not? Everything is important." I was dumbfounded.

"What for?"

As much as I was puzzled by his answer, I knew now that I couldn't stick around to find out why. I let it go.

"Never mind."

At least some of the awkwardness between us had dissipated.

I became as restless as Claire must have felt before she left England. I wanted action, needed to see detective Sibeko again. Something. Anything.

I knew it was high time to leave Palapye. Only a few weeks left, I said to myself. The exams would soon be over.

On the spur of the moment I decided to phone Kgomotso Min and Emily van Heerden. They had worked with Claire, knew her well. I took Tony's car one day and drove to the Hotel. Kgomotso wasn't there, so I spoke to Emily.

She was surprised that Claire's sister was in the country, but we arranged at once to meet in Gaborone on Saturday.

"We could meet at the Gaborone Sun Hotel for a drink," she suggested. "It's always full on a weekend, but we can sit somewhere private and chat. How does 10 o'clock sound, can you make it by then?"

No problem. I was determined.

Surprisingly, Tony agreed to drive and Neo also wanted to come. We were almost punctual. 'African time'. Being about 30 minutes late, was still quite acceptable after all. They dropped me off at the main entrance to the hotel and went to see friends. I would then find my way back to the Mall and meet them for lunch. Perfect.

Emily sat in a corner with a view of the swimming pool. I knew immediately that it was her. She was as pretty as Claire had described her, wearing a cool linen shirt over white capri-pants with her sunglasses pushed on top of the light brown hair. A confident young woman.

We talked for a while – with interruptions. She greeted people all the time. Apparently, she knew almost everyone in Gaborone.

Emily introduced me as a visiting friend without missing a beat and deftly blocked off lengthy small talk.

I decided to trust her and Emily responded with open frankness. She told me what had happened at the office in July. At last, I could fill in the blanks.

The staff at Packer Engineering had been questioned by the police. They had been instructed to keep quiet about the details about the case with outsiders, until investigations had been concluded. That basically meant forever.

And it explained why the news hadn't reached our remote Palapye. Emily was making an exception with me, because I was family and tried to find my sister.

"Does anybody else know why you're here?" She took a sip of her rock shandy.

We had already thrashed out the possibilities of Claire's whereabouts and had come to the conclusion that my sister was probably unconscious and cared for by good people in a very remote place. It was just speculation, of course. It didn't matter. It was a relief to talk straight about everything with somebody.

"There is Claire's husband, Tony Stratton. I'm sure you've met him before. He lives in Palapye now. That's why I'm there. We are pretending that I'm his girlfriend and I thought he was as keen as me to find more, but I can't get through to him. He doesn't seem at all interested to help find Claire."

Emily knew of course that Claire was married.

"Shock probably," she suggested and finished her orange-coloured rock shandy.

"Could be...I also have nightmares sometimes."

"Sorry. That will take a while to come right, I guess. Did you see anyone about it – the nightmares, I mean?"

"In Palapye?" I asked.

"No, back in England," she laughed when she saw my face.

"To be honest, I didn't even give it a thought," I said. "With Mom being so cut up about the whole thing. And then I had to prepare so quickly for Africa. And Dad was so... bitter. Men have a funny way of showing emotion. Just look at Tony."

"Tony might still come around, you know," she said.

"Let's hope so. I thought it would be easier with his help. Palapye is so close to Bobonong and all. But it's tough on my own. Frankly, I don't know anymore what I'm doing in Palapye."

"Welcome to Africa. It would be better if you move to Gabs. Don't you know somebody where you can stay?"

The glare of the swimming pool prompted Emily to put her sunglasses on.

"Tony mentioned a family he knows."

"Then what are you waiting for?"

"The exams...and, oh I don't know. I thought that things would just fall into place," I wailed.

"Well not just like that, all by themselves, that's for sure. Would you like another Coke Light?"

Emily gave me her private number. I was to call her, in case I found the courage to move to Gaborone. A quick look at my watch confirmed that it was time to leave. I wasn't sure how things would turn out. At least I had kicked things off And found an ally in Emily.

That weekend I also finally met the Winckler family in

Gaborone and fell immediately in love with them.

Rita Winckler, tall and elegant with long greying tresses, didn't give a damn about etiquette or what others thought of her. Her natural composure surely kept the common species of gossips in check. And there was apparently an entire army of them in Gaborone.

I liked Rita from the start and we should gradually become close friends. While helping with plates of food in the kitchen, I explained to her the real reason why I had come to Botswana. Her husband Uli, Tony and Neo played ball in the garden with the girls. We could hear them shriek with delight through the open windows.

"You must be a little patient," Rita said. "Otherwise nothing will come of it."

"I know, but I'm battling with that."

"Still, it's a good start to move to Gaborone and I will help you wherever I can."

"Thank you." This was a great weekend!

She promised not to tell anyone and never did. I had made a second friend in one day and my Gaborone network was growing. It was the closest thing to what I had left behind in England.

When Tony told them during lunch about my plans to move to Gaborone, Uli immediately agreed to take me in. The Wincklers didn't seem to mind the temporary extension to their family and vowed on their honour to protect me from gossip mongers.

A constant flow of friendly banter between them kept everyone in stitches, while their two daughters were rolling their eyes in teenage mortification.

Twelve-year-old Jasmin wore braces and took after her mild-mannered father. Thirteen-year-old Adrienne grappled with the endless demands of puberty. The Wincklers had adopted her in Thailand und she was just as German as the rest of the family.

Uli Winckler was an engineer and instructor at the

Gaborone Automotive College.

He stood as tall as his wife, but was stout and very blond. Uli wore khaki suits on a daily basis. In the eighties, they were the acceptable work uniform. Uli was a genius in communication and turned out to be rather well-connected.

When we check the time, it's already too late to drive back to Palapye, and the Wincklers invite us to stay overnight.

No matata.

The two boys share the guest bedroom and I sleep in Adrienne's bed. I felt part of the family already.

The last few weeks in Palapye flew by.

Summer was upon us with a vengeance now. That meant heat and rain. And lots of it. I had learned from Neo that Pula was the Setswana word for rain. Pula also means 'blessing' and was the Botswana currency.

One could expect at least one shower a day and it never just rained. It rained cats and dogs, regularly flattening the flowers I had coaxed from the sandy soil.

Even without fierce thunderclaps and lightening that made people jump out of bed at night, the rain was a force of nature no umbrella had a chance against. Sink-holes appeared even in newly tarred roads. And the sandy roads that everyone used, turned into impassable mud.

A charming bedroom companion had moved in with me. A tiny gecko began to patrol the ceiling, spying out intruding insects.

I named it Hubert.

Every day Hubert inhabited a different corner of the ceiling, looking at the world upside down. A welcome guest, as Tony assured me.

One night I had gone to bed and as I nodded off into dreamland, something plopped into my water glass on the bedside table. I suspected that one of the large moths managed to slip through the window's fly screen. I switched on the bedside lamp and discovered that it wasn't a moth at all. It was my little friend the gecko thrashing about wildly.

Hubert splashed around in desperation. How could a light-footed gecko lose its grip on the ceiling? I couldn't bring myself to touch a lizard, so I quickly picked up the glass and chucked the water with gecko out the window.

I missed Hubert, but soon another gecko moved to my bedroom ceiling. Perhaps it was the same one. Who could tell the difference? Having a gecko slip and fall on my face while I was sleeping didn't exactly rank at the top of my list of favourites, but the new Hubert balanced cleverly and took care of the mosquitoes at night.

During exam week, little Samantha Jones was born in Cardiff with a birth weight of 5 pounds, as her proud father Alfred kept reminding everybody. Judith and Samantha would arrive as soon as the baby was big enough to travel.

The new Dad was showered goodwill. Poppelmeyers summoned him to dinner and Mr. Pielsticker, the good-humoured manager of the Botsalo Hotel, treated us teachers to a bottle of Montaigne Brut champagne.

But there was more celebration planned. Alfred Jones had purchased two goats for Friday night through Mr. Matija. The goats were barbecued on a spit-braai and eaten Botswana-style, together with steaks, beer and salads.

The cleaning ladies offered to help against a good salary. The barbecue was to take place in one of the halls on the school grounds. Tradition demanded that everybody - invited or not - was welcome to participate in the joyous revelry.

Many participated.

Nobody quite understood why so much fuss was made about the birth of a daughter. But incidentally it was also National Independence Day. And that had to be celebrated.

The Matija children danced and sang traditional songs all day. Their effort was echoed by festive noise from the village that lasted all night, robbing poor Ethel Poppelmeyer of her beauty sleep.

There was so much food, that the school messenger's wife waited outside for her husband to bring scores of raw steaks. She hid the meat in plastic bags and carried it off on his bike. That was teamwork if I ever saw one. Half of Palapye enjoyed steaks on this National Independence Day.

I was late for the party, because my concerned parents still phoned every Friday night at 8 o'clock sharp to check if I had not...well... disappeared.

The celebrations didn't stop.

On Saturday, all the morutis at the training centre had been invited to the funeral of a high-level village elder. At a village not far from Bobonong!

"Can't I get out of this funeral, Tony?" I moaned. "It feels so morbid after all that's happened. And I'm only a substitute teacher anyway."

"Why, do you think that something bad has happened to Claire?" Tony asked.

"No, of course not," I quickly changed my tune. What else was I supposed to say?

"Then I don't see why you shouldn't want to go. It's an honour for us to be invited by the Kgosi."

I relented, although it meant getting up at the crack of dawn for the bumpy ride to the remote village. I climbed sleepily into the back of the school's pick-up truck, called a bakkie. We had to be there by 7:00 am. Everyone was covered in blankets against the cold and huddled together. The bakkie rattled past quiet homesteads while I tried to make up for lost sleep. Luckily it didn't rain.

We arrived when things were about to begin. We sat down with all the other guests in the sandy gathering place in the middle of the village. A tall young man in a white golf shirt walked past and I had to look twice. But it wasn't the man, who had been to Tony's house.

The speeches dragged on. Perhaps it was a good thing that I didn't understand a word. I sat in the cold sand and looked around. To our right, a number of village wives stirred the food in large, black tripods over open fires.

African hospitality knew no bounds and everybody, invited

or not, would get their share of the funeral feast later.

I desperately wished I could stand up and stretch my legs, but I couldn't let our Kgosi down. So I tried to look as solemn as possible, while shifting my weight ever so elegantly from one butt cheek to the other.

The speeches took more than two hours. We stood up on wobbly legs. Everyone lined up outside one of the huts I had studied during the endless address. So we did the same.

I began to wake up and realized that we were expected to file past the open coffin! A proper moruti had to show respect for the dead. Creepy.

A woman in traditional garb with heavily beaded braids walked around between the huts. I caught a glimpse for just a moment, then she was gone.

"Who was that?" I whispered to Neo behind me in the queue.

"Who?" Neo whispered back.

"The woman with the long, beaded hair." I described what I had seen.

"Sounds like a sangoma."

"A sangoma? What is she doing here?"

"Helps the spirit of the dead join the forefathers," Neo answered.

My very first witchdoctor. Somehow she looked nothing like the wild-eyed sangoma in 'Shaka Zulu'.

I wondered why she didn't queue with the rest of us, then it was my turn to enter the hut, where the vigil was held. The deceased woman lay in state inside the coffin, with her hands folded on her chest. She seemed to sleep. It wasn't pleasant, but also not half as bad as I had imagined.

There was a sudden high-pitched screeching outside. I left the hut quickly and saw three young women throwing themselves around in the sand. Screaming and crying with the white of their eyes showing as if they were in a trance. Others tried to help them up, but the women were beside themselves.

It was a sight the expatriates among us were unprepared for.

"This is quite normal at Tswana funerals," Neo put us in the picture. "It's even expected from female relatives."

"Really?" I said.

"Yes, I hope it doesn't upset you guys."

"Bit strange, I'll say," Alfred mumbled.

Next thing we knew, we were stumbling up a stony footpath to a piece of ground shaded by thorn trees. A simple graveyard.

Pallbearers solemnly carried the coffin to an open hole in the ground. While the coffin was lowered, the three noisily grieving women tried to jump into the grave.

They were firmly taken away by villagers and a priest spoke a few winged words. As soon as the coffin was safely in the ground, the wake festivities began.

We teachers were directed to an elevated platform under a makeshift tent of red fabric. The other guests had to queue by the tripods for plates of food in the hot sun. The Kgosi and other dignitaries sat down with us and tried to make conversation to their best ability with Neo's help.

The Kgosi saw to it that our plates were refilled with samp and goat's meat that had been pounded into long fibrous strands. To my dismay I couldn't eat the toughest, driest meat I had ever come across. So I praised the goat's meat and stuck to the familiar coleslaw.

The sun was still high in the sky when we returned to Palapye. The kraals that had been so quiet in the wee hours of the morning were now teeming hives of activity.

Women carried firewood and water pots nimbly on their heads. Children ran alongside our bakkie, cupped their hands and called: "Ke batlá mádi, ke batlá mádi!" I want money, I want money.

At a crossing, the bakkie had to wait for a herd of goats and the children climbed onto the tires. A little boy of about six held up a meter-long snake.

"Oh, yuck! That thing is as long as the child," Tony cried.

"He wants to show us how clever he was, killing the

snake," Neo said.

"Wonderful. I hope it's not poisonous."

"No, it's not a poisonous snake."

Neo scolded them in a strict tone of authority. They immediately jumped off the car and ran back into the village.

He taught me to say 'Ga ke ná mádi', which meant 'I don't have money', to get rid of the little rascals in the next village.

I relaxed a little and took note of our surroundings. We were out in the bush, not in the Tuli Block, but close enough.

No chance of finding anything out about now. Perhaps it was my imagination, but I could feel Claire. How she laughed with us at the children's shenanigans.

I was stunned. Claire had to be here somewhere.

Close by.

# CHAPTER 5

My parents were understandably anxious. What was I still doing in Africa, if my efforts weren't showing any results?

How could I even begin to explain? I simply had to stay. I couldn't give up now. What if Claire was suddenly found somewhere in the Tuli Block and needed me? And there was still this very strong feeling that she was with me.

At the end of November, the year-end exams had been marked and Tony helped me move to Gabs.

My Gaborone-life began.

In Gabs, I no longer had to make my way through deep sand to get to the mall. In fact, I had to get used to being spoilt for choice. I got used to it quickly. After a few weeks I felt no longer like a country bumpkin in the big city lights.

The heat was also more bearable in the city. The Winckler residence was spacious and airy and a public swimming pool beckoned in walking distance across the field.

I still woke up to the crowing of roosters and harsh braying of donkeys and there were just as many spiders and cockroaches around. There was also a lot more entertainment. Pubs and restaurants vied for the attention of well-heeled customers and there was even a cinema.

You couldn't miss Rita walking down The Mall, wearing her flowing kaftans and the long locks, barely tamed with broad hair bands. She kept telling me that she tried to smoke less, while lightening up another cigarette, handling her two teenagers at the same time.

It was these little inconsistencies that made her even

more interesting. She took things in her stride and was a respected pillar of the fickle expat circles.

After two weeks Tony came for a visit. He kept some of the boxes with Claire's things in an outside room behind the garage and wanted to take something with him.

I decided to stay away from the room.

Princess the maid, lived with her daughter Mpho and one grandchild in the quarters adjacent to the storeroom. She clearly hoped that Tony would take his boxes so that her other two children, who wanted to find jobs in Gaborone, could move in. But her hopes were dashed when Tony took only one box with him to Palapye and she was grumpy for days.

Tony also took one puppy from the family dog's recent litter. A cute black Labrador backstreet special, we named Gina. Now that I no longer lived in Palapye, the little mutt with the white stripe on her chest, would keep him company.

Chunky, the bitch, cried for her puppy and Pauli, the Dad, howled when Tony pulled out of the driveway. Family or not, I felt relief.

I was certain Princess saw me, the young unmarried woman, as the third child in the family. Right down there in the hierarchy with Adrienne and Jasmin. She was a big Tswana woman of about fifty, always in a spiffy light-blue maid uniform that gave her an air of authority. She was very different to our gentle Tsanana in Palapye and ruled the Winckler household with an iron fist.

Princess had Uli and Rita well-trained. Besides paying her monthly salary, it was Uli's job to switch on the geyser in the kitchen, whenever Princess decided to wash the dishes, or he could very well do them by himself.

Rita had to cook dog food twice a week in a large aluminium pot. Mieliemeal mixed with so-called dog mince. The whole house stank during the procedure, but Princess didn't tolerate objections.

Rita also washed the family's underwear in the machine,

especially that of the females.

In Princess's belief, the mere sight of a slightly blood-soiled undie might start her periods again, and she would have none of that. Her daughter was called in to clean the windows and pack away towels into the upper cupboard shelves, because Princess was too plump and dignified to climb on a chair. As the head of her own family and being beyond child-bearing age, she could expect due respect.

Luckily she never commanded me around, but I stayed well out of her way when she was in a foul mood. Just to be on the safe side. On the other hand was Princess very proud of her heritage and patiently answered my questions about Tswana culture.

"What do you know about sangomas, Princess?" I asked her while she ironed Uli's dark blue safari suit.

"There are good sangomas, madam, and bad one. They kill and make muti with body part of children." I held my breath as she re-tied her light-blue headscarf. "Not medicine muti. Magic muti for success."

"But - how do they get the... the - body parts?"

"They steal young children and put hex on people. Bad, very bad people. Careful madam, not talk to bad sangoma."

Spine-chilling. According to her, wealthy and influential people made use of such services. I could only hope that Claire had not fallen into the claws of a bad sangoma. Stop thinking the worst, for goodness' sake! I scolded myself and stopped asking questions like that.

Princess taught me a thing or two about city customs. I was not allowed to rudely say 'Ke batla' (I want), if I wanted something. This was for uncouth country folk. Instead, I had to use the polite 'Ke kopa' or 'I would like'. 'Ketumetsi' meant 'Thank you', but the word 'please' didn't seem to exist in Setswana.

After a few days, Rita had sent me to her hairdresser. I inspected the results in the passage mirror. Not bad!

My hair was cut fashionably in dark layers bleached by

the sun. But there was something else. My eyes challenged me now. Yes, I was different.

One evening during dinner, we heard a pained cry coming from the garage. Then shouting. Alarmed, we stormed outside.

Princess came huffing and puffing up the driveway to tell us that someone had tried to break into the store room. She added triumphantly that the thief had met with a mousetrap set up by herself, the maid of the house. He had taken off, with his fingers still caught in the mousetrap. Uli was concerned. "Shouldn't we call the police?"

"No, master," Princess said determined. "Nothing missing here. She will not come back. Or his brothers. I told her a spook is looking after this house. He will kill all, who come here to steal. She will not come back!"

She grunted satisfied and went back to her room. We were speechless, but Princess's strategy seemed to work. There were no more trespassers.

The problem had been handled African style.

Rita didn't lose time to introduce me to her social circle. Carol Jenkins, a delightful working-class Geordie from Newcastle had invited us to her pre-Christmas party.

Carol was around thirty and rather beautiful with her blonde locks and delicate features. In Gaborone, she was a socialite of sorts. Devoted to her husband Len, who worked for an insurance company, and her two young sons Callum and Shawn, she led the existence of a typical expat wife.

The party was in full swing when Rita and I arrived. As far as I could tell, there were only women present. Oh joy, the dreaded Gaborone gossip machine at work!

"Ah, aren't you Emily's friend?" Perhaps she recognised me from the Gaborone Sun Hotel.

"Yes, actually," I said.

"Well, come along then Bridget, come along. Welcome to my modest home," Carol said in a broad Geordie accent.

The Jenkins lived in a crescent opposite the Gaborone Sun Hotel. The modest home was a quaint double-story house set in an English country garden.

Satan, the ancient beagle, barked hoarsely in one of the guest rooms as we walked to the back of the garden.

I found out soon enough that it was socially unacceptable not to be married or at least engaged. But Carol meant well and was determined to integrate me, the single gal, for Rita's sake.

The conversation revolved around children, teachers and what other Moms were doing wrong - and their husbands, of course. At first I was just standing around listening.

Lorato Sepeng, a mafuta (portly) Tswana woman in her late twenties with three children to her name, had been chatting animatedly to Carol, when Rita introduced me. Then Rita and Carol walked off to mingle with other friends and the conversation immediately focused on me.

"Wena, Bridget, you are not married and you don't have children?" Lorato didn't seem impressed with my lack of accomplishment in the family department. I'm sure she tried to be polite by not asking why I had left my boyfriend behind in Palapye. The rumours had made the rounds with flattering speed.

"No, I don't," I said.

"Howe! But you are already 22 years," she said, laying into the favourite subject of all Tswana matrons. I knew this just too well from experience.

"That's not very old where I come from. See we don't have nannies to help us raise the children and it's a lot of work." I looked for support, but Carol and Rita were moving on to share gossip with other decently married mothers.

"You don't have nannies in England?" Lorato asked with an incredulous expression.

Apparently, it had never occurred to her that in England, the motherland of all civilization, maids or nannies weren't freely available to run after a growing brood.

"No, only the very rich people do."

"Howe! That's terrible. So sorry."

"No, it's okay. People just don't have that many

children, not like here."

"Wena, that's terrible, mma," Lorato repeated and shook her head with feeling compassion. Such a heartless lifestyle was beyond her comprehension.

"Aah, Lebo!" she called out to a friend and anointed member of the mother club, and walked away with a brief nod in my direction.

I made my way to Carol's group. She stood with Tessa, who co-owned an African curio shop in the mall. I saw Emily van Heerden from afar, but we only greeted each other. No chance of having a meaningful conversation today.

"Ah, Bridget. Let me introduce you to Jennifer Harland. She has also just arrived from the UK," Carol trilled and pulled me to the other side of the large snack table.

Jennifer was a waif of a blonde girl, who looked about sixteen and forlorn. It turned out that she was older than me. Her husband had taken up a post with Barclays Bank in Gaborone a couple of months ago, and Jennifer had just joined him. She was still rather pale, a dead give-away that she'd arrived only recently. She made me feel like an old hand in Africa.

"Isn't this just a dreadful place? So dirty and uncivilized."

She clearly expected my backing, from a member of the 'British Sisterhood in Foreign Lands'.

"I actually quite like it here." Why did I have to think about Ethel Poppelmeyer?

"Oh." Jennifer seemed disappointed.

Rita Winckler stood chatting by the kitchen door. She waved to me without losing her momentum.

"I like the space and peace we have here. And the people are friendly."

"I see. Where in Britain are you from?" she ignored my praise.

"Cambridge," I said with pride in my voice.

"Oh really?!" Jennifer frowned. Apparently, there was

something wrong with Cambridge.

A woman, who stood nearby joined in the conversation. "What a coincidence. My cousin went to college in Cambridge. I've forgotten the name of the college," she informed us and shook her dark curls. "By the way, my name is Henriette. Henriette Milton." The ring on her pudgy left hand gave Henriette away as a married woman.

I sighed.

"Did you know that a girl from Cambridge, who'd lived in Gaborone for a few months, suddenly disappeared in the bush?" she gossiped. "What was her name again... Clara, no wait, it was Claire. Claire Stratford. Yes, that's it. Never found out what happened. Poor girl." It was jarring to hear about Claire in this way.

"That's my...my goodness. That's so sad."

I swallowed and caught myself in time. No use in telling her that she'd gotten Claire's name wrong. I was still incognito.

"Disappeared? How horrible." Jennifer's hands trembled.

The mere thought of this dreadful country her husband had made her come to!

I wanted to tell them all about Claire. What a wonderful person she was and that I, her twin sister, had not given up on finding her. But that, of course, was impossible.

"Yes, it's sad," Henriette said and walked over to the snacks. We were quiet for a few moments, while she loaded her plate with devilled eggs and sausage rolls.

"So, what does your husband do?" Jennifer tried to change the unpleasant subject to something normal. I realized that she was still unaware of the gossip surrounding me. Claire and I would have had a good giggle. She had written in letter no. 3 that the other wives could not imagine for the life of them that she brought home the main bacon, and not her hubby.

"I'm not married."

"Oh," Jennifer said. She looked nervously at Henriette.

Unused to speaking to an eccentric woman, she ran quickly out of topics.

"Ah, plenty of time for marriage at your age. You're a mere spring chicken," Henriette Milton said. Another devilled egg went into her mouth. Bless her!

"So you came here with your fiancé then?" Jennifer Harland tried again with hope in her eyes. Of course this had to be the solution to her conversational dilemma.

"No, Jennifer, I don't have a fiancé either," I laughed.

"Oh my. You're all alone here in Africa? That's very brave of you." I could tell from the tone in her voice that she thought I definitely had a few screws loose.

"I don't think I have to be married to live here in Africa."

Wrong answer.

"Look at the lovely snacks Carol made. I wonder if she'll give me the recipe for those divine crostini..." Jennifer changes the subject. She had obviously given up on me.

Ah well, I had an illness called 'single' and perhaps it was contagious.

She was right about one thing: the buffet looked rather inviting. Finger foods, salads, pâtés and breads, a cheese platter and bowls with fresh fruit. I took some of the devilled eggs and canapés and sat down on a chair against the house wall, watching and listening to all the chitchat around me. I would eat up and then thank the hostess for the pleasant afternoon. It was probably best to go for a walk until Rita was ready to leave.

Then Helen Rossi sat down next to me. She looked rather boyish and angular with her short dark hair. Rita had told me that she was an engineer of Italian descent from Australia, who worked for Len Jenkins' company. And she was one of the rare female 'singles'. It was obvious that Helen also felt out of place.

"Can I stick you for a drink at the Sun Hotel across the street?" she asked and winked at me.

"Yes, that sounds like a good idea," I said. "After all,

that's what singles like us do, isn't it?"

"Exactly."

Rita agreed to pick me up later and we left the gossip-machine behind. We had gin and tonic at the bar outside and I complained about the lopsided party talk.

"I can't figure out why they don't like me. Maybe I'm contagious or something."

"Oh, don't mind them," Helen said. "Lorato can't imagine, not having a hundred children and being spoilt by her maid. Most of the expat wives are plain scared. That's all."

"Scared of what?" I was genuinely surprised.

"To lose their husband's to an attractive single girl, I suppose," Helen guffawed.

"But that's ridiculous! Have you seen those husbands? I mean, even if they looked like Tom Cruise —"

"Remember, you come with a reputation." Of course, Tony!

"I see. But that doesn't mean…"

"Didn't you know that married couples have often problems when they move abroad?" she asked and ordered another double G&T. "That's what they mostly talk about."

"No, I didn't know that," I said and tried to ignore another guest, who kept staring in our direction.

"Especially here in Gabs. Any unmarried woman is a threat to the unhappy union."

"What makes them think we can't wait to drag their precious husbands into our lair?"

"Beats me. Self-preservation probably." Oh dear, no wonder then! My unsavoury past didn't seem to be much of a problem.

Before I could say 'socialite', I had become part of the inner circle in Gaborone.

Rita also found out through the grapevine that the CEO of the German Volunteer Organization was looking for a new Personal Assistant.

According to her informant, the job was available from the beginning of February and I was quite suitable. Up until now housewives, looking to supplement their allowance, had applied.

"With a work permit in your pocket, you needn't worry about staying in Botswana," Rita said. It made sense.

And more good news: a colleague of Uli Winckler's at the Automotive College was leaving and his flat became available.

The teacher was returning to England, because he missed his girlfriend. The fully furnished ground floor flat with its small porch at the back was not far from the mall.

I would be able to take over the flat in December - after Christmas.

Uli made an appointment with his colleague and drove me into town. Uli was very persuasive. The teacher accepted me as his 'successor'. The well-maintained 'Acacia Court' housed mainly foreigners. There were 12 flats in the building and loads of parking. We sealed the deal. I took over the remainder of the contract.

My own place!

The place was big enough, with two bedrooms, a kitchen, bathroom and lounge. Unfortunately furnished in the timeless style of the seventies. At least I didn't have to worry about buying furniture.

I could just come and go as I pleased, cook and invite friends over — provided I would make friends — and it cost a mere 200 Pula a month. The flat was only available for 9 months, which wasn't really a problem, since I wouldn't need it for long anyway.

Next was the interview at the German Volunteer Service. I was nervous. It was only the second job interview I'd ever had. The first one had been with a translation agency. There I had proved too inexperienced.

It was hot, so I donned my most formal summer outfit – a beige pencil skirt and a black figure-hugging blouse.

All I had to do now was to make a good impression. It hadn't rained for a few days and I could only hope to stay sweat and dust free. Luckily, I had packed a résumé and my certificates in England.

Like so many other offices in Gaborone, the German Volunteer Organization operated from a converted private house. A receptionist directed me from the small entrance hall to the waiting room. A number of curiously carved Malawi chairs were scattered around low coffee tables. They were surprisingly comfortable.

Mr. Köhler spoke English with a heavy accent. He kept studying me critically over the rim of a pair of glasses on the tip of his nose. Everything went fine, until in the middle of the interview, somebody walked into the waiting room with a mumbled excuse.

My focus shifted to a good-looking, tall young man in beige shirt and shorts and with dark wind-blown hair. Muscles rippled in his tanned arms and neck. He walked past. Even from behind he was a dish and carried an air of adventure into the stuffy waiting room.

He turned around and lit the room up with his broad smile, setting off a swarm of butterflies in my tummy. No wedding ring. Pull yourself together, Bridget; that has nothing to do with your interview, I scolded myself. The young man disappeared into a small room at the back and I could concentrate again on Mr. Köhler's question.

"Have you ever lived in Germany?" He looked at my papers.

"Yes, I spent some time with relatives in Berlin for about one year to complete my training. I also have an uncle in Cologne."

"Vielleicht sollten wir auch ein wenig Deutsch sprechen." Mr. Köhler suddenly switched to German. "Nur um zu sehen wie es damit noch klappt." I understood: perhaps we should speak some German, just to see how it goes.

"Das is kein Problem Herr Köhler," I replied. "Ich glaube mein Deutsch ist noch recht gut." No problem, Mr. Köhler. I think my German is still quite acceptable.

But he had already heard enough. Did that mean I had taken the hurdle?

"It's important that you are familiar with the German

mentality. You'd be working with German volunteers and officials here," the CEO of the GVO said in an accusing tone.

"Yes, I'm sure I can do that, Mr. Köhler." What did he expect me to say?

"Oh, that's wonderful, just wonderful, Miss Reinhold." He seemed delighted with my answer.

A short man with crooked teeth and oily hair entered the room and whispered into the CEO's ear. A tad bit more intimate than appropriate for an employee, perhaps. Kurt Köhler nodded. The little man left the room with a frown on his face, just as the muscular dish walked past with a stack of letters. Oh dear, those stupid butterflies!

"Ah, our male model Benjamin Glasberg from the Kalahari Desert." Kurt Köhler introduced us. The young man was a volunteer.

"Ben, come over for a moment and meet Miss Bridget Reinhold. She is interviewing for the PA position."

"Oh, you're not saying that Margaret is leaving, are you?" Benjamin Glasberg seemed concerned. "I'm always the last one to know about such things."

Margaret Marducci was the current and obviously very popular PA. She had introduced herself briefly before the interview. An attractive woman of about sixty, she was tanned and had the walk of a runway-model. Her grey hair was streaked with natural blonde and gathered in a loose Victorian bun on the top of her head.

"Yes I know. It would be easier if there were telephones in Kang. It's a catastrophe that she's leaving! Her husband's contract has expired and they are going back to England at the end of February. I will miss her terribly." Kurt Köhler threw his arms up in an exaggerated manner.

"Everybody here will. She's such a gem. What a pity."

Benjamin Glasberg bowed slightly and smiled. He looked at me. I felt all flustered, because his dark brown eyes held a question.

"I hope you will employ this young lady, Kurt. I can tell

that Miss Reinhold is right for the job." The handsome volunteer charmed his way right into my heart. I dropped my eyes instantly. It was dangerous to look at him.

"You think so Ben?" Kurt Köhler seemed to ponder the possibility. Then he blurted out, "ah, it's too bad you are straight. Not even a little bit of batting for the other team?"

I was taken aback. He waved his arms around and looked at me briefly in a theatrical sort of way. *If I want the job I better get used to this sort of thing*, I thought and smiled back.

"Most definitely not." Benjamin Glasberg brushed the question off with a most charming smile. Come on Bridget, this guy surely has a girlfriend and you won't see him again anytime soon. My thoughts were wandering again. *Concentrate*, I said to myself firmly, *the interview is more important!*

"Ah, too bad. I think you may be right there, Ben." Kurt Köhler eyed me again, letting his spectacles slide down his nose.

It felt awkward, how they both stared at me now. Then the moment passed.

"Phone for you Kurt!" The little man peeped in and made his presence known.

"Oh, this is Hansie by the way. He also works here," the CEO said. He walked out of the room and I had barely time to nod. Oh no, they were leaving me alone with the model volunteer!

"Hmm, I just came to check my mail," he mumbled. "Must go now and take my stuff to the Radovics. I'm staying with them tonight." He offered the unnecessary explanation with far less self-confidence, while playing with the envelopes in his hand. I had no idea who the Radovics were.

"Right. Bye then." I didn't know what else to say. I turned around abruptly and took a magazine off the table.

"Well, goodbye and good luck – with the job." Ben walked out without looking at me. Oh dear, he doesn't like me anymore, my foolish heart whimpered.

I sat glumly on the wooden chair and waited, paging through the reading material. Mostly official gazettes and magazines aimed at volunteers.

Kurt Köhler took his own sweet time. I was reading an article about this new disease called AIDS, when he walked back into the waiting room at last, only to wave me out into the hall.

"We will let you know by next Monday, Miss Reinhold. I must consider every single application, you know." He took my application form off the reception desk. "You are staying with the Wincklers, I see. Brigitte will give you a ring."

"Thank you for your time Mr. Köhler." I formally shook his hand and he waved me out with the application form.

I left the office and saw a large new Nissan bakkie, parked at the bottom of the driveway. The male model Benjamin shifted some boxes around on the back-seat. He wasn't in that much of a hurry to leave then. Should I just walk past the truck and leave quietly? There was still time to get away unnoticed. But then he pulled himself up and stared at me through the windscreen for a second. He climbed down and stood in front of me grinning charmingly. My heart jumped. I came from cold and rainy Britain after all and was not yet used to tanned and sexy men. Not yet.

"Oh, you are still here?" I said clumsily.

"Yes, I needed to find some string to tie the bushman bows together." Bushman bows? What was he talking about?

"Well then." I hoped that he didn't hear my heart thumping as I pushed past him.

"So, how do you like Botswana?" Benjamin asked quickly.

I had to smile. Almost everybody I'd met so far had asked me that question.

"I love Botswana," I launched into my standard answer, avoiding his eyes.

"You get that question a lot, don't you?!"

"Yes, I do. Everybody asks me that."

"Okay, how did you like Kurt Köhler then?" That question was more to the point.

"I quite like him actually, he's funny," I said.

"Yes, I suppose you could say that," Ben laughed. "Needs some getting used to."

Did I detect a touch of sarcasm in his voice?

"Hmm, you think. I really don't mind that he is gay, if that's what you mean."

"Direct — I like that! Although Kurt can be quite moody. Nothing you couldn't handle, I'm sure."

"Sure." I coughed a little, feeling embarrassed.

"I'm just stocking up on supplies in Gabs. Must go back to Kang tomorrow."

He changed the subject, clearly not prepared to let me go just yet. I felt flattered. Benjamin liked me.

"Where exactly is Kang?"

"In the middle of the Kalahari Desert, halfway to Ghanzi." He smiled his charming smile again.

Kang was in the middle of the desert, how exciting! Oh no, these dumb butterflies!

"I see."

"How long have you been in the country?" Benjamin wanted to know. There we go, another standard question. But at least we were talking.

"Since September. And you?" It was my turn to ask questions.

"This is my second year. I'm on a three-year contract. Feels like I've been here forever. Will probably extend my contract."

Two years in the Kalahari Desert! It made Benjamin seem even more attractive. "So you know Botswana quite well then?"

"Yeah, I guess I do. I prefer the desert to the towns. The Kalahari is a magic place. You should come and see it some time!" That sounded a lot like an invitation.

Was I already fantasizing about climbing into the bakkie with Ben Glasberg? Pathetic!

Before I could say ostrich, he had torn a piece off an envelope and wrote on it.

"Listen, if you feel like it, come to dinner at the Radovics' tonight. That's their phone number. Just in case you feel like it."

"Thanks, but I'm busy tonight," I pretended and took the paper anyway. Our fingers touched for one electrifying moment. He cleared his throat.

"Do you have a phone number then?"

"I'm staying with friends in town." I rolled the paper with the Radovics' phone number into a tube.

"Next time then, when I'm in town again," Ben said. He jumped abruptly onto his bakkie, where he started to rummage around boxes in the back of his truck.

Not very smooth. It didn't matter. This had been about as much excitement as I could take for one day.

"Yes, maybe. Bye," I said. I walked down the driveway and stood for a moment on the hot, dusty street with my eyes closed. Oh why did I have to play hard to get?

Because you are here to find Claire! Not for romance, a little voice said to me. The little voice was right. I walked away from the office with firm steps.

Over dinner, Uli told me about Billy Ansell and his sister Gertrude. Billy worked with him at the College and Gertrude had been visiting her brother in Gaborone for almost a month now.

She was dying to see the Victoria Falls in Zimbabwe, before taking a flight from Harare back to London, but didn't have the guts to travel on her own. She needed a travel companion. Me. So Uli asked me if I minded terribly going to the popular holiday resort of Vic Falls with her.

"I've only met her once, but she seems quite nice," he said and chewed on a chicken drumstick. Then he tackled the buttered gem squash.

Perfect. After today's episode with Benjamin, I was in the

mood for something spontaneous. Besides, I needed a change of scenery to clear my head. I hadn't even told Rita about him.

"Shouldn't I rather stay? Kurt Köhler might want me to come back for a second interview," I objected half-heartedly.

"Nonsense. The job with the GVO isn't going to run away. Here have some more." My motherly friend Rita dished up a good portion of her cheese-sauced broccoli. "Just go and see a bit of Africa, it'll do you good. We'll handle Kurt Köhler this side."

"He's a bit…" I began.

"Odd?"

"Impulsive."

"Yes, he's known for that. His PA gets on with him just fine, because she is never seriously bothered by anything. Margaret's been with the GVO for at least 17 years and she's seen quite a few CEOs come and go. She takes Kurt's lapdogs to the parlour, fetches his clothes from the dry cleaner, dropping whatever she's doing. In other words, she couldn't care less."

"I didn't know that. Dog parlours?" My heart dropped. I'd have to work as a personal slave! Well, one could get used to anything. Waking up to sunshine every day, for instance.

Finding new friends, eating squash and liver and things like that. Even the flat, harmless spiders that lived behind virtually every picture on the wall didn't bother me anymore. Why not get used to a slightly odd boss?

"It's not the most demanding work. If you're determined to make the best of it, it will be fine. Can you handle that?"

"I think so," I said and meant it. *I'm doing this for you, Claire!* It made everything worthwhile.

"Good. Go to Vic Falls and think about it. I can tell you now that you top Kurt's list." Rita didn't seem to doubt my interview success for a minute.

If I wasn't mistaken, Maun was close to Victoria Falls and Claire had been to Maun. Perhaps I should also stop over in Francistown on the way back and speak to Pierre and Karabo Boucher. And pop in to see Tony in Palapye.

Uli had invited Billy and Gertrude Ansell for tea after dinner so that we could meet. How on earth did he know that I was going to say yes? Was I that transparent?

Gertrude wore thick glasses and seemed to have a preference for Indian cotton tops. My travel-companion-to-be reminded me of my good friend Diane back in Cambridge with her unassuming manner and shy smile. We decided to make the bookings at Thebe Travel the following morning and to get malaria tablets from the pharmacy.

On Thursday afternoon we would board the train to Plumtree, a town on the border. There we'd take a slow train all the way to Bulawayo and board another train to Vic Falls. A week at a budget hotel was booked. Afterwards we'd go our separate ways. I phoned Tony to let him know that I would visit him on my way back from Zimbabwe.

'Just tell the conductor that you want to get off in Palapye. It's a very small station, you might miss it otherwise,' my brother-in-law had said.

Perhaps we could have a real talk about Claire this time. I had less luck contacting Pierre and Karabo. The Scottish house-sitter told me that they had taken the baby to England to meet the family there and would only be back in January. That was a setback, but what could I do?

One more thing I needed to do, was phone detective Sibeko. To tell him about my information campaign idea in the Tuli Block. Perhaps he could also look into my mother's abduction theory. The secretary told me that he would be away until the following Monday to attend a funeral. That was too late.

"No, nobody else knows anything about this case. Would you like to leave a message for detective Sibeko?"

"Thank you, but no. I will phone him when I'm back from Zimbabwe," I declined.

Thursday afternoon arrived. We were dressed like regular tourists. Gertrude in an ankle-length Indian dress and I in shorts and colourful halter neck top. It turned out that to travel on a slow-moving train was the best thing we could have done. Many tourists booked one of the regular flights from Gaborone to Victoria Falls, but from the train's perspective we were able to see the African landscape in all its glory.

The colonial steam train was something else. A zinc washbasin and a mirror decorated our compartment. We would sleep on the train and arrive in Plumtree in the morning. No elephants, zebras and lions just yet, but they weren't difficult to imagine in the vast golden savannah outside. Dusk fell as we passed through Palapye. There were the familiar kraals again, surrounded by motsetsi hedges in the deep sand. The village had been my home for 10 long weeks.

Gertrude was impressed when I told her about my brief stint as a teacher.

"Wasn't it terribly boring to work in a rural village?" she asked me, taking off her glasses to clean them. "There isn't all that much around here."

"Depends on how you look at it. Got sort of suckered into teaching, while visiting a friend. Palapye was actually quite interesting."

I told her of my informal language lessons with Tsanana, the funeral in the countryside and Mrs. Poppelmeyer.

Flakey soot from the locomotive's chimney flew through the window as the train negotiated a curve and we pushed it closed. Soon it was too dark outside to see anything. Gertrude shared a bunch of grapes with me and we had some Fanta for an improvised dinner.

Somebody came to prepare the bunks in our 'first class' compartment for the night. There wasn't much else to do, but to go to bed. We discussed politics, what we thought of Africa and the growing ozone hole until we dozed off. I had hardly thought about Benjamin Glasberg at all. The rattling noise didn't disturb me for long, but now and again random jolts of steel wheels on steel tracks pushed me one way or the other.

We awoke to the smell of fresh coffee just before the train reached Plumtree. We rolled to a standstill and passport checks were thoroughly conducted aboard. The landscape didn't change much behind the border. Then we arrived in Bulawayo.

The town wasn't as grand as I had imagined. Seven years into independence, Zimbabwe wasn't doing so well, it seemed.

The station teemed with Zimbabweans, who camped around the Gaborone train station with their huge white, blue and red-striped bags full of provisions. Many of those border-hoppers got off the train, pushing past us.

Gertrude and I handed our luggage over to a smiling clerk in uniform at the old-fashioned cloak room and went into town. We had the entire day to explore and followed the other passengers, who obviously knew the way. There were far fewer shops and many more potholes than expected.

One Indian shopkeeper was overly eager to sell us his wares at inflated prices, so we quickly crossed the road. At every street corner, well-spoken men accosted us. They wanted to change Zim Dollars into Rand or Pula, or better still US Dollars and Pound Sterling. We were easily identified as tourists.

Uli had warned us about exchanging money illegally. We didn't want to be jailed by the police and exchanged a few Pulas for a thick wad of Zimbabwean notes at the next bank we saw.

"Where do we get something to eat around here?" Gertrude asked with hungry eyes.

"I'm not too keen on shebeen food," I answered and pointed to a few tables and chairs in the street. Gertrude looked at me blankly and I told her about my shebeen experience in Palapye, about mieliepap and fatty meat.

"What do you think of going to the hotel over there, then?" She pointed to a green façade with café-house curtains in the long windows.

A brass sign was swinging above the veranda read 'Hotel', so we gave it a try. It wasn't half bad. One could observe the street from here and we kept ordering pots of tea and plates of English cucumber sandwiches.

We were back at the station in time, but the train to Victoria Falls left Bulawayo only after sunset with a two-hour delay. A troupe of soldiers suddenly boarded the train, scaring the passengers. Even before the train left the station, machine guns pointed out of windows and doors. Nobody bothered to explain the 2-hour delay or the presence of armed soldiers.

Gertrude and I finally learned from the conductor that trains were sometimes attacked by rebels in the troubled Matabeleland. The soldiers were on the train for our protection and had been a trifle late to arrive in Bulawayo.

Oh happy holidays!

If one ignored the soldiers, it was a time travel experience, straight from the movie 'Out of Africa'.

Passengers were soon called to dinner in the dining car by the clangs of a brass bell and the delicious à la carte meal and distinguished ambience — all inclusive — were nothing short of surprising. Outside, a setting sun bathed the landscape in orange light. Would the rebels attack us while I was far away in dreamland?

Sadly, we slept through the famous Hwange National Park with its incomparable wildlife in our beautiful mahogany and brass compartment. It had been a peaceful trip and in the morning, our steam train pulled into the no-less-colonial open air Victoria Falls station.

The area around Vic Falls was unmistakably tropical, so different to the dry savannahs of southern Botswana. Our hotel was situated near the station, right next-door to the classy Victoria Falls Hotel. We walked the short distance, taking turns carrying Gertrude's suitcase.

We shared a twin room at the Makasa Sun Hotel for a week. Breakfast and dinner included. All we had to do was buy lunch at a sparsely-stocked supermarket nearby.

First we wanted to see those famous waterfalls. The receptionist told us that it hadn't rained much of late and the falls had dwindled to a mere trickle. Nowhere near the usual roaring surge of water. It didn't bother us at all. We wanted to see the falls and could unpack later.

The water spray still reached the slippery board walk on the opposite cliff that all tourists used as a viewing platform. The noise was tremendous.

"That's interesting. The locals called it 'the smoke that thunders'," Gertrude yelled over the din, while she held onto the railing. She read the wooden plaques along the board walk through foggy glasses.

"Yes, and it's not even the rainy season yet," I yelled back.

"What?"

"Never mind!"

"Amazing, just look at all that water." Gertrude pointed to the massive white cascades rushing into the gorge below. "I want to know what it's like when the rains start."

"That's a whole huge river coming down there," I cried at the top of my voice, "the Zambezi River. Must have been an earthquake or something, forming that abyss."

Gertrude stood right next to me now and we could talk almost normally. A couple of tourists made their way past us and disappeared in the spray.

"I want to go see the Livingstone monument," Gertrude said.

"Do you know where it is?"

"I think it's on the other side." She pointed across the gorge.

"Maybe we should ask somebody for directions."

"Okay, let's go then!"

We slid along the walkway back to the road and located the bronze statue. Impressive. Then we went on to the local craft market, where we soon found out that articles of clothing were more sought after than American Dollars.

The following day, Gertrude was the proud owner of two colourful, woven baskets and a wooden mask. All of that for a pair of old shorts she wouldn't need in wintry

Britain anyway. I purchased a highly polished, fat wooden hippo for a t-shirt that had shrunk in the wash. Claire would have gone mad for it.

Claire. A wave of guilt washed over me — and ebbed away. Where was she, while I was having fun? I'd had no nightmares since we'd left Gaborone. I will talk to you later, I said to her in my mind and was surprised how easy it was.

Gertrude and I listened to a marimba band that played at the elegant Victoria Falls Hotel. No fence or wall separated the two hotels. Although we couldn't afford the pricey 'high tea' for affluent tourists, the waiters let us listen to the music for free.

We passed the swimming pool as we walked back through the gardens to our own hotel. A long black snake slithered across the swimming pool. I blinked and the snake disappeared into the bushes. Gertrude was just looking the other way and I left it at that, but didn't feel like swimming in the pool for a while.

Our next visit to the cataracts was unexpectedly unpleasant. We made it through the undergrowth by the footpath to a great baobab tree. I touched the smooth bark in awe, when a large baboon jumped right in front of us and let out a mighty scream.

We jumped in shock. A menacing show of teeth was enough. We shrieked and ran back to the safety of the board walk as fast as we could. The whooping monkey didn't follow us all the way and we leaned panting against the railing.

Rolling thunder alerted us that a storm was brewing. The sky over the falls had turned a chilling black colour. In stark contrast, a dark cloud blanket lay over Victoria Falls, the rainy edges feathering out into a lemony sky.

It was best to hurry back to the hotel as quickly as the slippery wooden planks allowed. The rain came pouring down as we reached the hotel. We spent the next few hours in the Summit Bar on the covered roof terrace. The pouring rain was relentless and the bush now looked like an impenetrable rainforest.

"Oh bummer. What are we going to do now?" I complained to the barkeeper about the weather. "A rainy holiday is no fun." He just gave a guttural laugh.

"Ah, it's not going to rain for long. Can I get you ladies a drink?"

He mixed us two Makasa Sunset cocktails, the specialty of the house, and we chatted to the other guests about our terrifying monkey encounter. Free roasted peanuts saw us through the afternoon until it was time for dinner. The barkeeper was right. The rain was done by the morning.

A mock African village, called The Craft Village, had various African huts and artefacts on display inside its brightly painted walls. Three witchdoctors plied their fortune-telling trade for the grand sum of four Zim Dollars per sitting.

Princess and Tsanana had told me so much about sangomas that I wanted to meet all three of them! Gertrude had only the courage to consult the first sangoma, who hailed from Malawi.

The fur-clad man told her that her boyfriend would want to get married when she returned home. He also saw twins in her future. Gertrude was stunned by these revelations and recovered on a chair in the yard, while I consulted all of the witch doctors, one after the other, in their respective tents.

"You have no health or money problems. I see four children, two boys and two girls." After making me blow on the bones in his hand again and throwing them expertly on a woven floor mat, the soothsayer from Malawi told me: "You meet one man with dark hair and one man with light hair and not marry any of them."

"What about my sister?" I demanded to know, feeling my heart thump in my chest.

"Your sister will have three children and live happily with her husband," the alleged sangoma prophesied. Really?!

I went through similar rituals with a sangoma from Zimbabwe and learned that I would meet a man of my own tribe with grey hair and marry him and that I would move to another country after living in Botswana for some time. This time I'd have three children, two boys and a girl and interestingly, that my sister and I would be re-united. I wanted to believe him so badly!

By that stage, Gertrude probably thought that I'd lost my marbles. She wanted to leave and refused to crawl with me into the third sangoma's hide tent. Maybe she was right and I was a little obsessed. I managed to appease her and she waited one last time.

I promptly banged my head on a brass can, hanging from the low cross pole by the entrance. After paying the required fee over to the assistant, I blew on a handful of little bones and other curious objects before they rolled across the mat.

The sangoma rhythmically shook a small pot with a long handle that contained a short black horn. Then he studied the arrangement and collected the bones back into a dirty pouch. The procedure was repeated - and he gave me a strange sideways look.

"Not possible," he said with determination.

"Not possible, what?" I was expecting a standard prophesy.

"The ancestors are upset. It's taking too long."

"Which ancestors?" I was stunned. "What is taking too long, what does it mean?"

"Means nothing. You will marry a rich man and have three children. Two boys, one girl."

"But that can't be all! What are you trying to say?"

But his assistant ushered me out of the tent, before I could ask any questions about missing sisters. Gertrude looked at me crossly as I emerged.

"I'm hungry. This hocus-pocus is taking too long," she complained.

I was still wondering why the witchdoctor wanted to get rid of me so quickly.

"That was odd just now. He said the ancestors are upset."

I began to talk like a pro.

"I'll say. What are you doing going to all these shamans anyway? It's all nonsense," she said and pushed her glasses right up to the root of her nose.

"Why is it all nonsense?" I asked as we walked through the 'Lion's Den', between rows of knitting and weaving women. "Don't you think it's fascinating?"

"No, because my boyfriend broke up with me before I left London."

"So?"

"So? I don't think he is ready for anything close to marriage."

That sounded pretty final. And logical.

"Hmm, okay. Point taken. Where do you want to go?" I began to lose interest in the topic. There had been far too many contradictions in the prediction, so why should I defend the shamans?

"What?" Gertrude was still tense.

"You said you were hungry. Don't you want to get some food?"

"Ah yes, let's have sandwiches at the hotel."

Good sandwiches were reasonably priced at the hotel restaurant, so off we went. Gertrude was set to leave for Harare the following day and we celebrated her last day in Vic Falls with coke and sandwiches. After a while, the hotel receptionist summoned us to his desk. We were notified that we still owed a large amount of money.

"But we paid the full amount when we booked with Thebe Travel in Gaborone," Gertrude objected.

"I don't know about that. You must pay this. The amount is in American Dollars, not Zimbabwe Dollars," he insisted. I became suspicious. "American Dollars? I don't think so. The receipt clearly states Zim Dollars."

"No, I need American Dollars," the receptionist repeated stubbornly.

"I wish to speak to the hotel manager," I demanded.

"You must pay the invoice first."

"I refuse. Gertrude, please fetch the receipt from Thebe Travel in our room. It's in my backpack."

"Oh let's just pay him the money," Gertrude said. She wasn't happy about making a scene, but I was adamant. I would prove this sneering man wrong.

"No, please get the receipt. We are not paying one cent more."

Gertrude reluctantly set out to find our proof of payment, while I stayed behind, stubbornly oozing refusal. Then by chance, the hotel manager walked in.

"Mr. Solomon!" I called across the small lobby and he approached with a smile on his face. "Ah, Miss Reinhold, good day. You are leaving us tomorrow. Everything all right?"

"Yes, we are. There's just a small problem. Your receptionist is demanding that we pay extra for a fully paid booking. In American Dollars."

"We are usually paid in American Dollars."

"But we paid the full amount in Gaborone."

The hotel manager stared at the receipt that Gertrude now held under his nose. He read the document, frowned and conceded immediately.

"I'm very sorry about the misunderstanding, Miss Reinhold." Mr. Solomon said politely and glared at the receptionist. "Can I treat you to drinks at the Summit Bar?"

"Yes thank you, that wouldn't be such a bad idea." I heaved a sigh of relief. Mr. Solomon escorted us to the roof terrace and gave instructions to the barkeeper.

"I hope you have an enjoyable afternoon, ladies," he said and left. My holiday mood was somewhat restored.

"I didn't know you could be so fierce, Bridget," Gertrude said over a second round of free Makasa Sunset cocktails.

"Honestly, I'm not usually like that at all. But the cheek

of that guy. I'm sure he was trying to cheat us."

"I would have paid." Gertrude slurped the drink sullenly through a straw.

"That's exactly what he wanted us to do. And besides, we don't have that kind of money left." I felt a little self-righteous, no doubt helped by the cocktails.

"I know, but I don't like the way people stare at us."

"What do you care?"

"I just don't like it. It wasn't that much and I'm leaving tomorrow anyway."

"Crummy. But I still have to pay the National Parks Board for two nights and then for the trip back to Gaborone."

"I guess. Now you have at least enough money left."

We sipped our cocktails and walked around the peaceful hotel gardens one last time. No water snakes or baboons were anywhere in sight. The jasmine bushes exuded a heady perfume and orange-flowering flame trees stood out against the pink clouds in a deep blue sky. We were in holiday heaven.

Gertrude took a taxi to the airport in the morning and I made my way to the National Parks camping grounds. After sharing a cramped hotel room for a week, it was great to have a spacious chalet all to myself. I watched from a safe distance how a troupe of small baboons searched rubbish bins for food, banging the chained-on lids around. Then they raided a mango tree. None of the monkeys attacked.

A few tears rolled down my cheeks as I surveyed the beautiful landscape around me. Claire would have loved it here.

"Just look at that, Claire," I said to the mango tree, "Have you ever...? That little naughty one at the back there!"

Once I found Claire - and soon - I'd make her come here on holiday. I didn't do much in those two days at the camping grounds. Except for writing postcards and talking to the

young couple next door. Sam and Jenny were from New Zealand and travelled through Southern Africa.
They had already been to Europe for three months. I also met a South African teacher, who was planning to drive to the Chobe National Park in Botswana the following day. He reluctantly agreed to give me a lift across the border. I wouldn't have to worry about a bus connection after all.
"I prefer to travel alone," the balding South African said grumpily. "But I can take you as far as Kazungula. You can hail a minitaxi to Francistown from there. My name's Jacques Mellert by the way."
"Bridget Reinhold." We shook hands.
Jacques Mellert was obviously a bit of a loner. An art teacher from Durban, he was on his way back home after touring the ruins of Greater Zimbabwe, Lake Kariba and now Victoria Falls. A trip with virtually no planning.
I pushed my European way of thinking aside. The African 'tomorrow's another day' attitude to life seemed more appropriate right now. Claire would surely have done the same. No big deal, standing by the side of the road, taking a mini-taxi back to Gaborone. I had played with the thought of going to Maun in the Okavango Delta, but that was probably too much trouble without my own transport.
"I want to leave first thing at 8 o'clock in the morning," Jacques said. "Better be ready." I was ready and waited for him by the reception.
"Just throw your stuff in the back," Jacques instructed me curtly and off we went.
Not far down the winding country road, he was forced to stop his land rover for a herd of majestic elephants. No more than a hundred feet in front of us. The huge animals came out of the jungle and randomly crossed the two-lane road, taking their time. The sight was unbelievable. Jacques grabbed his camera and clicked away. Wasn't this sort of thing only supposed to happen on safaris?
Here I was, an absolute greenhorn in a land rover on a remote

stretch of country road in Africa, staring some grey behemoths with flapping ears right in the eye. It was thrilling.

Suddenly I understood why Jacques Mellert had gone on his car trip alone. And why Claire had wanted to see the elephants in the Tuli Block so badly.

# CHAPTER 6

Thanks to the cooperative guards at the Kazungula border post, we were in Botswana within minutes. As promised, Jacques dropped me off on the main road to Francistown. It was one of those days, when the air above a hot tar road seemed to turn liquid like water.

Opposite the junction, a road sign with Maun written on it pointed to a side road. Feeling adventurous, I asked Jacques on a whim what he thought about me taking a detour to the Okavango Delta. I probably thought that I would be able to take up Claire's scent like a lioness. As I said, it was rather hot.

"Not a good idea," he discouraged me. "You can get stranded out there in the bush on your own. Much safer to go straight to Francistown."

It was sensible advice. Apart from the fact that I didn't know a living soul in Maun and had just enough money to make it back home.

Bye, bye boat safari, hippos and exotic bird life. Goodbye, lion fantasy. My spontaneity had definite limits. Jacques Mellert lost no time and continued his journey to Chobe. I was left standing by the roadside under a tree with my backpack and a wooden hippo. So what now?

It was getting hotter by the minute. In the air-conditioned hotel the heat had been quite bearable, but next to the road I was mercilessly exposed to the elements. Other people turned up one by one with their luggage and became quite chatty, wanting to know where I was headed. Everybody was going to Francistown just like me.

The first minitaxi stopped after thirty hot, long minutes, and we embarked after paying 14 Pula a head.

Most of our luggage was fastened onto the roof and bits and bobs stuffed between the seats and various legs. We were about 15 passengers not counting the small children. Soon, my elation at the prompt ride made way for unpleasant discomfort. It became rather stuffy inside the van and everyone, including myself, was sweating profusely. Despite the air coming in through opened windows.

Jacques Mellert had given me two soft drink cans as a farewell gift, which now saved me from certain death by dehydration.

If it hadn't been for the repetitive, ear-splitting music and a man reeking of beer to my left, the trip would have been more bearable. In between emptying beer bottles, the man jabbered relentlessly of how he would marry me on the spot and look after our beautiful children, while pushing against me.

I stopped smiling and just stared stoically out of the dusty window. The heat made me sleepy and I nodded off a few times, taking care not to lean against my beer-swilling neighbour.

It wasn't all unpleasant, though. I saw elephants taking a dip in a lake on the Zimbabwean border, adjacent to the Hwange National Park. Just that very sight was worth the uneasy ride in the crawling van. Wild animals didn't care much for man-made barriers, it seemed.

Judging by the occasional glimpse past people and pieces of luggage, the scenery on the other side of the road must have been breath-taking, too. We were leaving the Okavango Delta and Chobe National Park behind and I hadn't caught as much as a glimpse of it.

Our minivan was rather rickety and almost certainly would have pulled of the street in England. No wonder then that the vehicle broke down halfway between Kazungula and Francistown. We were not far from a routine rest stop, where the passengers could purchase oily doughnuts with spicy mincemeat and cold drinks. I was surprised at the hostile stares I received.

The woman behind the counter wouldn't even sell me two cans of coke, until my drunken 'protector' demanded it. After meeting only friendly locals in Zimbabwe and Southern Botswana, this hostility was a new experience. There was no explanation for it and I decided that it had nothing to do with me.

In the meantime, our driver hailed down another minitaxi and after some haggling, we were ordered to climb into the new van with all our belongings. Nobody asked why. No matata!

The music in the new minitaxi was just as deafening, but at least I managed to sit between a window and an overweight matron this time.

Eight hot and tiring hours and an inevitable roadblock later, the van dropped us off at Francistown station. Magically, the next train to Gaborone left just 15 minutes later. I was starving by now, and once I sat in my compartment, I wolfed down the squashed sandwiches in my backpack. Then I fell asleep.

When we were about to arrive in Palapye, the conductor woke me up as promised. It was 1 o'clock in the morning.

I was the only passenger, who clambered down the train steps in bright moonlight and found myself promptly on the wrong platform.

There was nobody waiting for me. I had no choice but to climb across the tracks and make my way through the deep sand past quiet kraals towards the housing complex. A full moon shone down on the village, helping me choose the correct turns.

I reached Tony's house after what seemed an eternity. Banging on the door didn't show any effect.

Only after I'd knocked on Tony's bedroom window for a while did the lights come on and the key turned in the door lock. As so often, Tony had overslept.

I spent two pleasantly uneventful days in Palapye.

Alfred Jones' wife Judith and baby Amanda had moved in next-door. Judith was not a very friendly woman. She seemed to resent being stuck in this place at the end of the world with a newborn baby to care for. Amanda on the other hand, was the cutest little thing and slept most of the time.

Mrs. Poppelmeyer observed all of us from behind her famous lace curtains, but thankfully stayed out of my way.

Dinner at the Botsalo Hotel felt like old times. I told Tony and Neo about Zimbabwe and the interview with the German Volunteer Organization and that there was a good chance of me getting the position.

They in turn reported that Mr. Poppelmeyer had been rather annoyed with my choice to perfidiously run off to Gaborone. The regular English teacher had decided to stay in her home village after all and it had been a problem to replace me. Not much else had changed in Palapye and Tony was still unwilling to speak about Claire. Well, nothing new there.

I knew with every fibre of my being that Claire was alive, no matter what everybody else thought. There was just this nagging, helpless feeling that I still couldn't do anything on my own.

Back in Gaborone, I did get the job with the GVO and I spent the festive season with the Winckler family. Much to my parents' chagrin, who had hoped that I would come back to England for good now.

Gabs was rather quiet at this time of year. I missed my family, the British winter and the concert by the choir at King's College.

We celebrated the German way on Christmas Eve in soaring temperatures with all the shebang. With candles, carol singing around a plastic-pine tree and the exchange of gifts. Rita gave me a copy of 'Moll Flanders' by Daniel Defoe.

I could strangely relate to the hardships the 17th century

heroine. She also had to make peace with her circumstances and push back useless feelings.

'We cannot say, indeed, that this history is carried on quite to the end of the life of this famous Moll Flanders, as she calls herself, for nobody can write their own life to the full end of it...' I read in the preface. It had something encouraging about it. Then Rita called us for an elaborate dinner out to the veranda.

I carried on reading on Christmas day. Of course, circumstances had been very different in those days. I was not forced into relationships with men to get ahead in life, but the way Moll Flanders mastered hardship was an inspiration to me.

No doubt Rita had chosen the book for me for that very reason. To give me hope. And all I had given her was a pot holder set. Soon after Christmas I moved into the flat in Acacia Court. It was heaven, being in my own space and here in the centre of town, no roosters or donkeys disturbed my morning sleep!

The move took no time at all and with much time on my hands, I finished reading 'Moll Flanders'. Then I took out another book. 'El Jadida' - Grandpa's novel. The story set in Morocco in the year 1957 twisted and turned around a kidnapping case with an unexpected ending. Impressive. I decided to read all of his other books as well.

The small park at the back of the building invited me to sit and read in the shade. I spent as much time as possible outside between red and pink Bougainvillea bushes.

Yellow weaver birds made their bulbous nests from strips of palm leaves. I watched in amazement as the female inspected the finished domicile hanging from a tree branch. When she didn't like the nest, the male ripped it to pieces and started over.

The only neighbours I saw during those days was an elderly Indian couple next door in No. 2, who never greeted me. The wife was dressed in saris and walked a few paces behind her husband with their shopping bags. I would have liked to exchange a few words with her, but she ignored my attempts at conversation.

My life had irrevocably changed, no matter how temporary the situation was. A year ago, I would have thought it impossible to live in a foreign country. And now I had accommodation, a job and a modest social network in Gaborone.

The only thing I painfully missed was Claire.

Just before New Year's Eve, a parcel from Mom arrived. It contains a turquoise cashmere jersey and my favourite perfume. I could feel her love as I touched the presents. The jersey would have been perfect in winter.

I started mailing postcards and parcels with African curios to my family and friends in England. Even by airmail they could take weeks to arrive.

I had neglected my friends back home and was scolded without delay:

*Cambridge, 14 December 1988*

'*Hi Bridget,*

*Remember me? I don't hear from you for weeks and then you write postcards from Zimbabwe. Now you are settling down in Gaborone of all places. Why? Will we ever see you again? Who are you and what have you done with my old friend?* — '

Diane had a point there. Of course, I had changed, how could I not have?

I wrote long letters full of news to Diane and the others, to tell them about my trip to Zimbabwe, the new job and how different Christmas felt in the Southern hemisphere. I added that detective Sibeko was still on leave and that I had to speak to him soon about things I could do to speed the investigation up.

In the meantime, I spent some time to spruce up my new abode. The little wooden animal sculptures, I had bought at the museum in Serowe, looked sophisticated on the bookshelf next to family photographs. The fat wooden hippo from Victoria Falls, occupied a place of honour on the coffee table after I had carefully treated a broken leg with super glue.

A white, crocheted table cloth adorned the dining table and I stuck Botswana posters from the curio shop to the walls with Prestik. *Not bad*, I thought, *not bad at all*. The wooden hippo just stared at me accusingly with its wooden googly eyes.

"What are you looking at?" I scolded. "Nothing wrong with getting a little comfortable in here —"

New Year's Eve came and went quietly, but I didn't mind. With so much change lately, I really needed a break.

As it turned out, a number of global events should mark the year 1989. Coastal California was to be shattered by an earthquake, the stock markets took a knock and the Berlin Wall came down. These events should also affect me. The Californian earthquake made me realize how lucky I was to live in remote Gaborone. The stock market crash put a dent into my modest investments in IT stocks. And the fall of the Berlin Wall - well, I will get to that later.

I phoned Pierre and Karabo Boucher in Francistown in January. Once again, I only had the house sitter on the line. They had decided to extend their visit to Britain, I was told, so there was no chance of visiting them anytime soon.

I eventually spoke to Karabo at the beginning of March.

"Claire wanted to see the elephants in the Tuli Block and as far as I know she had booked one night at some game lodge outside Bobonong. We gave a report to the police. I'm really sorry she disappeared, Bridget, but I don't know what else we can do to help." She did not invite me to visit them in Francistown and I didn't ask.

I already knew about the game lodge booking and that Claire had never showed up there. Karabo seemed to feel guilty and pushing her too hard would just close that door for me. Another dead end. I was frustrated. Of course, I didn't have a clue yet, what was really behind it.

As scheduled, I began to work at the beginning of February and was faced with a whole new set of challenges to keep me on my toes.

"My worker bees, my little ants, how are things getting along?" Kurt cooed as he checked in on us once again at Margaret's office. Then he danced into the room and massaged my shoulders. Then Margaret's. His long-serving secretary seemed used to it and just smiled.

"Everything's just fine Kurt. I'm showing Bridget how the filing system works."

I was rather less comfortable, having my shoulders massaged by my new boss.

Margaret and I got on like a house on fire. We also spent time together after work and on weekends. Her British-Italian husband John had retired as an engineer for the electricity department in Gaborone. So they were going back to London for good. *What a pity that the two of them were leaving so soon,* I thought.

Margaret led the double life of a nature enthusiast or more specifically, a cactus enthusiast. A collection of succulents shared her garden with prickly plants in all shapes and sizes. Not to mention a variety of potted specimen on the veranda.

"What are you going to do with all those plants when you leave Gaborone?" I asked her during my first visit to the cactus house.

"Oh, some friends are taking the pots and I'll just leave the other plants in the garden. The next owners must decide what to do with them," Margaret said simply.

She never seemed flustered about the future and her quiet husband was just as uncomplicated. Not surprising then that it was peaceful at the cactus house.

I soon opened up to her about Claire and told her about my inexplicable feeling that she was still alive and all the difficulties

I had encountered. Margaret had lived in Africa for a long time and didn't find this sort of thing strange at all.

"You should go and see a sangoma for advice." She said matter-of-factly after listening to my story.

We had early supper at the cactus house and were planning to go for a walk later.

"I don't know. The sangomas in Vic Falls weren't exactly convincing. Every one of them told me a different story - mostly what they thought I wanted to hear. The last one couldn't wait to get rid of me."

"Maybe they weren't real ones. Just a tourist attraction or so."

"Possible. The three of them in the Craft Village were naturally there for the tourists."

"Do you think they were genuine?" Margaret stacked the dishes.

I thought for a moment. "Probably not. The last one said something about ancestors. That they were annoyed for some reason. I don't understand what he meant. Maybe I'm just not ready for witchdoctor talk."

I studied the large saguaro cactus and the prickly green ball next to the veranda stairs.

"Ancestors? Sounds about right. But they were probably just fakes. Actors, for the tourists. What about the police?"

"They don't seem very interested." I snorted with disdain. During the last visit at the police headquarters, my hopes had gone up in smoke again. "I told you, detective Sibeko doesn't take me seriously at all. Just what choice do I have?"

"Look, it's a question of how quickly you want to find your sister. A sangoma talks to spirits, the police doesn't. You should pick yourself up and speak to a proper sangoma." Margaret took the dog leash from a hook on the wall and called Tennessee, her dog. "Come let's get some exercise, it'll do you good."

The matter was crystal clear to her, but I wasn't comfortable talking to spirits. Didn't that mean the spirits of the deceased? No, Claire was alive and well. There was certainly no need to contact her spirit.

That's how I thought back then.

As so often, we walked Tennessee, the huge Great Dane, to the Gaborone Dam for a walk. The park behind the dam was a large nature reserve and one of my favourite places in town. There was always a cool breeze over the water, a welcome treat in this dry, sweltering climate.

It took some getting used to seeing giant Tennessee breaking through the undergrowth, galloping towards me in full speed. He looked more like a small horse than a dog.

But then all he wanted to do was lick my toes and push himself up against my legs like a little puppy. It was Tennessee's way of letting me know that I'd better pat his broad back. He would be looked after when Margaret left. One of her friends had agreed to adopt the gigantic lapdog.

I'd suggested a picnic by the idyllic dam one day and Margaret just laughed.

There was much grass around, just not the smooth blanket of lawn one could expect in an English park. This kind grew in coarse tufts, clustered over the hard red soil. As if that was not deterring enough, large black ants crawled all over blankets and food in no time. And termites. No picnic then.

Margaret loved to watch birds and never left the house without her binoculars. I had never been exceedingly interested in that sort of thing, but my new friend turned bird-watching into an interesting experience.

She knew the names of nearly all the birds we encountered. There were Madagascar bee-eaters on some bushes and the blue, iridescent roller birds and circling raptors in the brilliant blue sky.

I also saw small springboks and large lizards in the reserve and once we found a long dead snake as we walked the dog along the edge of the water. Creepy. I was quite intrigued by large butterflies and the red dragonflies that seemed to stand still in the air.

"Did you see the dassie over there by the rocks?" Margaret asked and pointed to an animal that, even through binoculars, looked rather like a large rat without a tail.

She was also an expert at removing ticks from Tennessee's paws and neck. The tiny spidery insects turned into small, grey rubber pears when filled with blood,

"Don't just pull them out," she cautioned me. "Use alcohol, glue or oil on the head. Then you carefully twist it out. If the head stays in, it causes infection."

Margaret knew what she was talking about.

I'd heard from Rita that Carol Jenkins had a nasty run-in with a tick and that her knee was red and painfully swollen. I visited Carol after work and saw that her knee was in a dreadful state. The tiny black head was still lodged in puffy, red skin.

"Got infected somehow," a pale and gaunt Carol said. "The doctor lanced the abscess and put me on a second course of antibiotics yesterday. Says he'd seen worse. And that with my knee looking like a balloon. I didn't know tick bite fever could be so nasty." She ignored the chocolates I handed over. No appetite, obviously.

"You poor thing!" I commiserated. "Do you feel very sick still?"

"Ach nay, it looks so much better already. Headache's improved too and I don't feel so nauseous all the time anymore," she said bravely and I shuddered. I would be hellishly careful about ticks from now on.

Her gardener Phineas was busy cutting the white rosebushes in the garden. Satan, the ancient beagle, barked half-heartedly whenever Phineas moved too close to his spot in front of the kitchen.

"Sorry Bridget, my headache's come back. I think I'd better go and lie down for a bit, before the kids come home from school," Carol said.

By mid-February, I had learned my way around the

office. Margaret had also managed to induct me into the essential who-is-who of the diplomatic circles in Gaborone and in Berlin. Then it was time for her to leave for England and I missed her sorely.

The two of us had become good friends even if just for a short while.

My peaceful existence ended abruptly as soon as I took over my new responsibilities. As Mr. Köhler's new PA, I was constantly invited to fancy dinners and functions. I was now apparently also on the radar of the Gaborone singles scene.

One of those singles was Gabrielle Habenicht from Munich, who worked in the passport section at the German Consulate. She was not much older than I, had frizzy dark hair, slightly crooked teeth and loved to play tennis.

Her sense of humour was priceless, especially when she skipped into a Bavarian accent, and she was forever on her way to some party or other. Just Gabby to her friends, Gabrielle was always cheerful and extremely popular. We soon became great pals. I needed new friends badly.

We went together to one of the more formal events. The Gaborone premiere of the spectacular movie 'Gorillas in the Mist'. I had read the positive reviews in the latest edition of 'Times Magazine' and looked forward to making the acquaintance of a very different Africa on film.

We stood outside the only cinema town in our cocktail dresses — both of which came from Gabby's wardrobe. Gabby told me that a grey-haired and very dignified woman was the famous Lady Khama. A few dignitaries kept her polite company. She was the widow of Sir Seretse Khama, the first president of Botswana and a huge celebrity.

I had read about their early romance in Britain, their marriage and the difficulties they had to endure in Botswana, because she was white, and he black. They had prevailed and raised four children. The current president was Quett Masire, but Lady Khama was a legend.

We strolled through the cordoned-off area and had some sausage rolls before being ushered to our seats inside the theatre. Suddenly, everybody stood up and clapped. The president had entered the building. As soon as he had taken his seat, the audience was allowed to sit again. The lights went out and the movie began with a murmur of awe in the audience. 'Gorillas in the Mist' did the film critics proud.

Gaborone began to draw me into its spell and I began to enjoy myself. I danced and chatted at parties and met more singles by the day. It must have been around this time that I slowed down my ambitious search for Claire. I had achieved absolutely nothing and ran out of energy to carry on. Perhaps it was true that I was running after a spectre. I was here and alive and wanted to enjoy life. The partying gave me a perfect excuse and it was suddenly so easy to let myself go.

I should have known right there and then that this wasn't like me at all.

And then I saw Benjamin again — quite by chance. My motherly friend, Rita Winckler, wanted to meet me for drinks and a bit of overdue natter on the terrace of the President Hotel.

It was getting late and I knew that Rita had to fetch her children from choir practice. I bumped into someone as I was hurrying up the stairs. I didn't even look up and just murmured 'Sorry about that,' ready to hurry past.

"Ho, hi there, don't run away." I would have recognised this deep melodious voice anywhere. I looked up, trying not to show my delight.

"Oh hi, it's...Benjamin, isn't it?" I feigned indifference.

"Yes it is, and I hear that you are Kurt's new PA now." He seemed genuinely happy for me and kept smiling, clearly expecting some small talk.

"That's right. Margaret and her husband went back to England last week."

"I also hear that you left your boyfriend in Palapye."

Benjamin blurted out and caught me by surprise. I swallowed. He was interested in me! Why else would he ask something like that?

"News travel fast," I said and leaned against the handrail by the stairs.

"Forgive me that was rude. It's a small community and people talk about things like that," Benjamin apologized. Apparently he was not quite the hermit he wanted me to believe in.

"To be sure. I'm still learning about Gaborone ways."

"Touché. Any chance of you getting back together?" he carried on all the same. Should I encourage him? This was taking too long, I had to go and meet Rita upstairs. I made a snap decision.

"No, no chance at all right now."

"I see." Benjamin seemed to wait for an explanation.

"Tell you what, why don't you pop into the office tomorrow? I'm really late meeting a friend for a drink."

I looked up at the terrace and saw Rita at one of the front tables, holding one of her ever-present cigarettes. People were pushing us aside now on their way up. It was a busy time at the President Hotel after all.

"Perhaps I can come with you for just one moment," Benjamin offered. Wasn't he crossing some boundary there? Oh what the heck, I was late and the sooner I could get to Rita, the better.

"Okay, but just for one moment," I agreed and raced up the last few steps.

Rita sat at one of our favourite tables by the railing. From here we had an excellent view of the mall for people watching. She had a coke in front of her and waved me over languidly.

"Sorry I'm late, had to do a last minute thing for Kurt at the office," I said out of breath.

Then Benjamin caught up with me. He made way for a waiter, who balanced his tablet past us with drinks for the neighbouring table. Then he stood next to me and waited to be introduced.

"That's quite all right. We still have about...42 minutes. Come sit down." Rita was the most patient person I knew. She looked at her watch again and took a long draught from her cigarette. Then her gaze fell on Benjamin.

"Oh yes Rita, this is Benjamin Glasberg, a German volunteer. Benjamin, this is Rita Winckler. We just bumped into each other at the bottom of the stairs. Literally."

"Nice to meet you." Benjamin turned on his charm and bowed slightly as he took Rita's hand. I could tell that she was impressed by his manners and his smile.

"Nice to meet you too," she said in a friendly, interested tone.

"I'll be on my way then," Benjamin said and turned towards me. "I just wanted to tell you that in case you feel like joining me and a few friends at the Chinese restaurant tonight for dinner, I've booked a table for seven."

I felt steamrollered, but managed to say casually "I'll think about it."

"Excellent, goodbye now." He bowed slightly and smiled at each of us.

"Goodbye." I sat down and ordered a rock shandy.

I had just discovered this refreshing, virtually non-alcoholic drink made with Angostura bitters, ice, soda water and lemonade and ordered it at every opportunity. Benjamin Glasberg disappeared down the stairs and walked in the direction of Corner's Supermarket. I followed him with my eyes.

"Ding dong!" Rita could be so coarse sometimes. "And?"

"And what? I only met him once before," I defended myself.

"Really? Quite a dish!" this pillar of Gaborone society said with admiration.

"Oh is he? I hadn't noticed." I lied of course.

"Go to the Chinese restaurant tonight. Have some 'Ants

on a Tree' and get to know this lovely man." Rita referred to a spicy lamb mince dish, one had to spoon into crisp lettuce leaves and fold into parcels. A popular dish with expatriates.

"Rita, I don't even know the guy. It's not the right time to even think about starting a relationship. It will just distract me. Have to see the police commissioner again next week," I argued weakly.

"Oh give it a rest, Bridget. He is into you, I can tell. A bit of romance will do you good," my motherly friend sweet-talked me with a meaningful stare.

I sighed resignedly. "Oh Rita, stop it. I'm not ready for this."

But I went to the Chinese restaurant anyway. Just after seven.

Benjamin bounded towards me as I stood looking lost by the entrance and escorted me to the table. He introduced me to his friends. Mette and Thorsten were Danish volunteers from Kang, Rudolph Haase, an older German volunteer and Roz Williams came from America.

Mette was a sturdy blonde girl with a healthy appetite. Her boyfriend Thorsten was tall and Nordic-looking and very quiet. Rudolph Haase's nose twitched nervously like a rabbit's. He seemed too bashful to look women directly in the eye. Roz was a corporate lawyer, now in the Peace Corps on a mission to help suffering Africans. She admitted to being in the wrong African country, because there was not as much suffering in Botswana as she had expected.

After the introductions, it seemed that everybody talked in code. About things, they had experienced together and I had absolutely no clue about, and people I had never even heard of. I didn't understand a word. Ben noticed my discomfort, called them to order and the conversation turned to the progress or the lack thereof in their respective projects.

I gathered that Benjamin was upset with some villagers,

who worked for the school in Kang and siphoned off building materials for their private use. Apparently they also treated expensive 4x4 vehicles in their care with disdain.

"If a truck stops working, that's it. They just leave it by the side of the road to rot, until somebody remembers to ask about it. Same goes for water pumps. Stops working? Just ignore it and carry on without one," he laughed bitterly. "Usually I'm the one, who ends up fixing everything." Benjamin was obviously a mechanic.

"Oh yes, I know about that sort of thing," Rudolph moaned.

"Why do they do that?" I asked incredulously. "Don't these people need a car or water pumps?"

"Too lazy maybe. Generations living in the desert did just fine without all that technology. Why start now?" The others seemed to agree with Ben's view.

"Yes, before I came out here, I met a volunteer, who had just gone home to Denmark. She said that the best way to describe the Tswanas was that they sit under a tree and said ehéy, ehéy all day long," Mette informed us.

"Not so much the women. Especially not those in the towns. But many of the men... definitely. Women often do all the hard work and men drink beer," Roz backed her up.

"Two of my apprentices have already left after the first trade certificate. And there are three certificates over three years. One single certificate seems to be enough to get a well-paid job. So why slug it out for two more years just to get the full qualification?" Ben complained some more. The others nodded.

"Yes, quite. With one certificate hanging on the wall, you just sit on your butt and order everybody else around," Rudolph added and scratched his nose.

"I taught English for a while in Palapye. My secretaries weren't anything like that," I threw in. They all stared at me.

"That's different," Rudolph said, but didn't explain why it was different.

"Yes, that's rather different," Roz seconded.

My own positive experience was not in demand, it seemed. So I rather listened to the other stories. Mette and Thorsten worked with Bushmen, or Khoi San, in the Kalahari Desert. That sounded interesting. It was one of their tasks, to regularly supply the San with drinking water in large containers. This surprised me, because I had assumed that Bushmen were able to find water in the ground. Digging up roots that contained water and the like.

"So does somebody else take over from you when you come to Gaborone or go on holiday?" I asked Mette.

She just shrugged her shoulders and told us about the engraved ostrich eggs that the Khoi San sold to her. I ordered such an egg and a necklace for 10 Pula each.

Rudolph Haase soon had a few beers too many and began to speak in an rambling way about a weavers' project he oversaw. He lost me halfway through his account and the conversation changed once again to insider talk. I gave up trying to understand and turned my attention to the wordless dialogue Benjamin had started. Looks and smiles and touching my leg with his foot under the table. I liked the 'Ants on a Tree' and I liked Ben.

He stole a kiss from me that night when he dropped me off at Acacia Court and I didn't mind. It felt rather romantic. I walked in the door just in time before it started raining and my heart was thumping in unison with the splatter of rain on the tin roof.

By the following day, my mind had cleared again. I couldn't give myself over to romance right now, despite a nice, warm feeling in my stomach. Other matters demanded my attention. Work of course. And then I needed to employ a maid.

Up until now, the previous tenant's maid had done a spot of cleaning for me, but I soon found out that she used the flat for trysts with her boyfriend while I was at work. Foolishly, she had left her underwear lying around in the lounge and I had to fire. No problem I said to myself, I can do my own housework. Not so!

Tswanas apparently regarded it as selfish, if persons of certain social standing did not share their income with someone who could do the rough jobs around the house. I didn't know that of course, when a young Tswana woman knocked on my door at the weekend.

"Koko! Koko!" she called in the Tswana way to get noticed. I was surprised. Locals weren't usually so forward. Except the occasional beggar, who demanded to be fed. Everybody fed the beggars. The woman was certainly not a beggar. She was well-spoken and demanded employment as soon as I opened the door. Somebody had tipped her off, that the Lekgoa woman in No.1 Acacia Court, had fired her domestic worker for misconduct.

"No, thank you for asking, but I really don't need a maid. See, it's only myself here. Why don't you try the couple in No.8 upstairs? Perhaps they are still looking for somebody to clean," I suggested. The young woman was incredulous.

"They are black, madam," she whispered. The woman seemed well-informed.

"Excuse me?" Now it was my turn to be incredulous.

"I'd rather work for a white madam. Like you," she explained.

"But what is the difference? They are really nice people," I said clumsily.

"Black madams make you work long hours. No extra money. The maid must be ready all the time, when the madam rings the bell. The whole day! Eish."

"Really?" I didn't know that. Ringing a bell sounded very old-fashioned.

"Yes, my sister's black madam even hit her — like that." The woman demonstrated a smack in the face and I took a step back into the lounge.

"Why?" I forgot to close my mouth.

"My sister, she wanted to take weekend off," she said

simply.

It took me a moment to regain my composure. Why was she telling me that? She must be thinking that white people were real fools to believe her stories.

"Sorry to hear that, but I still don't need a maid. So, good luck." I wanted to close the door and get back to my magazine.

"Howe! Please madam," she pleaded with me and put her foot in the door.

"Look, I just told you that the couple in No.8 needs a maid. I don't. Good bye."

I pushed her foot back and closed the door. The young woman must have stared at the closed door in disbelief for a while. Then she abruptly turned around and I saw her walking across the parking lot into the street. She didn't even give the couple in No.8 a try. Odd. I told Gabby later about the incident and my friend informed me about the cultural ins and outs of employing household staff in Botswana.

"She was probably exaggerating, to soften you up. But I've heard of cases like that."

"You have?"

"It's not that straight forward to employ somebody here. As an employer you are regarded as a parent."

"You are joking! I know about the whole respect thing, but parents?"

"No seriously. A domestic might lie about having to go to another funeral — her grandmother' third, but, you are expected to help her out of a tight spot. And just like some people slap their children around, they think they can do that with their maids." Gabby was dead serious.

"Crikey. What if I'm in trouble? Doesn't it work both ways?"

"Sometimes maybe, but it's usually the other way around." Live and learn Bridget.

"But I can't believe that they prefer Lekgoas to Tswanas."

"I've heard Lorato admit that her maid works all hours for next to nothing. That's how the hierarchy works. Young village cousins usually don't get paid at all."

I remembered that Mrs. Matija had brought such a young cousin along to Palapye. On the other hand, Princess firmly ruled the Winckler household. Well.

Gabby knew of a university lecturer, whose part-time maid needed a 'piece job' twice a week. She urged me to employ Hilda to avoid any more 'interviews' and gave me advice on working hours and payment. That's how I became Hilda's 'mother' on Wednesdays and Saturday mornings. Hilda soon became not only my cleaning lady, but also a trusted confidante. Hilda was petite and attractive and wore a headscarf at all times. She immediately took control of my neglected residence and always left it in a sparkling state of cleanliness. Hilda was bright as a button. My very own Tsanana.

It felt strange to be an employer, but it could be far less pleasant to live with one's neighbours.

As so often, I sat outside in the complex garden under a tree one day. A large bougainvillea bush in need of a haircut gave me some privacy and I read my book while listening to music on the walkman.

When I looked up by chance, the lady from No. 2 appeared on her porch and quickly walked over to mine. My underwear was drying on two washing lines, hiding the open back door. Was she coming for a visit? Then I realized that my usually so elusive neighbour had something else in mind. I watched her thoroughly fingering my bras and panties. This didn't look like an unannounced visit to me.

"Excuse me, what are you doing there with my underwear?" I jumped up and dropped my book and headphones. Before the surprised woman could slink back into her flat, I'd planted myself bravely in front of her.

"Why were you just searching through my underwear?"

"No speak, no speak," she wailed and tried to push past me.

"Not before you tell me what you were doing there on my

porch."

"No speak, no speak." The woman kept adjusting the fold of her sari. It was absurd. I would not find out this way, squabbling with a woman, whose name I didn't even know.

"Don't you ever do that again, you have no business with my underwear," I said in my best teacher tone and let her pass. Then I checked my washing, but couldn't detect anything out of the ordinary.

"Why would anyone in their right mind inspect their neighbours' underwear?" Gabby was astonished. "That's sick."

"How must I know? The woman is Indian and she isn't my enemy or anything. She's not the friendliest neighbour, but I don't think she wanted to harm me," I replied. "And I didn't find any muti or stuff like that."

I had learned that one could harm enemies by strategically placing objects.

"She must have seen Benjamin around and your neighbour's curiosity got the better of her," my worldly-wise friend suggested. "Your neighbour must have tried to find out, whether the two of you live together." It was a plausible, if bizarre explanation.

"Well, I never! Maybe that's why she sat with some visitors directly in front of my bedroom window and had a full-blown conversation on Sunday morning. She spied on me."

"Was there anything to spy on?"

"No, not really. I was on my own until breakfast."

"Shame on her then."

"Yes. Shame on her. She should get a life!" My anger had dissipated. People could be strange sometimes.

Slowly, but surely I settled into the routine of my new African life. There were so many changes, but I had given up fighting against them. I began to dress differently. In England I would never have dared to wear a figure-hugging dress to work, printed all over with large purple fruit. In Gaborone I felt comfortable doing just that. I was living in a town where women waited at the bus stop, dressed in shiny evening dresses ready to go to the office.

The corporate dress code in grey and black seemed boring in comparison. In England, I had never noticed this lack of colour. Perhaps the lack of sunshine had something to do with it.

Work was also a different experience in Gabs. I'd leave early and walk along the sandy pathways that the local people used, enjoying the cool morning air. A more relaxed way of starting the day.

The job wasn't too tiring and I was part of the social scene after hours. Not because Claire would have done it that way, but because I enjoyed it. And I decided to give romance a chance and my reputation changed. No longer the sad spinster Bridget, who had left her supposed boyfriend in Palapye. I was now Bridget the gal, who worked for a reputable volunteer organization and partied the nights away. Bridget, who had captured the heart of one of the most eligible bachelors. I began to like my new role.

"Ah Bridget, I hear your attractive boyfriend is back in town. What is it like to kiss a model man?" Kurt salivated.

I couldn't believe my ears, although I must admit that I was a tiny bit flattered.

"I'm not sure I want to talk about this."

"Oh, you spoilsport, don't be such a prude. You are sooo lucky." Kurt waved his hand around and gave me a scolding look.

"So are you, Kurt, Hansie is very nice," I quickly changed the subject. It worked.

"Yes, I know," he said a trifle theatrically.

"Do you still need the two folders you asked for earlier?"

"Yes, yes. Mustn't dawdle, Berlin is waiting for my weekly report." He looked markedly at his gold watch.

"Oh, Kurt don't forget your doctor's appointment at 10:30." I called after him as his back disappeared into the passage.

Kurt's head reappeared in the door. "You are so efficient

my little worker bee," he sighed and went back to his office.

Kurt Köhler was getting used to me not being Margaret. The neck massages had stopped. I chuckled to myself and gave the two folders my full attention.

It wasn't always easy to handle my boss's ever-changing moods, though. There were weeks of peace and then suddenly he'd snap. Margaret must have been immune to this. I wasn't. Kurt had given me a tongue lashing just the week before, because I'd carried out his instructions to phone all the volunteers in the country for some survey. I was halfway down the list, when he complained that I had the audacity to waste the budget.

Defending myself with facts was futile. He was also incensed by the fact that volunteers started coming into my office to meet the new PA.

"They must come into my office first. Then they can go to yours. That would be the proper thing to do," he lectured me as if I had been luring the volunteers on purpose into my den.

"I don't know why they do that, Kurt. In the future, I'll tell them to go and see you straight away," I promised and my boss seemed appeased. For a while.

"Oh Foompy. What a jerk!" I would complain to Claire's picture in my desk drawer, as soon as Kurt was out of earshot. "As if I wanted his job! There's just no pleasing the man."

Rita joked about the whole thing and Gabby showed sympathy, but I sulked for a while. Then I resolved it in my stride. Anyway, Benjamin was coming back to Gabs for a weekend, so what did I care about Kurt Köhler.

I could understand now why Margaret had welcomed the occasional excursions to the dog parlour and dry cleaner.

"Say Bridget, is your boyfriend as sexy as he looks?" Gabby blurted out after lunch two days later. We were at The Parks Restaurant in the African Mall, mostly frequented by the younger crowd.

"What? Can you keep it down please?" I could feel the colour rise to my cheeks. "And it's none of your business anyway," I added annoyed and looked over my shoulder. Gossip-mongers were around every corner, especially in places like restaurants.

"Yoh, may. Come on." Gabby pleaded in her comical Bavarian as if I was telling her about the next instalment of a popular TV soap. I didn't see why I should indulge her.

"No, it's none of your business. And if you must know, we just kissed a little and went to the movies. What do take me for?"

"I see," she said pursing her lips, clearly not believing me and took a toothpick.

"You see what?" I was still annoyed. "Why is that so interesting for you?"

"Animal magnetism! Benjamin Glasberg is just about the cutest guy around and you want to push him away, because you're scared you'll fall in love." I gasped.

"No, that's not it at all," I huffed, although it probably was. "I only just met him."

"Okay whatever you say, got to beetle, duty calls," Gabby said offhand and picked up her fashionable red handbag. "If you don't want him, just say the word."

My face felt as red as the bag by now. Gabby could be so crude sometimes. She air-kissed my cheeks and swanned out the door. I thought about Benjamin for a moment and that I couldn't waste too much of my time with even the cutest guy.

He would be in Kang for the next two weeks at least and I had enough on my plate. But the harder I tried to fight my feelings, the more I was drawn in. It felt good to have someone else so close to me again. To be so desirable. I began to include Ben more and more in my thinking. What would he have said to this and that or how would it have felt, had he come to that party with me.

Another appointment with the police was around the corner. This time a British agent deigned to see me. His name was MacDonald, like the hamburger. Grandpa must have been in contact with the MI 5 somehow and pulled some strings.

"Do you see these files over there?" he asked as I sat down. His manner was as brash as his crew cut. I saw stacks of green files and folders against the opposite wall atop a shabby table.

"I have to go through about 30 unsolved cases every year. We do not have the manpower to follow up no end on each individual case. With most cases we get help from tribal leaders." He took a deep breath. "In your sister's case, we went out of our way to get results because she is a British citizen. And to do your Grandfather a favour. But, the locals did not exactly cooperate and there is nothing we can do about it." The hamburger didn't mince his words.

"But why not?" I didn't have the impression that anyone was going out of his way.

"We don't know why. We are in Africa. But there is only so much we can do, Miss Reinhold. Please don't get your hopes up. I'm really sorry, but chances are extremely slim that you will see your sister again. We will soon consider this a cold case."

Very subtle, thanks. It took me a few minutes to digest the harsh news. I felt hopelessness wash over me. Was I really in denial? Didn't I want to see the truth of the matter?

"What do you expect me to do? Drive around the Tuli area by myself, looking for her with no police backup, no plan? I need your help with this."

"Honestly Miss Reinhold? Pack up and go home. There is nothing more you can do here. Or drive around the Tuli area. It's entirely up to you. As long as you stay out of trouble and don't get lost yourself in the process." He scribbled something down on his exam pad.

"Will you release her car then?" I don't know why I had asked that.

"The car has already been handed over to your brother-in-law. I believe he wanted to sell it." More news, but then I hadn't spoken to Tony for a while.

The police couldn't - or wouldn't - help me find Claire, so what were my options? I needed to get in touch with Tony again. He had to still care about Claire! Organize a meeting with a tribal leader or even - a sangoma. *I'm not giving up,* I thought grimly to myself, *I'm not giving up!*

Agent MacDonald had left his office to attend to some urgent matter and walked back in, nose in another green file. He didn't exactly pay attention to me.

"Oh, you are still here, Miss Reinhold. I'm sorry, but I've got so much..."

"Well, excuse me for living, but my twin sister is very important to me and I'd appreciate it, if you could give me a few more minutes of your precious time." I raged helplessly.

The green file snapped shut and landed with a thud on the big desk.

"Fine, what would you like to know?" he looked at me with tired eyes.

"If I have to search for Claire myself, I need to know where to start. Where exactly was my sister last seen and when?"

Agent Hamburger sighed, but I was determined not to let him off the hook.

"Very well. Here is what we know. Mrs. Reinhold-Stratton left Francistown in the early afternoon, after spending the night at her friends' house, the..." he had to look the name up.

"Bouchers. She then headed for the Tuli Block and got as far as Bobonong. It grows dark early in winter and she most likely drove in the dark."

"But the cows and goats are lying in the road..."

"Precisely. She could have hit the goat in the darkness. We don't know where, because no reports of such an accident were received." He closed the green file and spelled the facts out. "We believe she lost her way on route to the nature reserve. It is unlikely that your sister then drove all the way to Mochudi and into the field where we found her car with a near-empty petrol tank.

There was nothing else in the car to give us a clue. It's probable that the car was stolen and the thief took to his heels when he ran out of petrol. In other words I'd start looking in the Tuli Block area. Forget about Mochudi."

Okay, nothing new there. I could have figured that out by myself.

"And who should contact there? The local police?"

"I wouldn't bother m'am. I know I shouldn't say that, but if I was you, I'd rather speak to the chiefs in the area. Again, we are in Africa and you don't want to waste your time."

The police were a waste of time? I tried my best to understand that.

"Thank you agent MacDonald," I forced a smile, "I guess I'll have to think about that, before I do anything."

"Good luck to you m'am. Be careful, whatever you do."

"I know, we're in Africa."

"Just try not to disappear or better still, go home to England."

"Goodbye then."

"Goodbye, m'am."

He politely opened the door for me and I stepped into the green passage. Then agent MacDonald had surely forgotten about me and Claire as he gave his attention to the new green file again. It should be my last visit. Would I have to come to terms with the fact that I would never find Claire?

He had told me to speak to the chiefs. Margaret Marducci had said long ago to speak to sangomas. But I pushed the thought aside - again. Defeated, I trudged over to the Mall in slow motion and sat down on a bench. A street boy followed me around, wailing "Batla mádi, batla mádi!" I want money,

I want money. I gave him 50 Thebe and he ran away.

I had to think things through. My doubts had been confirmed once again. The ambitious plan to work with the police had gone up in smoke and what could I possibly expect from the High Commission. There was little I could expect from Tony and it would be too much to expect help with this from my new Gabs friends. It would be madness to go and drive around, looking aimlessly for Claire all by myself. I simply couldn't grasp another solution.

This was not something I could simply power through. It was too big for me. Then a question encroached on my mind. A very selfish question. What about my life and what if Ben was the ONE after all? Our relationship began to blossom. My energy had its limits. So why did I feel so guilty even thinking about him? I didn't want to admit it to myself as I sat on this bench in the Mall, but I had to make a decision how to best apply my energy.

I managed to hitch a ride by truck from the water affairs department's car pool bound for Ghanzi, just as Ben had told me to. The driver would drop me off on the main road in Kang and Ben had described in detail how to get from the main road to the brigade compound.

I was spellbound by the open space and the ever-changing landscape. There was a good deal of sand, red and white and yellow dotted with tough, thorny plants clinging to the sparse ground.

*Perhaps I am falling in love with the Kalahari more than Ben,* I thought and smiled to myself. Wild ostriches sprinted elegantly alongside the truck, not far from the dirt road, like dolphins of the desert.

I watched in amazement how they took turns with little springboks that darted through the air, before running this way and that. It was not a normal dirt road for normal cars. One could only make the distance in a truck or 4x4 at high speed, in order not to sink into the sand or get stuck on the hump in the middle. Countless tires had eaten relentlessly into the soft ground over time and the level of the road was sometimes below the surrounding desert sand.

The hump in the middle of the single lane road had to be graded on a regular basis. The grader vehicle and oncoming traffic announced themselves in a cloud of dust, which was a sure sign for the driver to make way in time. Overtaking a slower vehicle was also a mission, but somehow we made it to Kang in one piece. Despite the breath-taking view, it wasn't a comfortable trip and only the seat belt prevented me from being knocked against the roof or windshield. No chance to have a conversation either. We arrived after dark and I immediately made my way to the brigade compound.

"No, that's not cycads, Bridge," Ben said when I asked him early in morning about the chirping sounds. "Those are lizards. Come I show you."

We walked to the bush on the outskirts of the town. In the early hours of the freezing desert morning, before a flaming red sun began to scorch the day, lizards were bouncing on the tips of long grasses and twigs, 'singing'.

*Oh Foompy, I wish you could see this!* I thought enthusiastically. The mere thought of Claire hurt and I pushed it impatiently aside. On the other hand, the thought of Ben felt warm and comforting.

"How can they sing like that?" I asked impressed.

"They don't really sing. Mette says it's got something to do with raising their body temperature after the cold desert night. The lizards sometimes do that in the evening as well. Especially in winter."

"That's amazing," I marvelled and watched the funny little critters bounce on their grasses and twigs. "Do you think that's true?" I blinked into the rising sun.

"I have no idea, but Mette is usually clued-up on stuff like that."

There was still so much to learn. On the way back to the compound, I walked barefoot next to the path and let the fine sand flow through my toes.

"Ouch, what's that?" I hadn't expected the cutting pain.

"I told you to wear sandals, Bridge," Ben scolded and helped me pull out tiny round seeds, the feared devil thorns, hiding in the glinting sand. They had lodged themselves painfully into my soft-skinned soles.

"Only hardy Bushmen with their callused feet are immune to the sting."

"Ouch, that's really sore." I watched as Ben unhooked another devil thorn.

"That'll teach you to wear proper shoes next time when we go into the bush and to stay on the footpath."

The 'singing' lizards didn't cease to fascinate me. Whenever I visited however, I managed to get painful devil thorns stuck in my soles. What I learned was that not everything is what it seems in the Kalahari. What resembles lakes is nothing of that sort. These pans are the remains of an ancient inland sea and contain a bitter cocktail of salts. Totally undrinkable. But if you dig deep enough, you'll find much drinking water underground. The Tswanas call this desert Kgalagadi and the harsh syllables describe it perfectly.

The Okavango Delta to the east is a totally different world. A wetland forged by a massive land slide ages ago, that forced the Okavango River to empty its waters inland instead of into the ocean.

In this Everglade-like paradise you find the zebras and giraffes, hippos and tiny vampires in the clouds of annoying mosquitoes.

But only the dry Kalahari, pure and starkly beautiful, became part of my world. I went to Kang as often as possible and soon knew all the different sections of the Trans-Kalahari Road like the back of my hand. The changing shades of sand from red to grey to yellow and white at different times of the day. The low hills, the thorn trees and settlements we passed.

Kang wasn't very big and it must be one of the remotest

towns on earth. A trade post with warehouses, a post office and bottle stores. No motsetsi hedges anywhere in sight and only dirt roads between the simple, one-story houses. Not much that could be called a garden.

Growing flowers or vegetables was a mission in itself. The sun reflected brightly from the white sand, barely shielded by the shade of thorn trees, and a constant breeze swept the empty streets. I remember the distinct smell of smoke, thatched roofs and creosote, used to paint wooden poles and fences.

Washing shampoo out of one's hair wasn't so easy either, because the water was extremely soft. But I didn't want to drink anything else than this very soft water, whenever I was in Kang.

The silence was sporadically disturbed by the yelping of a stray dog or the drone of passing cars. Despite these bleak surroundings, the Tswana etiquette in the street was intact even here.

"Dumela, ra."

"Dumela, wa tsoga, wa tsoga."

The frugal supplies in the few shops explained why the volunteers came to Gaborone to buy their provisions.

To the right of the main road, the high school and brigade were right next door to each other, run jointly by different development organizations. Inside the complex, the houses were rather modest, just sufficient for one volunteer. The conditions were not suitable for volunteers with families. Thatched rondavels on the other side of the Trans-Kalahari Road were the actual Tswana village. In the rainy season, it wasn't unusual for the daub and wattle huts to get washed away during violent rainstorms, only to be stubbornly re-built in the same place to the same fate the following year.

Lucky then that the buildings at the brigade training centre where Ben worked, were of a more sturdy built. I never witnessed a heavy storm that did more than rattle on windows and doors and caused the tin roof to leak.

A few weeks later I was on my way to Kang again. As always, many thoughts wandered through my mind during the eight-hour drive. I could only stay three days this time. The last time we'd had four. I would push the question aside, whether Benjamin and I had a serious relationship. I wanted to immerse myself in the simple life and the peacefulness of the Kalahari.

To be swept up in an intoxicating whirlwind of love and laughter, a few days at a time. I had never felt like that with David. Or Mark, my first real boyfriend. I vibrated to a different tune now.

Ben came to Gaborone about twice a month. On those occasions, we went to dinner at the Chinese restaurant or the new Korean place in Ramotswa, to the swimming pool at the Oasis Hotel or to one of the frequent parties. It was great to do fun things together and to ignore the worries of daily life. I just snatched the moments as they presented themselves.

And when we were separated by a hellish 8-hour drive? Instant communication was out of the question. There were no telephones in Kang, so we resorted to writing letters that other volunteers carried for us. My life began to revolve around asking for rides to Kang and writing letters to Benjamin.

I sometimes resorted to hitch-hiking from the diamond town of Jwaneng, where the Trans-Kalahari dirt road took over from a coarse gravel track north of the town. The things we do for love...

Then Ben was gone. He had gone on home leave to Germany for six weeks and I missed him. Him and the Kalahari Desert. I'd had no idea that I was capable of pining so much - for a man and some sand.

"So, suddenly I'm good enough again for you." Gabby teased me, when I begged her to come to a concert at the Maitisong Hall with me.

I didn't want to be alone on my birthday. The Gaborone Choir presented 'Carmina Burana' by Carl Orff, a collection of medieval songs. It sounded promising and had nothing to do with Africa at all. Probably better suited to a Cambridge concert hall than Gaborone. I couldn't wait.

"How often must I apologize for neglecting you, you know how it is..."

"Actually, I don't. Men don't seem to find me attractive enough to ask me out."

"Or...they are just intimidated, because you have such amazing self-esteem," I objected. "They don't dare ask you out."

"Yeah, well, I can't help that."

"Don't grow jealous on me now, Gabby. I'm not exactly asking for male attention. Ben just happened." Why did I keep apologizing?

"I'm not jealous, just stating a fact. Are you serious about Ben? There seems to be going on more between the two of you."

"I don't know, but I think...he might be the one." I stuttered.

"Do you have doubts?"

"I don't know," I repeated. "Not much time to think. And now I miss him so much that I can't think either," I sighed. "What's a girl to do?"

Of course Gabby came with me to the concert at Maitisong. We were early and sat down in the first row.

"I wish I could give you relationship advice," Gabby said randomly.

"My sister Claire would have known what to do. Boy magnet." Oops!

"Your sister? I don't think you've ever talked about her." Gabby was understandably surprised.

And that's how I told Gabby about Claire. What had happened and why I was here in Botswana. Words were gushing forth and Gabby listened open-mouthed.

Then people were sitting down around us and the

moment of privacy was gone. I hadn't even told Benjamin, my boyfriend, about it yet.

# CHAPTER 7

"Koko, koko!"
I gently touched the frosted-glass door. "Don't go away, Claire, I'll be right back," I said. Or maybe I just thought that I said it. I hardly dared turn around and leave her there on her own. "Don't go away."
"Koko, koko! Madam!" Hilda knocked louder against the front door now.
I didn't want to open my eyes, didn't want to leave Claire, but the sun shone so brightly through the cream-coloured curtains and chased away the last bits of my dream.
Hilda was by the back door now. "Madam, madam, you still sleeping?"
I looked over at the clock. It was 8:31 am. And it was Saturday morning. Hilda must have been waiting already for half an hour. I had been so close this time - so close.
Claire wanted to tell me something, but I couldn't hear her properly. Because of the glass door between us and then the noise Hilda made. Now it was too late.
"Coming!" I croaked and choked back the tears.
"You very tired, madam. Sorry," Hilda apologized when I opened up yawning.
"It's alright, Hilda. Come in. Sorry you had to wait."
"Madam is working too much. Too much!" Hilda opened the kitchen cupboard. "Ah madam, you forgot to buy dishwasher and bleach. I need bleach to clean the bathroom."
Reality had caught up with me again.
I hadn't had nightmares for so long. Why now? And

Ben was still away in Germany.

Then for weeks nothing remarkable happened. My dreams came and went, but they were never as clear as the one on that Saturday morning.

And then this thing with Ronnie Immelman happened. Ronnie was a young, light-haired South African with a brand new bachelor's degree in entomology from Oxford. Entomology - yes exactly, insects!

I had never heard of Ronnie Immelman before. But Emily had. His parents in Johannesburg knew Emily's Mom, who had given them my address in Gaborone. Although I didn't know Emily that well, she thought that I might be willing to help him out.

Ronnie Immelman was not allowed to go back to South Africa and needed a place to stay. Only for a few days. And there was no space at the company house where Emily lived. She told me about it afterwards.

So one evening in April, he knocked on my door. As a former ANC member, Ronnie's name had ended up on some Secret Police hit list when he was only 17 and wanted to change the world. That had been five years ago. Emily told me later that his motive for joining the struggle had stemmed from teenage rebellion rather than political conviction.

Anyway, Ronnie had suddenly found himself between a rock and a hard place in South Africa and needed to leave his country in a hurry. After staying with political supporters in Botswana for a few months, he'd left for Oxford on a British student visa in order to explore the world of insects.

Ronnie looked innocent like a choir-boy and the connection to Emily's mother was enough of a reference for me. Big mistake!

I should have asked the one question - why none of his former friends had taken him in.

Instead, I spontaneously offered Ronnie my spare

bedroom for a couple of days, because it was virtually unused. In my charitable state of mind, I didn't consider that Ben might not approve of another man sharing my flat when he returned from leave. Or that I didn't know Ronnie for a bar of soap.

The following day, I found out that my new flat mate was big on reading. To my shock and surprise he arrived in a pick-up truck with a duffel bag and hundreds of books he had stored in somebody's garage. The books were neatly stacked against the guest room wall, which suddenly looked a lot smaller.

I also found out that Ronnie was big on other things. I had returned home late from work one night and searched the fridge for something edible. The leftover rice and stew from the night before had disappeared. The fridge was as empty as political promises. Not even a piece of bread. So I decided to fry the last egg in the fridge.

Ronnie sat on the floor by the coffee table, leaning against the couch, staring out the veranda door. That should have set off some warning bells. The floor was littered with empty beer cans and dirty plates. Hmm. I stood by the kitchen door with the saucer in my hand and hungrily wolfed down the fried egg. And I was annoyed.

"Ronnie, you promised to buy some food."

"Ah man, no time. Looking for a job and then I came home and relaxed," he said lazily without looking at me once.

There was this smell. He took a long drag from a small pipe, blowing out sickly sweet smoke. Great, my new flat mate wasn't just a messy and unreliable sponge, he was also into drugs!

"I don't want you to smoke dagga in here," I told him firmly after I had watched him light his pipe for the third time. I had learned recently that dagga was the local term for marijuana.

"Don't be so straight-laced. It's harmless, you know. Want a beer?"

"No I don't want beer." I swallowed the last morsel of my egg.

"Why not?"

"I just don't like beer. And I don't like dagga either. So smoke it somewhere else, if you absolutely must."

Ronnie contemplated this outrageous statement for a while and kept on staring at the veranda door. Then he turned around to face me.

"No beer and no dagga, hey?" His eyes were red-rimmed.

"No dagga in the flat and beer in moderation. And please clean up this mess in here." I used the firm voice my Dad would have used.

Ronnie mulled over my words.

I walked into the kitchen and put the saucer into the sink. Surely there was some chocolate left in my room! I would have to stash some food in my room as long as Ronnie stayed in the flat. I was disappointed. He was turning out to be quite the opposite of the spunky young graduate, who had knocked on my door just yesterday.

At last, the penny dropped. So that's why nobody wanted him around!

I didn't know half the story yet.

"I just like being stoned." I jumped. Ronnie stood leaning against the door frame. "Coffee didn't keep me awake all night when I had to study for exams. Speed is better, but dagga is harmless just like coffee."

"Whatever. Just don't smoke it in here," I said.

He didn't like that. "F***! Who do you think you are? The queen of the flat?" he snapped at me.

"What?"

"You heard me! Just leave me alone. I can do what I like. And your maid's coming tomorrow anyway. It's her job to clean up, not mine." Ronnie threw himself into a tantrum that made Rumpelstiltsken's look pale in comparison.

"F*** this sh**! I do what I like!" He boxed against the door frame and blew smoke in my face. I admit, it was difficult to stay calm, but somehow I managed.

"I hate to break it to you, but this is my place and I'm paying for it. You are just a guest here and only for a few days tops. So behave like a good guest and don't talk to me like that."

"F*** you! You are not my Mom!" He slumped halfway down the door frame. I'd just about had enough! Was he only smoking dagga in his pipe or something stronger?

"F*** yourself... and that will be the day —".

Had I really said that?

"But, you are a witch," he said in a menacing voice. "And do you know what they do with witches - in Africa?"

I gasped. This sounded much like a threat.

"What did you just say?" I flew at him. I could only imagine what they did with witches in Africa.

"Who me?" His eyes narrowed and he grinned insanely.

Ronnie pulled himself abruptly up and strutted to the back door. Here he began smoking through the fly screen into the cool night air. So at least something had filtered through his thick skull. Too little too late.

"Listen Ronnie - that goes too far. You can't talk to me like that. I want you out of here by tomorrow." My voice trembled with anger.

"F*** you! I have every right to stay here," he ranted. Enough with the F-bombs already!

"Oh no, you don't." I was determined to put an end to this living arrangement as quickly as possible.

"Witch!" Ronnie yelled and stomped his foot.

"By tomorrow you're out of here."

I had enough of this surreal conversation. Besides, I was still hungry and there was chocolate in my room. I left him standing in the lounge and went to bed.

Ronnie murmured to himself for a while longer and I locked my door twice. Just in case. Ronnie Immelman, insect-lover, was apparently intent on ridding himself of witches. I couldn't tell anybody about this at home! My mother would have a dozen kittens and my Dad might just start a search and rescue operation.

Hilda, my loyal maid stood in front of me the next morning and shook her head in disbelief. The lounge looked as messy as it had the night before.

"The man who stay here. Roanee. She's no good, madam," Hilda whispered in my ear. "He is very dirty and talk funny things."

I saw that Hilda was genuinely frightened. We carefully checked the guest room door. Ronnie wasn't at home. Hopefully, he had gone to organize a car for his things.

"What did he say to you, Hilda?" I pushed a couple of plates aside and sat gingerly down on the couch. Hilda busied herself with picking up the trash.

"He says Monday... a little birdie told her that you, madam, you are witch and you must disappear." She stopped and looked up. "You were not home when I leave. Eish madam, sorry!"

I shuddered. Was Ronnie going around, telling people I was a witch? And what did he mean by that - that I had to disappear?

"Why did he say that to you?" I queried Hilda.

"I don't know, but please say she must leave, madam. He is no good," this usually so confident woman begged me.

"I'm sorry he scared you, Hilda. He told me the same thing last night and I told him to leave. I think he's - mad."

"Howe! You better change the lock, madam!"

To be honest, I was also frightened by now. Whatever may have been wrong with Ronnie Immelman, I didn't want any part of it.

"Good idea, Hilda. I'll go to the mall and ask the locksmith what to do. No matata."

"Yes, madam, I lock door on inside. You must knock. Come back quick."

She looked at me with relief and began to scrub the floor. She must have thought that the solution to the problem with the mad Lekgoa man was firmly in madam's hands now.

I went to the Mall and bought an inner lock. Then I phoned Emily to tell her about all the trouble Ronnie was causing. But Emily had left for Johannesburg to visit her family. I couldn't get hold of anybody else. So I had no choice but to handle this on my own.

When my erstwhile flat mate returned home late that night, he found that his key no longer fit into the door lock. I heard him stomp on the gravel to the back door.

He obviously hadn't noticed that it only opened from the inside. Ronnie stomped back to the front door and began to swear at the top of his voice.

"F*** man! Let me in, you witch. That's my flat!" He yelled angrily and probably stone drunk through the locked door.

"I can't do that. You no longer live here," I yelled back over the banging noise against the door.

"You just want to steal my books." He tried to kick in the - luckily - sturdy door. "Hey everybody, she's stealing my books!"

"If you don't stop it, we'll call the police!"

The noise stopped.

The neighbours wisely decided to stay out of the argument, but I could just imagine them eavesdropping. Especially the lady next door in No. 2.

"I told you to move out. Get your friend to come with his truck tomorrow and fetch your damn books."

"Winston doesn't like me anymore," Ronnie complained in a teary voice. Oh dear!

"Not my problem. Make a plan," I said roughly and realised only afterwards that I was risking an even less agreeable house mate, like a fat tarantula. Crunching gravel. Then it went quiet. Only now did I notice that my whole body was trembling from all the tension. Who was this alleged friend he had stayed with, anyway? A couple of weeks I found out, while visiting the Winckler family. I met Winston

Mokoena, the previously good friend of Ronnie Immelman. On that occasion, the former ANC operative shared with us that Ronnie had also threatened his wife.

"She just wanted him to pick up his towels in the bathroom. He became abusive and was going to get her killed, because she was a witch," he said.

Gaborone was apparently full of witches. Winston had kicked Ronnie out.

"He threatened me with the same thing. Why didn't you tell anyone about it?" I asked with a hint of accusation.

"I'm really sorry. Didn't know he'd behave so badly. I would have warned you through Uli. Ronnie said that he'd known you for a while and that Emily's a mutual friend. I thought you knew —"

There was no use being angry with Winston as well.

His former comrades had turned their backs on Ronnie for some time now. Because of the drugs and his mental issues. No guessing that they had been only too glad to wash their hands of him and what's more, secrecy was really important when you moved in political circles. That's why nobody had said anything and the problem had quietly shifted to me. Thank you kindly. His parents were just as clueless - as was Emily.

Right now I knew none of this. I sat down. The crunching of the gravel still rang in my ears and I got a fright at the slightest noise. Perhaps it was a good idea to make myself a cup of tea. With a bit of luck, this unpleasant matter would be over by tomorrow.

Unfortunately I had no such luck. Ronnie didn't come on Sunday to fetch his books. He came to my office on Monday morning. Kurt Köhler was one of his acquaintances and was clearly unaware of Ronnie's state of mind. He ogled the good-looking young man fondly while listening to his insane story of witchcraft, theft and deceit. I was sure that my boss knew better than to believe his ramblings and tried to get some work done. I was wrong again.

## SINGING LIZARDS

After a while I was called into his office. Hansie, Kurt's boyfriend, skulked to the left side of the desk. A sneering Ronnie sat in front of Kurt. I walked into a courtroom!

"Miss Reinhold, I hear you have been misbehaving," Kurt Köhler scolded.

He mustered me over the rim of his reading glasses and shook his index finger. "You must give this poor man his books back," he commanded sternly.

It would have been funny, but I was getting angry now.

"Mr. Köhler, I don't want Ronnie's books. The sooner he fetches them, the better."

"I don't have a car," Ronnie wailed.

"Then organize one," I snapped at him.

"Tztztzt, Miss Reinhold. I'm very disappointed in you." Kurt looked dotingly at Ronnie. "This young man needs a place to stay. You cannot just turn him cold-heartedly out on the streets." He gave me a disapproving look.

"Oh, really? He calls me a witch and threatens my life when he's on drugs. So forgive me if I don't want to share my flat with someone like that."

"Ronnie wouldn't do such a thing," Kurt protested in an over-the-top voice.

"Well, he did."

"I don't believe it for a moment!"

Kurt's vehement answer made Ronnie sneer some more. No, I wouldn't suggest that Kurt take him in. That was probably exactly what Ronnie wanted.

"I can't help that," I said instead. "He must let me know when he wants to come and fetch his books. The sooner the better."

What was wrong with Kurt? Was I speaking Chinese all of a sudden? He patted Ronnie's hand reassuringly. Hansie squirmed at the sight of it and I nearly laughed out loud. This was all too much. Pure comedy. Just that it would have made things worse.

"We'll see what we can do," Kurt comforted our friend-of-insects. He had to be quite mad himself to believe in all this hogwash. "You can go now," Kurt dismissed me rudely and I trudged glumly back to my office.

Who knows what other nonsense Ronnie dished, while he was being so nicely entertained? By midday Hansie informed me that a bakkie would come to my flat at 7 o'clock that evening. Success at last! The little truck arrived three hours late, but I didn't complain. Hurray, I was rid of Ronnie Immelman! Better still, I never heard from him again. Perhaps he'd gone back to Britain or to South Africa. I didn't care. I didn't care.

But Kurt Köhler never forgave me for attaching this nice young man' books, even if it had been only temporarily. This was the second strike against my name. The first one had been my inappropriate popularity with visiting volunteers. The atmosphere at the office had changed. Kurt was in a bad mood more often now and things became rather unpleasant. A scorpion couldn't have done a better job at injecting an effective poison than the mad entomologist had.

Nothing I did made the slightest difference. The third strike was waiting just around the corner.

'Bridget, I asked you to sort this in descending order. Do I have to repeat everything ten times?' or 'Why are you on the phone again? Don't you have work to do?' or 'You are five minutes late, did they make you eat a horse for lunch?'

Then it happened. Our new staff member, Manfred Raab, had forgotten to pass the message on to Kurt that I needed to go to the bank in the morning before work. I arrived to an icy reception. Judging by Kurt's stony expression, he was unwilling to let it slide. It was time to rid himself of this troublesome worker bee. Manfred Raab was called into the court room - I mean office.

"No, sorry, she didn't tell me on Friday about going to the bank before work today." Manfred squirmed in his chair.

I was shocked. "Manfred, that's a lie and you know it!" To think that on Friday I had patiently listened to Manfred lamenting about his Tswana girlfriend called Sophie, who had set his car on fire out of jealousy!

"Miss Reinhold you are hereby dismissed," Kurt began. "Not coming to work in the morning without a valid excuse and insubordination. Of course, we will give you a month's notice, which you are expected to work, until we have found a suitable successor..." he droned on. I just stood there and listened to the blood rush in my ears. Then I pulled myself together.

"You will place an ad in the paper tomorrow..."

I turned around and left the room without another word, packed my few belongings into a box and parted with the GVO. Out of the corner of my eye, I saw a small fur pouch hanging on the hedge. No concern of mine, I decided and took a deep breath before I stepped out onto the street.

My secure existence in Botswana was over.

Manfred showed up at the flat that evening and apologized that he had forgotten about my errand. He had been afraid that Kurt would load it over him. It didn't make a difference now.

"Please come back to work until we find another PA. Kurt doesn't want to ask you directly. You know how proud he is."

"In a year of blue moons, Manfred," I said with a note of triumph. "Go and tell Kurt the truth, then we'll see."

But Manfred did no such thing and I never went back to the GVO office. I got a doctor's note, stating high blood pressure due to stress (which was true), and Beate Belseck, a friendly volunteer, regularly checked my mail in the little backroom. What if I missed one of the letters from England? Or Benjamin's? He was still away on leave and didn't know what was going on.

I slept a lot, but those eerie dreams were giving me thankfully a break for now. A couple of days later, Beate brought me unexpected mail. A letter from Palapye. Tony wrote that the Bouchers had invited us to Francistown for a weekend! I was wondering why they would invite us now of all times and Tony couldn't have cared less about Claire's disappearance when I'd left Palapye. I wrote back that there was no reason for me to see the Bouchers but if Tony felt like it he should go right ahead and visit them. They couldn't tell me anything new and I really didn't feel like socialising.

I had other problems now and soon heard through the Rita-grapevine that my dismissal had caused a minor scandal in Gaborone. All that drama! Oh well, I didn't feel like going out anyway.

There was just this eenzi weenzi question of my residence permit. What was I supposed to do now?

# CHAPTER 8

A small parcel arrived from Stuttgart. I knew Benjamin was there, visiting his parents. The parcel contained a music tape - nothing else. Gabby gave me her tape deck so I could hear what was on the tape. I felt butterflies in my tummy as soon as I pressed the 'Play' button. But there was no music, just Ben's voice - a 'spoken letter'!

'I'm sitting here in my parents' dining room, looking out the window...' the voice said to me, 'I've been here for two weeks and I'm counting the days...'

The 'spoken letter' droned on, but Ben could have recited the telephone directory and I would have been on Cloud 9. He went on to assure me, how much he missed me and said jokingly that by the time I received the parcel, he would be most likely on his way to the airport. *That's funny, Mr. Glasberg*, I thought.

There was a knock on the front door.

I reluctantly paused the tape and checked my watch. Gabby wanted to pop in only during her lunch break. I reluctantly pressed the 'Pause' button. Perhaps just somebody looking for a job again.

But it was Ben, who stood grinning in front of me!

I gawked at him in disbelief. He had just said on the tape that he might be on his way to the airport and I thought it was a joke. He was only due back next week, but the post took ages to arrive. Now he stood there in the flesh — a lot paler than about month ago.

"How did you get here so fast?"

"What?" Now it was his turn to look all confused.

"Nothing. You're back!" I tried to fumble the screen door open.

"Aren't you happy to see me?"

"Of course I am. Of course. Come in." The screen door snapped open at last and Ben swept me up in his arms. My pent-up tension gave way to tears.

"I thought you were happy to see me…" my returning boyfriend laughed.

"I am!" I wailed.

He pushed his duffel bag into the lounge with his foot and closed the door behind him. I sobbed on his shoulder while Ben calmed me down. He deposited me on the couch and made tea. Then he sat down by my side.

"So, what happened? Those are not just tears of joy or are they?" He asked gently.

"No," I admitted and cried a little more. How was I supposed to put all the things that had happened while he was away into words? Where did I even begin?

"How is it going at work?" he asked cautiously.

I sniffed and wiped my probably red and swollen eyes from all the crying. "I'm no longer working for Kurt," I confessed.

"I know. I went to the office first to fetch my Nissan bakkie and to see you. Kurt and Hansie told me some story," Ben said.

"What story?"

"That you didn't come to work on time and then just upped and left…" His eyes held a question.

"You should know that it isn't true!" I replied heatedly and wiped my tears.

"Hey, I just came back from Europe. Give me a chance to understand."

"Okay, I'll tell you later then."

"No, I want you to tell me now."

"Fine." The story poured out of me, interrupted only by a few sniffles. Everything I went through with Ronnie Immelman and with Kurt and Manfred. Ben studied my face the whole time.

"Kurt's story sounded convincing too," he said drily and looked away.

"I can't believe you just said that. Do you believe Kurt over me?" Ben looked out of the window as if the answer lurked there in the bushes and trees.

"I don't know what to believe." I moved away from him just a fraction.

"You better believe me, if you know what's good for you," I said half-jokingly. "In any case, there's now this problem with my residence permit."

"You think we should get married so you can stay?" he blurted out.

"That's one option, don't you think?"

Ben pulled a face. "Okay, I guess it's not a good idea then," I said and couldn't help feeling a little disappointed.

"Know what?" Ben suddenly asked spontaneously. "If you aren't too busy, come to Kang with me. Just for a long weekend, to get you out of Gabs for a few days."

That meant that Ben believed me and that he wasn't jealous of Ronnie Immelman, didn't it? As I wasn't exactly busy working right now, so I welcomed a visit to the Kalahari. To help me clear my head. Suddenly I longed for peace and quiet. Ben went out on some errands and I began to pack my things. Gabby arrived a bit later and wasn't exactly thrilled to hear about my plans.

"If Ben believes Kurt Köhler over you, it's probably not such a good idea right now," she said. "What if you two have a fight? Then you sit around in Kang all by yourself."

"Don't worry, I'll convince him. Ben isn't like other men."

"I'm not so sure about that..."

But being a good friend, she encouraged me regardless to take a well-deserved break.

I don't remember the car trip, but the quiet mood was just wonderful and made me feel immediately at home again. With all this space around, there was no space for pessimistic thoughts.

The mornings in Kalahari-country were far from quiet, though. Donkeys brayed and roosters called at the crack of dawn. It was the usual early morning soundtrack.

I knew the small bedroom with the short orange curtains so well and stretched myself contentedly under the blanket. It was April now and cooler at night. The farm animals took over from the nightly village-disco. A male lead voice and a monotonous female chorus to stomping rhythms. I had fallen asleep to the Dum Dum Dum. So repetitive...

Everything was familiar: the sounds, the sandy wind, the smell of the thatched roof that mingled with the creosote of the wooden beams - glorious.

One couldn't hear them in the compound, but lizards were surely singing again in the dawn and little meerkat were inspecting the surroundings above their burrows.

The morning sun sneaked through the closed curtains. I lightly kissed the fine blond hairs on Ben's neck. He stirred and turned around grinning sleepily.

Yesterday we had been so lazy. Ben had prepared a Kudu pot roast in his tiny open-plan kitchen with Tanita Tikkaram and Joe Cocker singing in the background. Just for the two of us. There were still signs of former girlfriends around. The turquoise nail polish between toaster and windowsill and the pink razor behind the toilet bowl. I'd decided to ignore them long ago. While the Kudu leg was roasting away in the oven, Ben had cut my hair. He was good at cutting hair and at cooking - among other things.

Mette came around to give me the decorated ostrich egg and a necklace I had ordered from her months ago. She often bought things from the Bushmen she cared for. A Khoi San hunting scene was scratched into the smooth surface of the ostrich egg then coloured-in with blue shoe polish. Stunning.

To prevent me from getting bored, Ben gave me his favourite novel and I began reading 'Love in the Time of Cholera' by Gabriel Garcia Marques. My boyfriend was surprisingly well-read. He instructed his local students in auto mechanics during the day and read novels after hours. As I turned the pages, I pictured myself and Benjamin - instead of the main characters - in undying love that matured over time. How romantic!

"Do you want to seduce me with your pretty, long legs?" Ben grinned. He had taken his shirt off and looked rather sexy.

I put my wineglass down and considered my legs. I had put my feet on the table and there was absolutely nothing enticing about my legs sticking out of grey shorts.

"What's so attractive about that?" I giggled.

"Do you want me to show you?"

"That will have to wait until tonight, I'm afraid."

Ben pulled a face and I had to laugh. He looked so handsome without his shirt and his hair still tousled from taking a shower. Muscles rippling under tanned skin. Pull yourself together, Bridget! I busied myself paging through an old women's magazine that I had found lying around.

"When exactly were you born, Ben?" I knew that he was 27.

"2 December '62."

"Then you are, wait —"

"Sagittarius!" we said in unison. Hmm.

Ben was checking on the roast and basted it with some of the red wine he had bought in Gaborone.

"Let's see. Aries and Sagittarius: 'The Sagittarius man is too complicated for the lively Aries woman and much too passive this summer. Better suited to…' Hmm, doesn't sound very promising." I saw the date on the cover. "But that's a while ago; the horoscope is from last year. I was born on 22 March, which is only just Aries. I always look under Pisces as well," I prattled on, "That suits me better. But Claire is a true Aries." I stopped and swallowed. Too late.

"Who is Claire?" The question was inevitable.

"Oh, just a friend back in England. We share the same birthday," I lied.

"I see."

I felt a sudden twinge in my chest. Sorry Foompy, sorry Ben! I wasn't ready to tell him yet why I was here in Botswana. Couldn't remember properly myself. Claire's letters were packed away and I rarely looked at the pictures now. I was tired of being sad all the time.

The Kudu roast tasted wonderfully of garlic and red wine and fresh thyme – and the Kalahari. And I'm not just talking about the crunch of desert sand between my teeth. Later, Roz Williams, the Peace Corps lady, had dropped by to ask whether we felt like going horseback riding in the Kalahari. Imagine, horseback riding in the Kalahari!

Her Nigerian boyfriend Wilfried, also a teacher at Kang High School, had a Tswana friend who owned a cattle post not far from town. I'd met Wilfried only once. He was a big, burly man with a gentle manner.

The farmer had introduced him to his Khoi-san horse handler by the name of Andries. Andries looked after five beautiful horses in the middle of the Kalahari Desert. Wilfried was constantly at the cattle post now riding the horses and Roz came with him on weekends.

We went to fetch Priya, an Indian volunteer from Bangalore. She was a strong-willed woman with severely combed-back hair. Then we were off to the cattle post. Priya came from a wealthy family, who did not approve of her choice to teach in Africa. As we sat in the back of the bakkie that Wilfried steered down a rough dirt track, she told me that her contract was ending in two weeks' time.

"So what are you going to do when you get back home?"

"My father wants me to get married. He says I'm already too smart and soon too old for a good marriage. He sent a picture of the man he wants me to marry."

"What are you going to do?"

"Don't know yet, but I won't get married. I could try to find work in another country. Australia maybe." We sat silent.

"Is it safe to ride horses in the desert?" I interrupted the silence. "I've already made the acquaintance of meerkats and lizards. But what about predators?" The others laughed.

"Don't worry we won't see lions or hyenas around here," Benjamin assured me, "Not even giraffes or zebras. Here in Kang you find mostly smaller animals like bucks and ostriches and some warthogs. And they are rather shy."

The bakkie stopped next to an enclosure marked with short poles and a thorn thicket. A primitive hut, roughly made from branches, was inside and large garbage heaps rotted away in front of it.

One heap consisted of desert melon halves scraped empty that a thousand flies called home. Many of these small, bitter-tasting melons were lying around in the sand between the thorn trees. They were part of the Khoi-san staple diet. The other heap consisted of empty Chibuku beer cartons. Wilfried told us that Andries was paid in food items by his Tswana boss, as was still common practice in rural Africa.

Andries, the Khoi-san horse groom soon appeared. He was quite dirty and couldn't be as old as his wrinkly face led to believe. He didn't speak English, so he communicated with gestures, some Setswana and many click sounds.

He took the two Pula note Wilfried handed him with a toothless grin and gently untied the front legs of the horses. When I saw the steeds close up, my heart sank. They were so incredibly tall!

But before I knew it, I sat on a chestnut mare and we were trotting along the shady trail that Wilfried so often used. It took me a queasy moment to get used to the dizzy height. When I managed to take my eyes off the mare's neck, I was amazed at the beauty that surrounded us.

From up here, the Kalahari presented itself from a totally different perspective. Andries was barefoot, leading Wilfried's horse on a leash. Our tame mounts sauntered placidly behind. The soles of his feet had to be incredibly hard.

The afternoon sun bathed the sandy landscape in a golden light. Clouds moved along the blue sky and the shadows and colours kept changing constantly. We left the shady thorn tree lane and the horses trotted past a small saltpan. What an experience!

On the hill behind it, I saw meerkats weasel in and out of their burrows. Standing on their hind legs, they sniffed nervously the air, scanned the area and I was sure they watched us too. It was so peaceful, as the sun sank lower.

Andries guided the horses back north in a drawn-out loop, while we watched how other Bushmen herded cattle into a big kraal for the night. The heat of the day was already making way for cool evening air, before our steeds took us back to the two unappetizing rubbish heaps.

Roz, Priya and Wilfried had some party to go to afterwards - Ben and I went home. Now it was morning in the room with the short orange curtains.

"Did you sleep well, my darling?" Ben asked lazily and looked at me tenderly.

He used the German word Schatz and my heart melted. This had to be true love! He nuzzled his mouth along my jawline. Our lips locked. His hands moved down my neck and came to rest on my breasts. I gave up thinking and surrendered to the magic of the moment.

Again, I pushed that little voice aside, warning me relentlessly: don't fall in love with him; a man for bed is not a man for life. I was just so happy when he was with me, happier than I had been in a long time. I didn't want to listen to the voice. Nobody could fake love like that. We were meant for each other.

When I left Kang, I was ready to face the world again. The Kalahari therapy had worked its magic again. Back in Gaborone, I began to line up interviews. When one door closes ten others open, my Mom always said, and opportunity soon knocked.

The incomparable Uli Winckler had heard that Rockhill Primary, the private school his daughters attended, was looking for a French teacher. I just gave it a shot and made an appointment with the headmistress. Mrs. Mulholland, a motherly, middle-aged woman, almost hugged me for joy. The second French teacher at the school had suddenly left and Mrs. Laville couldn't cope with all the classes on her own.

Rockhill Primary was nothing like the British schools I had attended. The classrooms were arranged in rows along broad, shady verandas lined with flowerbeds. There was a large sports field, a playground and even tennis courts.

"I see that you have some teaching experience, Miss Reinhold, you were a teacher at - the Vocational Training Centre in Palapye."

We sat in the principal's office and Mrs. Mulholland had my CV in front of her.

"Yes, I taught English there and enjoyed it very much."

"Excellent, excellent. Do you have any experience with children?"

"No, not really, but I love being around children. I sometimes babysit Adrienne and Jasmin Winckler. Surely, I could ask their parents for a reference."

The interview didn't last very long - then I was the new French teacher at Rockhill Primary School. Payment was lousy, but at least I had a job and I needn't worry about my residence permit.

"I'm Vanessa, nice to meet you Bridget. Just sit at the back of the class and watch what I'm doing," Mrs. Laville commanded when I arrived for my first day at work.

She was a petite, energetic woman from Yorkshire with

cropped dark hair. Vanessa's stern expression made her look older than her 32 years and everybody seemed a little afraid of her. Her husband was a charming Frenchman, who had lived in England all his life.

"All right. I'll do that." I followed her up the veranda stairs.

The children giggled at the sight of an adult at the back of the class, but Mrs. Laville didn't tolerate silly behaviour.

"Quiet please. This is Miss Reinhold. She will be teaching French at the school. Douglas, sit down immediately!"

The class stopped giggling. You didn't jest with Mrs. Laville.

"Good, that's better. Let's show Miss Reinhold what we've learned yesterday." She held up a flip card with the unmistakable image of rain.

"La pluie."

"La pluie," the class chorused.

"Les nuages."

"Les nuages."

I soon settled into my new role as a respectable French teacher. At first, it felt a bit odd to be greeted with a respectful 'Good morning madam' or 'Good afternoon madam' by school children at every turn. During assembly, I sat in the teachers' row, but it took a while for me to feel like a real French teacher. I adored my colleagues. They were so accomplished and sociable and nobody tried to interfere with my subject matters.

In the first week, Jasmin wanted to hold my hand and chatted to me during break. Adrienne thought it was totally uncool to know the new teacher and just greeted me like all the other kids. Albeit with a secret twinkle in her eyes. Lunch break in the staff room usually meant animated chitchat over coffee and sandwiches. It rained now regularly in the afternoons and I often prepared lessons in my classroom to avoid having to walk back to my flat at Acacia Court in a sudden downpour.

"Do you have any siblings, Bridget?" I looked at Vanessa in shock. The discussion the other teachers had been pleasant background noise and I had no idea what they were talking about. The worksheets on the table in front of me had kept me too busy to pay much attention to the conversation. Everybody stared at me in expectation.

"Ehem, no my only sister died some time ago." I stuttered. Why had I said that?

"Oh I'm so sorry I had no idea…was it an accident?"

"Ehm, yes. I don't really want to talk about it," I mumbled.

Close shave! I shivered despite my turtle-neck jersey and the blazing heater in the staff room. Bridget, how could you! You know that's not true! That little voice inside me hissed indignantly. The conversation turned to Rosemary Bennett's travel-crazy brother.

I got up and quickly left the staff room. The voices behind me morphed into intense whispers.

The fresh air helped me to regain my equilibrium. Only three people in Gaborone knew about my secret. I hadn't seen much of Emily since the Ronnie Immelman story. Gabby sometimes took me with to play tennis at the club and I still met Rita over lunch at the President Hotel.

But we never discussed Claire. The less I thought about her the better. Forget, forget, forget. If there just weren't those meddlesome dreams and that annoying little voice.

By the time I went back to fetch my things for the next lesson, the bell had rung and the teachers were trying to get to their classrooms in a hurry.

Summer was fading fast and Ben had sent only one letter since my visit. I had written four. Rita mentioned popular Setswana lessons by a private teacher called Agnes Müller. She thought it would be a good idea for me to enroll in the Saturday morning course and learn some Setswana. I think Rita wanted to distract me. I didn't mind.

Agnes was a bubbly, full-figured Tswana-lady, who didn't mind sharing titbits of her private life in class. She had lived with her German husband and two children in Wuppertal for 9 years, before eloping to Botswana with Robert, a turner from Leeds.

Robert had promised to marry her after her divorce and that they would live in the land of her forefathers. A step she soon regretted.

Not only did Robert have no intention of marrying her, he also drank like a fish and had begun to lock his girlfriend into the house after their rousing fights. Her long-suffering husband in Germany was no longer interested in a reconciliation. So Agnes didn't have much of a choice, but to stay with her new boyfriend. Despite her troubled home life, she tried her best to teach us her tongue-twisting mother language.

"Everybody listen up," she said jovially at the end of the first lesson. "If there is anything you need, you know where I live. Unfortunately, I don't have a phone here..."

I became friends with two of my classmates. Dieter Stoeckl, who insisted on just being called Stoeckl and his best buddy Herbert Schmitt.

The two of them were on short contracts and new in the country. Stoeckl worked as an instructor at the Automotive College, had a pleasant personality and instantly offered to repair anything from a leaking pipe to a flat tire.

Stoeckl was not the best looking chap around, with his bony frame, long nose and droopy eyes. But Tswana girls found him irresistible. Herbert Schmitt on the other hand was rather good-looking in comparison — at least by Western standards.

He was blond and well-built, but the girls made a wide berth around him. He was an auditor and would be in Botswana only for six months.

Herbert was fond of fish and invited us frequently to the new seafood joint in Ramotswa with the freshest Mozambican prawns and lobsters after our Saturday lessons. Benjamin avoided the get-togethers with my new friends when he was in town, but assured me that he didn't mind at all. Alright then.

I liked my work at Rockhill Primary. Being part of a lively school community was just what I needed. I was the only 'Miss' at the school and Mr. Green was the only male teacher. In sports of course. It was an undisputed fact of life that all female teachers were married, so the children called me Mrs. Reinhold. I didn't mind.

The only unlikeable teacher was Mrs. Pienaar. She had her classroom right next to mine. I felt sorry for the little ones, who were subjected to her screeching day in and day out.

Everything about Mrs. Pienaar seemed pinched. She walked around with her mouth pressed into a tight line, had tightly curled poodle hair and grey eyes that were too close together. I tried to ignore her most of the time, but I couldn't ignore her 13-year-old son.

Jan-Hendrik, from her first marriage, was a piece of work. The only pupil in grade 7, who dared to openly swear at me.

'Voetsek!' The Afrikaans version of 'f*** off' was his favourite expression to squeals of laughter by the other teenage pupils.

Unfamiliar with Afrikaans, I asked a mortified Mrs. Pienaar, what the word meant. She didn't want to use the f-word and gave me a long-winded description. In the meantime, Jan-Hendrik got a couple of girls in the last row to produce a note saying 'Mis Rynhault is a motherf******'. They had allegedly found the note on the floor. The ensuing investigation by Mrs. Mulholland revealed nothing about the origin of the note and the case was dropped with stern threats of punishment in case of a recurrence.

"Jan-Hendrik has been so difficult since the divorce. Please understand. I battle with his behaviour at home." Mrs. Pienaar pleaded with me.

That it might be unfair to expect other teachers to battle with her son's behaviour, didn't cross her mind. So, young Jan-Hendrik spent most of his French lessons outside my classroom, lolling about on the Veranda steps.

In June, wintry conditions set in for good. This meant dry air, sunshine and a drop in temperature of up to 30 degrees between day and night. I now understood what Claire had meant with chilly nights and warm days. Just that 'warm' didn't feel pleasant.

The air was arid and buildings remained frosty even during the day. I was told to get a humidifier, which was apparently as important as a heater. An excellent tip.

At some stage, Vanessa Laville mentioned that being a member of her running club would spruce up my social life and took me along to a meeting after school. I liked it and went running with Vanessa at least once a week.

The Gaborone Hash Harriers were a jolly bunch of people from all walks of life, who exercised together by running or walking in the great outdoors. In addition to the benefit of exercise, I got to see Gaborone. The great marula trees in the business district, fields and hills around. Once we were accosted by baboons in the hills. The monkeys formed a half-circle around four runners and chased us down the rocky path. We avoided the hills for a while.

Then things started to change. Just as I settled comfortably into Gaborone, my life came apart at the seams.

There were subtle changes at first. But I couldn't ignore it any longer that things between me and Benjamin were difficult. It was my turn to visit him, but I undertook the 8-hour trip to Kang with mixed feelings.

Thorsten and Mette picked me up in the Mall as we had arranged weeks ago. Just after Jwaneng, the Kalahari captivated me again and I was wondering why I had felt so ill at ease. We arrived after dark. As so often, I walked to Ben's cottage and passed two ground staff workers fast asleep in wheel barrows, despite the cold.

It didn't take me long to see that Ben wasn't happy to have company. He kept making sarcastic remarks throughout dinner and practically ordered me to wash the dishes and that, after I had come all this way to be with him.

"What is wrong with you today?" I asked.

"I want to be alone."

"That's no brain buster."

"I can't help how I'm feeling. This is my house and I have every right to relax after work without somebody making demands on me."

"That's so mean of you. As if I can read your mind all the way from Gaborone," I sulked.

What was I supposed to do now? I should have listened to my intuition. It was exactly what Gabby had warned me about. I didn't know anybody here well enough to wade through the deep sand in the middle of the night and ask for a place to sleep. Mette and Thorsten lived too far away and what was the point anyway?

My boyfriend took no notice of my dilemma. He sat at the table, reading letters. I suddenly felt claustrophobic and got up.

"Where are you going?" Ben demanded to know.

"I need - fresh air. Half an hour or so." I tried to sound composed. Of course, I didn't really feel like going for a walk on a freezing Kalahari night, but sitting next to an unkind Ben was even less appealing.

"Be careful." He looked up and then turned his attention back to the stack of letters I had brought with me from the city.

"Sure." I put on my jacket, opened the door and braced myself against the cold.

The air was surprisingly fresh and a near-full moon greeted me. I marvelled at the star-studded sky and trudged all the way up to the Trans-Kalahari 'highway'. The workers, who has slept in the wheelbarrows must have woken up and stumbled home. There was nobody else around, just me. But who knew what stalked around in the middle of the night.

I reached the Trans-Kalahari. Walking on the newly-graded road was better than wading through deep sand. I wanted to get away from Ben, the faster the better.

The stars in the dark blue sky seemed so close. The blue was translucent somehow and the sand glistened, reflecting the bright moonlight. Insects chirruped dreamily and in the village the Dum Dum Dum of the disco competed with sleepy-donkey cries.

I walked and walked into the night, farther out of town. The Kalahari was good to me. There was only me and a huge expanse of dark blue sky. Exactly what I needed.

The peaceful mood was balm on my wounded soul. My dark thoughts hovered somewhere in the air and couldn't reach me. I didn't mind the cold anymore. I felt like a tiny ant inside a gigantic dark-blue balloon with millions of glowing dots stuck to it. Was I dreaming?

Why don't people go out more often at night and look at the stars, I mused. Then my problem crept up on me again and a lonely tear rolled down my cheek.

It was a small problem compared to the magnitude of all this nature, but big for the tiny ant that was me. I dared to think. One moment Ben was all romantic and lovey dovey, the next he wished me far away. Was it possible to simply switch off love? Maybe he didn't love me after all.

Two light beams drew closer, encompassing everything around. Bright headlights cut through the darkness and preceded the sound by minutes. The trucks drove in convoy and fast, to avoid sinking into the dirt road.

All I had to do was step down onto the gravel and keep my balance, while the trucks blasted by. The light beams grew smaller and dissolved in the darkness. The road was mine again.

It must be getting late. I roused myself reluctantly and left the hypnotic sky and shiny road behind. At least I knew what to do now. It was best to get some sleep, if I wanted to catch an early lift bound for Gaborone.

Benjamin had been waiting up for me. "Where the hell have you been so long?" he flared up at me. "I was worried."

"Really? Must have lost track of the time. Nothing happened."

I didn't want to share my incredible waking dream of the Kalahari night with him. Instead I said, "Ben, I don't think you want me here right now. I'm going to leave again tomorrow morning."

Ben didn't protest. To my irritation, he seemed relieved. Why didn't he just apologize and asked me to stay?

"I'll take you to the pick-up point before work. I'm sure you'll catch a lift quickly."

"Thanks. Can I sleep on the platform under the roof? I don't mind," I offered, unable to spend the rest of the night close to him.

"No, you take the bed."

"Okay then, night."

"Night." There was nothing else to say.

I waited for the little voice, reproaching me 'See, I told you...'. But it stayed quiet.

Just after dawn, I left Kang behind on the back of an open truck in the company of 20 Tswana workers. I only saw Benjamin again in Gaborone on President's Day in the middle of July. We had drifted even further apart. Besides, there was someone else in Ben's life now, who demanded his attention.

Jörg Walter, a 53-year old wealthy entrepreneur from Flensburg, the latest addition to the volunteer community in Kang. He wanted to give his life meaning by working in Africa for two years – and get away from his life partner Karin. He wasn't even ashamed to say it.

Jörg had enough money to rent a flat for himself in Gaborone - which, I heard, led to some arguments with the

GFO. Ben also spent his time there, whenever he was in town.

We hardly knew each other, but Jörg had somehow jumped to the conclusion that I was the ball and chain in Ben's life. Being tied to just one woman was unacceptable to him. Ben had told me once with shining eyes about Jörg's opinion on marriage, but I had only half-listened. Nothing to do with me.

Mette had told me that Ben couldn't make it to Gabs on President's Day. But when Jörg Walter suddenly decided that spending the long weekend in Kang would be too boring, the two of them drove together into town.

Ben turned up and invited me to dinner at the town house of some friends of his. I was happy to see him so unexpectedly and was in high spirits. We didn't really break up. It was possible that he was sorry about his behaviour. And I didn't have anything better to do, anyway.

Jörg Walter already sat at the table on the narrow terrace of the town house. He had a chin that could have sunk the Titanic and an awkward balding pate. Perhaps he had a nice personality. If Ben liked him so much, he couldn't be so bad. A gentle rain soaked the garden, highly unusual for this time of year.

At first, we small-talked awhile. Then, for some reason, Jörg constantly made cynical remarks about women. Not very nice.

"So you prefer marriage to a simple living arrangement?" Jörg Walter challenged me. Just as Doris Radovic, our hostess, served up dry sausage rolls.

"Here are some starters, the chicken isn't quite ready yet," Doris said quickly. Then she disappeared into the kitchen, refusing my help with dinner preparations. Too bad.

"All I'm saying is that it's up to those individuals. You make me sound as if I had nothing better to do than forcing an innocent man into marriage. Like a spider trapping her prey in a net," I said and grinned.

To distract myself, I bit into a sausage roll. The appetizers were as dry as the conversation.

He didn't find my remark funny at all. "See, I knew it! You women are all the same. As soon as you have a poor bastard in your claws, you won't stop until you can drag him to the altar," he dressed me down.

I felt uncomfortable. Why did this Jörg guy try to pit himself against me? I looked at Ben for support, but he only smiled at his half-empty beer bottle.

"Wait, I didn't say that at all. And I meant it even less," I stammered.

Doris, who'd made a feeble attempt to join us while the chicken was in the oven, took to her heels. I didn't blame her. It was common knowledge in town that Doris had left her husband last year to marry Dragan Radovic. I would have liked to hide from Jörg as well.

*Ben is such a spineless rat*, I thought angrily. It would have saved me a lot of trouble to just get up and leave. But I stupidly tried to save the discussion. Soon plain words flew forth and back between us. Dragan tried valiantly to change the subject and failed. We exchanged desperate looks.

"You seem to enjoy twisting around every word I say. Why don't you enlighten us about the ideal partnership between two people?" I snarled.

Jörg's enormous chin trembled as he launched into yet another sermon. Ben nodded in agreement. I gave him The Look and hoped that he would get the message, but no such luck.

"Is that right?" I was beginning to lose my temper.

"Of course I'm right. After all, I have lots and lots of experience."

"Oh please! You are just a cynical old man, who hates women!" And from now on, the least desirable house guest in Gaborone, I added to myself. We carried on sparring. It was so not like me, but I couldn't give up now!

Then to top it all, I lost my voice and couldn't do more than croak pitifully. I finally realized that I had to end this argument and leave with my dignity intact.

I pushed my chair back and wordlessly rejected an offer by Benjamin to take me home. I'd had enough! So I marched down the dark road to Acacia Court by myself. I thought back to the night, I had left David at the pub. It seemed so long ago! And no stars or moonlight to keep me company this time. Here I was again, ending a relationship. Just that it wasn't over yet.

Ben arrived at the flat an hour later. Stone drunk. I had found my somewhat shaky voice again and told him off in no uncertain terms.

"How could you stab me in the back like that? I don't care what this old coot thinks, but what about you... you..."

"Why? He was totally right. I always let women wrap me around their little finger." Ben reeked of alcohol and sprang another surprise on me. "I wanted to tell you something else... Jörg says one should always be honest in a relationship."

"Jörg? So - what is it then?"

"I'm not proud of it, believe me... but well, I slept with a prostitute before we met," he blurted out.

What? Why was he telling me this now?

"Ah?" I tested my voice, "I thought you had a girlfriend."

"Actually I was between girlfriends. I didn't know that she was a hooker, until she asked me for money," Ben slurred and pulled a guilty face.

"Oh, that makes a world of difference! As long as you had protection," I said with a great deal of ice-cold loathing. In those days, nobody thought much about the impact of AIDS, but there were quite a few other nasties around.

"Eh, don't bite my head off," he chuckled. At this point things became unstuck.

"What you didn't? You've got to be kidding!"

"I had nothing with me," Ben chuckled again. He seemed to find the memory of it hilarious. I only felt hot anger.

"Are you crazy?"

Bang! There, I'd finally slapped him. This couldn't be the same man I had spent such wonderful, happy times with! Done, finished, over.

"Wow. I didn't know that she was a whore." he laughed the slap off. "And in any case, do I know for sure what you did with this Ronnie Immelman —" My hand itched to give him another slap, but I caught myself in time.

"How dare you bring that up! You know better than that. I didn't know what he was like. I took him in, because I didn't have much of a choice..."

"Why didn't you have a choice, did he beat you with a red-hot stick? You could have said no! And what about all the other guys?" Ben blustered.

"What other guys? Why are you acting jealous all of a sudden?"

"I'm not jealous, I'm disgusted with you! You're a slut!"

"You think you can turn it all around on me? Here, you're insufferable and totally sloshed," I pushed his bag into his chest and he tumbled backwards, "You can go now!"

Ben gawked at me wide-eyed. "So, that's what I get for being honest."

"That's what you get for being an utter idiot all night long." I was beyond livid now. I could have killed him.

"Okay then. I see you don't want me here anymore," he grumbled. "I'll go and stay at Jörg's flat tonight."

"See if I care. Thanks for the lovely evening!" I called after him. He tried to slam the door, getting the handle of his bag stuck on the door handle.

As soon as the sound of the truck's engine had faded away, I started crying.

*What is wrong with me?* I thought fiercely. *How can you miss somebody, who doesn't have the guts to stick up for me and just told me that he may have given me an STD? You need to get your head read, Bridget!* But I suddenly felt so lonely.

"So you think this is funny?!" I scolded the wooden hippo, "You just watch. Never again will someone do that to me. Never!"

The hippo kept smirking. Oh no, now I was talking to objects again! 'Hey don't start with me,' it seemed to say, 'you knew it was coming.' I hated to admit it, but the hippo was right.

Clinging to the shreds of my dignity, I decided not to contact Ben. For the rest of the long weekend I was torn between anger and guilt and longing. *I hate him, hate, him, hate him... I miss him... It was my fault... I should have left the dinner party sooner... He's such a coward!*

The thoughts went round and round inside my head. Why was I overreacting so? With David the relationship had sort of petered out. This was different. There was so much love and passion involved and I had no experience with that. Damn falling in love.

Listening to music helped. I belted out heartbreak songs with Linda Ronstad, Cat Stevens and good old Janis Joplin under the watchful eye of my trusty hippo. Nothing had been so agonizing since Claire's disappearance. *Oh no, I can't deal with this now!* I pushed the thought of Claire aside.

Dr. Murfin informed me that the STD tests had all come back negative. I felt immense relief. At least my health was safe.

Good luck to Ben's next girlfriend, it was her problem now. The good doctor gave me something to calm my nerves and a note for work.

"Madam, she is no good Mr. Ben. You must find new boyfriend. Boyfriend, who help you and not make you sad. She is no good!" Hilda shook her head unhappily. Her red headscarf came loose and she tucked the ends resolutely back into place.

"Oh you are right Hilda, but it's difficult," I mumbled, ashamed that I felt this way.

"Why difficult? You find a new boyfriend. Easy job, you are pretty."

"Hilda, it's not that easy for me," I said weakly.

She shook her head some more and carried on with her housework. Anybody try and understand these white folks! She didn't have to say it out loud.

I didn't understand it myself. The European way was so complicated: hankering endlessly for something that couldn't be changed. The African way was more straightforward: just find another boyfriend, who doesn't make you sad.

Why couldn't I be just a bit more African?

# CHAPTER 9

To say I was rattled would be an understatement. First my job with GVO was down the drain, then my relationship to Ben. What was happening to me? Alone and in a strange country, I was in serious trouble. It was a lot harder to fall out of love than I had imagined.

"Ben doesn't deserve you. You can't change people, you know," Rita tried her best to console me. "I heard it's kind of his usual behaviour with women. Best you write the guy off." She lit another cigarette. "What's the deal with this Jörg anyway?" The breeze played with her long tresses. We sat on the high wall of the Gaborone dam. One of my favourite hang-outs.

"What do you mean? Besides the fact that he is an asshole...?" Gabby flared up.

"Well, why does he try so hard to break the two of them up? Is he jealous or something?"

"Crikey, I hadn't thought of that. Wouldn't be surprised, though. I mean, he's rather odd," I said.

Rita inhaled the smoke deeply and blew rings into the air. "Hmm, maybe I should ask around..."

"Ben's a dog! I hope he gets the most horrendous STD rash ever!" Gabby grumbled and waved the cigarette smoke away from her face. "Why does he have to be so good-looking?"

"Animal attraction," Rita said and Gabby giggled.

"Oh bugger, I think I'm cursed with bad luck!" I moaned.

"Bollocks! How is that supposed to work?" Rita took a

last drag from the cigarette butt.

"Maybe Kurt." I watched the shallow waves glistening in the afternoon sun. Rita stumped out her cigarette on the stones.

"Kurt doesn't even remember your name properly. And besides he wouldn't know the first thing about cursing somebody."

"You simply got too close to that guy. And old Benjamin took advantage of it," Gabby said.

"You're totally right. Why on earth did I do that?"

Gabby thought for a moment. "It's like an egg and bacon breakfast."

"What?"

"You see, the chicken contributes, the pig is involved," she said with a serious expression. I had to giggle.

"Nice metaphor. That means - I'm the pig. Thanks so much."

Rita laughed her guttural laugh and coughed a little.

"Yes, that means you're the pig," Gabby sighed. "Why don't you just talk to the jerk and get it sorted out?"

It grew cooler now and we made our way back to the car.

"He's back in Kang and anyway, I want to cry when I just think about him."

"No, what I mean is you do it on tape. Just to let your frustration out. Play the recording back and repeat it, until you are happy with the results," said Gabby. "I read that in some magazine."

"Not a bad idea, actually." I should have done this with Claire, too - talk to her. But it just didn't occur to me at the time.

I then spent hours with Gabby's tape recorder giving Ben a piece of my mind. Mostly after class and as quietly as possible. Otherwise, my colleagues would have thought that I was going nuts talking to myself. After a week, everything I had to say had been said and it made me feel better.

"That was a super idea with the tape recorder," I praised Gabby on Saturday morning over coffee. She'd had an early-morning tennis match and still wore her white outfit.

"I could tell from the start that he had a dodgy character. The Prussian swine," she said with Bavarian vehemence. Gabby was the picture of vitality. I on the other hand didn't feel energetic at all.

"Don't be daft. What happened to animal attraction? You thought he was the most gorgeous guy around," I said.

Gabby took a sip of tea and loosened the elastic band in her tumble-weed hair. "Well yes, but he always had this look in his eyes."

"What are you talking about? What look?"

"You know... leering somehow." She stared out the window and her hands played with the white elastic.

"Oh really," I said.

"Enough with the moping already," she declared suddenly. "I'd take you out tonight, to take your mind off things. But I have to be at the ambassador's for his birthday bash at seven and I won't be able to get away early."

I was no longer part of the diplomatic in-crowd and - of course - not invited. "I don't feel like going out anyway. No energy..." I sighed.

Hilda was cleaning the lounge around us and gave me a worried look. "The energy will come back as soon as you start going out. You need to meet new people, talk about different things," Gabby pep-talked me. "Hanging around at home is not helping."

"You're right, but who would want to be around a sorry mess like me?"

"We will find somebody, who'll take pity on you." Gabby was determined to make this work. "Let's see what Emily is doing tonight."

I had last spoken to Emily van Heerden about the thing with Ronnie Immelman. It would be a bit awkward, but

Gabby insisted. She used my phone and chatted to Emily for a while. I had no idea that she knew my sister's ex-colleague so well. Of course, this was a small town and Gabby knew many people. I took our cups back to the kitchen.

"She said she'll pick you up at 8 o'clock tonight. Party at the Simmons. All set!" Gabby informed me briefly and left. Everything sorted.

At 8 o'clock, I stood waiting outside in the parking lot. It was a crisp, dark night and I shivered even in my warmest jersey. Emily apologized again for unintentionally saddling me with a sociopath like Ronnie.

"When nobody had space to take him in, I should have known something was up," she said.

"It's water under the bridge. I really like my new job," I changed the subject and told Emily about Rockhill Primary and why I liked teaching so much. Soon we were on the subject of Ben and why Gabby had ordered some entertainment for me.

"Boyfriend trouble is tricky. Gabby's right, some partying will do you good."

"It's not so easy to get over a broken heart and all those feelings. I'm afraid I'm in uncharted waters here," I said.

"You know Bridget, life isn't always supposed to be easy. If everything is always hunky dory, we wouldn't have a reason to do better. Don't keep thinking about what you did wrong or how good it could have been. I've made that mistake before. Just learn from it…better luck next time —"

"No thanks, I'm off men for the next two hundred years! There won't be a next time anytime soon," I said with conviction.

"Of course there will be another time," Emily said simply and turned over the Crosby Stills & Nash music tape. "Maybe sooner than you think."

While I mulled over the whole thing, our party plans hit a snag. Emily was lost. The Molepolole Road had suddenly grown more potholes and there were no longer any street lights around.

"Darn, I thought I knew this place." Emily searched for landmarks in the dark, while trying to avoid the potholes.

"Look, we could ask for directions over there." I pointed to a spot of light we were approaching fast.

We stopped at a brightly illuminated bar, which turned out to be a club for the Tswana in-crowd. Strings of Christmas lights were wound around the trees at the entrance to the parking lot and under their soft light stood a group of people dressed in cowboy outfits. I made the startling discovery that Gaborone locals loved Country & Western music.

Not so strange, when one considered the nation's fondness of cattle.

A real gentleman, unsurprisingly in a white Stetson, gave us directions. Emily turned the car around and we soon found the side road we were looking for. Another five minutes and we walked into a big, old-fashioned house.

It was freezing outside, so everybody piled into the spacious kitchen and the lounge, where a Hi-fi blared 'Crimson and Clover'. The house had an enormous veranda with colourful Tiffany glass doors. My mother would have been ecstatic to see the artwork here.

Kirsten and Peter Simmons from Western Australia were new in Gaborone. They didn't have children, but lots of issues to keep them occupied. Kirsten didn't leave out an opportunity to draw attention to the fact that she couldn't have children - and that she couldn't care less. Her red t-shirt read 'Oops I forgot to have children!'.

The more she drank, the crazier she acted. Everyone tolerated her behaviour out of pity and because the couple was already members of the party in-crowd.

I learned quickly not to look at her t-shirt (and Kirsten practically wore it to all parties). Most of us were single and didn't have children anyway, so big deal. But in

Kirsten's mind, everybody on this planet gave her reproachful stares.

"You know why I don't have children?" she addressed me in a not so sober state.

"No, Kirsten. Plenty of time for that, I'm sure."

What was I supposed to say?

"No... what's your name?"

"Bridget."

"No Bridget, no, I'm infertile, you see."

"Sorry to hear that."

Emily had already warned me, but I thought that Kirsten could do with a sympathetic ear. But Kirsten didn't want to talk. Kirsten wanted to play.

"No, no, no, no! Nobody must feel sorry for me. Let's pordee!" she yelled in a piercing voice. Kirsten didn't take no for an answer and dragged me onto the dance floor.

"That's my husband over there," she yelled in my ear. "He's such a hunk. Isn't he just gorgeous?"

Her husband Peter stood around sheepishly and pretended not to hear a thing. It must have been embarrassing to have his wife tell perfect strangers that he looked gorgeous.

"Like PI Magnum, Tom Selleck, you know," she carried on.

Peter looked nothing like Tom Selleck, apart from his height perhaps. Kirsten, however, just knew that all the women were after her precious spouse. They couldn't resist her magnetic hunk, she probably thought. And seemed determined to hold onto him for dear life.

"Hey, wah you staring at my husband?" she jumped at a girl in a pink t-shirt, innocently chatting to some friend. She gaped speechlessly at Kirsten.

"Yeah, I know you like him. He's good-looking all right." She turned abruptly around to delight other guests with her conversation-skills. The stunned girl fled the scene. If that was the kind of distraction Gabby had in mind for me, it was a resounding success.

I walked to the kitchen and filled a plate with salads. Emily was already there and introduced me to her friend Kgomotso. She wore a fashionable top and her hair was pulled back into a short ponytail. Kgomotso was short and slender and had the most dazzling smile.

"Are you enjoying yourself here?" she asked and smiled her captivating smile.

"Yes, just that Kirsten is so, so..."

"Ah, don't mind her. Everybody feels like that. Bit off the wall our Kirsten," Kgomotso said shrugging her shoulders. I liked her openness.

"You can say that again. Poor husband. I'm beginning to count my blessings that she didn't pick on me."

"Don't we all," Emily sighed.

Similar scenes played themselves out at other parties. While Peter preferred to chat to the guys about rugby and his new 4x4 truck, Kirsten informed the attending females that her husband was an irresistible hunk and belonged to her alone. The two of them were even going to renew their wedding vows soon. Ten years of marriage! Pity stood on the women's faces, but Kirsten didn't notice it. Jörg Walter would have had a ball!

"Don't look at him like that," Kirsten snarled at me a week later, as we all stood around the flickering braai at someone else's party, waiting for grilled chicken pieces. I grinned and ignored her.

"Stop joyriding on my husband's back!" Kirsten had crept up on Mette, the Danish volunteer. Mette looked puzzled.

"What's joyriding?" she wanted to know.

One of the other girls whispered something in her ear. Mette couldn't figure out which one of the men in front of her was 'the husband' and jumped away as if they had all turned into snakes. Everybody laughed and Kirsten stomped off red-faced.

Mette had told me just minutes before that Rudolph

Haase, the German volunteer I had met at the Chinese restaurant was in trouble, too. He had been told to leave the country within two weeks. Nobody seemed to know what had angered the authorities and Rudolph didn't want to speak to anyone. Apparently, Ben didn't seem too happy either and was always in Jörg's company. Thankfully, I never ran into them.

Parties were a great distraction once again and I went out almost every weekend. In addition, I still went running with Vanessa. and Andrea Fry, a Social Science teacher at Rockhill Primary, took me to her amateur theatre club. Except for a few Tswana enthusiasts, most of the theatre club members were British expats. POMEs - Prisoners of Mother England - as James Skinner, a lanky young man in his late twenties, liked to refer to us fellow Brits.

A Christmas pantomime was in the making and I was assigned to the props section. The troupe met on weekends at the MOTH hall for rehearsals and liked to hang out at the bar afterwards. My Setswana classes had ended weeks ago and I was free on weekends.

The panto was based on the story of Cinderella and a mishmash of other fairytales.

The dialogues were an absolute hoot and in the usual tradition, men were cast in the female roles. James Skinner played the lead. He was a rather manly Cinderella. Two older chaps were the ugly stepsisters. At the end of the second act, the audience had to sing along to:

*'Tom, Tom the piper's son, stole a pig and away he ran.*
*The pig was eat and Tom was beat.*
*Tom ran howling down the street.'*

The tune stuck with me and I caught myself humming it all the time. Between my work schedule, friends, running and rehearsals at the MOTH Hall, I had little time for anything else. Unpleasant things were just swept under the carpet. Benjamin for example.

He hadn't been back in Gaborone for three weeks. Then out of the blue, he contacted me. I was confused. Should I just kick him to the kerb as Gabby and Rita had advised me? But he seemed his old dashing self again and suggested that we go on a holiday to Namibia in October. I said I'd consider it.

"You want to consider it? Are you out of your mind?" Gabby bellowed. "How can you take him back after all he's done to you?"

"I don't know. I can't explain it," I whispered, "We are just friends now. Nothing else going on."

"Sure, that's all he's after. Friendship." Gabby snorted contemptuously.

"You are allergic to that man, Bridget, please stay away from him!" Emily begged.

"I need more time to think about it."

"Yes, without Ben. Have you forgotten Jörg Walter and the prostitute already?"

"Gabby's right. You're in denial," Emily said.

They both had an excellent point. Benjamin was not easy to figure out. He blew hot and cold all the time. So why was I even considering a trip to Namibia with him? A brief memory - of skin against warm skin - flashed through my mind. Come on, I said to myself, you can't be serious. Show some self-respect! The sensation vanished. It was only August and there was still plenty of time until October.

Party invitations rolled in, mainly from the English crowd. Any excuse was good enough for a braai or a movie or a dinner at some restaurant. My social life was blossoming and I hardly noticed how little I thought about my life in Kang or in Palapye. Or about Claire.

No problem... as long as I wasn't sad anymore.

I saw much of Gabby and Rita and Emily. Stoeckl and Herbert Schmitt had extended their work contracts and often tagged along, without their current girlfriends. Benjamin never showed up.

Suddenly it was September and the Wincklers were preparing to leave for Germany. Rita had invited me to a last chicken and vegetable dinner on the veranda. It was too hot to sit inside, even after dusk. The girls clung to me all evening and Jasmin showed me proudly that her braces had been removed

"Oh, Jasmin, your teeth look lovely now! Come give me a kiss." The little girl giggled and pressed her lips on my cheek.

"Auntie Bridget, I don't know why Cherise and Jessica are always so ugly to me," Adrienne complained. "All they want to talk about is boys, boys, boys." She called the popular girls in her grade 'possies'.

"Darling, I think the possies are just jealous of you. You are so pretty and the boys might be interested in you," I explained to the blushing teenager.

Bridget, the great expert in boys!

Oh, how I would miss the Wincklers! I couldn't imagine saying goodbye to the family forever. I hated the thought of losing one of my best friends so soon, but that's how it was for expats in Botswana. Rita was planning to organise a jumble sale and then the following week a farewell party for all her friends.

I promised to support Rita at the jumble sale and bought a tennis racket for 25 Pula that I didn't need. Carol Jenkins, Henriette Milton and Lorato Sepeng, followed by her nanny who carried the baby, put in an appearance. We chatted, but compared to Rita, I found them superficial.

When Gabby learned that I had bought a Wilson tennis racket, she assumed that I must have found my passion for the sport.

She was dead set on teaching me how to play tennis. I can't say that I took to tennis like a duck to water and had no idea how to hold a tennis racket and even less what the rules were. But despite my distinct lack of talent, I began to play tennis now and again at the Gaborone Club.

The farewell party at the Wincklers was quite a bash. Most of their belongings had been sold or already shipped to Germany. That didn't prevent us from having a terrific party. Everybody had brought a plate of eats and we ate from paper plates. Then we danced. Princess, the maid, sat in her place of honour in her Sunday best and supervised her daughters all night long, pouring drinks and cleaning up.

Gaborone had been the Wincklers' home for the past three years, with Princess as the head of the household the entire time. Pauli sat by my feet the whole evening. Pauli the dog. Rita Winckler asked me during the party, if I couldn't take him off their hands.

"He's adorable and very protective," she coaxed me into accepting the sizeable mutt. "Chunky found a good home, but nobody wants Pauli. Please, Bridget. You can pick him up tomorrow, if you want."

How could I not take him after all the Wincklers had done for me? The black dog with the white patch on his chest gave me a pleading look I couldn't resist. As if he knew that we would be together from now on.

I already missed the leisurely luncheons with Rita at the President Hotel and her motherly ways, but at least I would have Pauli. I didn't think for a moment about how it was supposed to work.

"You're lucky it's not a human dog this time!" Gabby joked.

"Ha, ha."

But a week later, Pauli was gone from my back porch at the flat! I called him, I searched in the bushes and in the neighbourhood, but Pauli had disappeared. I was devastated. Pauli was part of the Winckler family and I didn't want to lose him as well! Gabby and I drove around in her little Suzuki 4x4, but Pauli was nowhere to be found. Then Gabby had a brainwave.

"We should go to his old neighbourhood. Dogs and cats sometimes run back to their old home," she said.

"But it's on the other side of town."

"We can still give it a try. Unless you have a better idea."

I didn't. So we drove halfway across the big village that was Gaborone in those days. As we turned the corner, there he was, lying in his old driveway in front of the closed gate. I was so relieved that I cried.

"Pauli, what are you doing here?" I hugged him.

My dog wagged his tail and jumped docilely into the back of Gabby's Suzuki.

"Look at him! He's happy to see you," Gabby said.

"Such a cheeky chops. You gave me a big fright... you," I said tenderly and scratched him behind his ears.

"He probably noticed that other people are living in the house and that he doesn't belong there anymore."

"As long as I have him with me again."

Pauli pressed his head against my shoulder on the way back, as if to apologize for running away.

We settled into a pleasant routine, then came more change - and even world events caught up with us. The Berlin Wall fell and East Germany was free. I watched stunned as the pictures rolled by on the news. This new Berlin was so different to the city I had lived in for a year. The Iron Curtain was crumbling!

My father phoned and sounded excited. He had spoken to his family in Berlin. They had confirmed the reports and said that hope surged through the country. We were far away from the events in our sleepy part of the world. Europe felt like a different planet at times. I told him everything was fine on my side.

Gabby and my other German friends celebrated. They were absolutely elated at the reunification of their two countries. Others not so much, as I should find out.

On Friday, Kgomotso, Emily and I decided to have a

girls' night out. The choice fell on a pub, the Bull 'n Bush, near the town centre. The place was thick with smoke and packed with people. As we walked in, a group of drunks we vaguely knew, laughed insanely at some dumb joke. They calmed down somewhat and shot strange glances at us. That wasn't exactly unusual. As three single females we could expect to draw some attention. The guys yelled into each other's ears and broke out into more guffawing.

"Charming." Emily felt visibly uneasy and tried to push quickly past the group.

"Ooh, here comes Hitler's daughter!" Roaring laughter.

Fingers pointed at me. It was a known fact that my father was German.

"What? What did you just say?" Kgomotso flew around and hissed at the drunken dolt. It was Bokkie Wilkinson, a well-known mining engineer from Johannesburg with rather unpleasant manners.

"Come on baby, she's not proper English. You are just right for me. Or do you like her better than me?" His pals laughed uneasily this time.

"You are an idiot," Kgomotso said very slowly. "And I'm not your baby." She stood in front of them like a large cat ready to lunge.

Emily rolled her eyes. "You know what? Bridget's father was a toddler during the war. His father was in a concentration camp, because he didn't agree with the Nazis."

I had told her about my Dad's history in private. It would be welcome fodder for the Gaborone gossip machine now. But there was no stopping Emily.

"Oh and by the way, Hitler was Austrian, not German. And the British invented concentration camps in South Africa long before the Nazis had them. For Afrikaaners," she turned the tables on the bullies. "Didn't you learn that at school?"

Emily's great-grandmother had been interned together

with thousands of other Afrikaaner women and children during the Boere War. All that was too complicated for sloshed Bokkie. A quieter song began to play in the background.

"Oh yeah?! Ho, ho!" That didn't sound very confident. "Don't be cross with me, baby!"

"And lose the 'baby' crap, will you!" Kgomotso shouted over the music.

A few people turned around and looked at us. Somebody behind me seemed to have something to say. It was Andrea Fry, my usually so friendly and helpful colleague, who had introduced me to her theatre group. Her embarrassed-looking husband stood right behind her.

"My father was a British gentleman-soldier in WW2 and he told me that the reunification of East and West Germany will lead to WW3," she said proudly.

"With all due respect Andrea, how did your father figure that out?" I challenged her. "Isn't that a tad bit hypocritical, considering that Britain started a war with Argentina only three years ago — because of the Falkland Islands?"

"My father knows what he is talking about," she said. "And the Falkland Islands, that's a totally different matter."

"Oh my stars. I mean people change and countries change," I tried to reason with her. "The Germans are not a military threat anymore. In fact, when I lived in Berlin, the peace movement on either side of the border was so strong and…"

"You lived in Germany? How do we know that you are not some kind of spy?" Andrea looked around for support. What? As if somebody who lives in another country becomes automatically a double agent. Unbelievably, some of the other patrons nodded.

"Right you are Andrea," one of them bawled.

"Come on now, that doesn't make any sense," I said feebly. "I'm British like you."

"Are you, indeed?" Andrea said.

"Well, your father is Irish now, isn't he? What's the difference?"

"Come let's go," Emily said. "There's no point to this."

We began to push through the hostile group. The drunken guys, who had started the spat, didn't know what else to say and just laughed. As we retreated out to the parking lot, a Cyndi Lauper song rang out. '...True colours, true colours...'. Luckily, not too many patrons had paid attention to the scene. '...True colours, true colours...are beautiful like a rainbow...' The song followed us all the way to Emily's car.

Nobody else did.

"What jerks!" Kgomotso was still upset. "Damn hypocrites."

Emily searched for her keys. "Yes, die mense praat kack," she said drily. Those people talk rubbish.

"Not proper English! 'Come on, Baby'... my word, what does he think I am - a duck?" Kgomotso said in such an exasperated tone that we had to laugh and our tension simply dissolved into laughter.

"Let's go to the Korean restaurant in Ramotswa. You're invited." Kgomotso perked up. The new Korean restaurant was next door to the top notch seafood restaurant in town and all the rage.

"Good idea," Emily agreed. "Hopefully there are not too many jerks there on a Friday night. Besides, we must still celebrate that Bridget has kicked Benjamin to the kerb. There is no better time than right now —"

A stitch went through my heart. That was still a grey area for me... "All right then, Korean it is," I said a bit more cheerful than I felt.

We pulled out of the parking lot and onto the freeway. Large billboards along the main road warned about this new disease called AIDS and encouraged the use of condoms. A touchy subject with Tswanas. Hilda had told me that some people thought Aids was exaggerated and that it was more important to be able to make babies.

At the restaurant, we tucked into the marinated slices of thin beef that we fried on the cone-shaped metal stove in the middle of the table. The conversation drifted along effortlessly.

"I like your lip gloss Motso," Emily said.

Kgomotso took a tube of pink lip gloss from her purse.

"The latest fashion colour. I bought it in Joburg last week."

"Mhm, this Thai salad is to die for. Why is it called Thai salad, if we are in a Korean restaurant?" I wondered.

No one mentioned the scene at the Bull 'n Bush or Benjamin. *Just as well*, I thought. Why burden myself with unpleasant topics?

A few days later, a letter arrived from Rita Winckler. It brought back memories of her elegant movements, her long grey hair and how she lit up a cigarette.

*Hi Bridget,                      Husum, 13 November*

*Husum is sooo boring. The kids are back at school and so is Uli. I hope we'll leave again soon. Soon meaning in 6 months or so. They gave us a choice between Bolivia and Indonesia, but I think Uli would like to stay here for a while. For the girls' sake.*

*So, Pauli ran away? Bummer. Before we left, I tried to explain to him that he needs to look after you now, but I guess he didn't pay attention. Now that he knows we're no longer in Gabs, he'll surely think twice about doing that again. I'm sure you are a great dog-mommy.*

*How's everyone else? Gabby still playing tennis? Sure she is. Any interesting new arrivals? Male and good-looking? Go and play tennis at the club. The new ones always join the club! Got to rush, must buy something for dinner. Look out for those gossips, you know there's nothing I can do from here...*
*Love you, stay well*

*Rita, Uli, Adrienne and Jasmin.*

It was the only letter I should ever receive from Rita. Apparently, she wasn't much for writing.

The days grew longer again. If just the contract for my flat hadn't ended, things would have turned out differently. I didn't have a choice but to look for another place to stay. It would be better for Pauli, if we lived in a house with a garden anyway.

I placed an advert in the paper and sure enough, somebody responded. A British contractor called John Whitaker. He had lived together with his girlfriend Khetumile since his recent divorce. The house was way too big for the two of them, John insisted - especially now that his two grown-up children had flown the coop.

Khetumile was a beautiful Tswana woman with masses of hair extensions done up in a ponytail. She worked somewhere in government and was rather well-spoken. John Whitaker was more on the short and burly side with a moustache and a dated blond mullet. I could tell that he liked to think of himself as cool and easy going. Well then.

The room was down the hall from the other bedrooms. Just enough room for a few things, but that's all I needed. There would be plenty of space for Pauli outside in the garden. My new room-mates welcomed a dog for security around the house. No matata.

I was sad to let Hilda go, but another - rather timid - maid already cleaned John's house. Things went well at first. John, Khetumile and I even ate the occasional meal together. It was my first taste of commune life and Pauli enjoyed exploring the garden. I didn't see much of them. They went to work and so did I.

Rumours were flying around that Peter and Kirsten Simmons had returned to Perth and were getting a divorce. It was a sad ending to a sad relationship. My own dysfunctional relationship to Benjamin came to a sudden end, when I pulled the plug on our planned Namibia trip.

He had arrived from Kang in a bad mood. I introduced

him to Pauli, but that didn't go too well. Pauli didn't seem to like Ben very much and Ben felt miserable with a beginning cold and moaned all day long about everything. On top of it, he just knew from bitter experience with another girlfriend that this trip would end in tears. I'd finally had enough. Last time I checked, we were not boyfriend and especially NOT girlfriend anymore.

Instead of taking the couch, he slept outside in the back of his Nissan and left in a huff in the morning. Pauli put his head in my lap and looked up at me with his sensitive, black eyes. He knew how to make me feel better. Together we watched Ben's truck rattling up the road.

I got over Ben surprisingly fast this time. There was no time for wallowing. Word of mouth had travelled fast — that I was specialized in technical translations. During term break the German Economic Agency requested the translation of a study into German. *'Economic Viability Study of Silk Production through the Use of Mopani Worms'* to be precise.

In Botswana, Mopani worms weren't exactly valued for the coarse silk they produced. They were the height of sophistication in Tswana cuisine. The worms were usually enjoyed dried and salted or cooked in a stew.

The money was good. We were still a long way from the computer age, so I hammered away on John's typewriter, while Pauli slept on my feet. Before I knew it, it was back to school. I thoroughly enjoyed teaching French now and had grown fond of the children. They often gave me little gifts. Colourful drawings, an apple and once even a little blue Smurf figure.

My new home had a major disadvantage. It was in stray-dog country. We lived next door to a high-placed police official, who kept five famished dogs. It wouldn't have been much of a problem, if the gate had been closed and the holes under the fence fixed. But nobody complained about the mutts for fear of the police official.

The dogs were ill-tempered and often tried to attack people walking past the fence. Picking up stones seemed quite effective for the Tswana pedestrians, so I copied them. The movement alone was enough to make them scram.

It was scary after dark, but there was nothing I could do. I had to walk home from work and past the policeman's house.

On the other side of our house was an open field that everybody used for walking during the day. At night, however, it turned into a territory for strays and this was trouble waiting to happen.

One night Pauli was lying peacefully inside our gate, watching the lane, when a pack of roaming strays 'abducted' him. One moment he was by the gate, the next, I heard pitiful howling and caught a glimpse of Pauli following the strays through a hole under the house wall opposite ours.

"Pauli, come here boy. Come," I coaxed and whistled in a special way. But he acted as if he didn't hear me. It was bizarre. Pauli was in the paws of a canine mafia.

"Pauli, come here, now. Come!" I kept calling and whistling. Nothing.

The neighbours across the lane were not at home, so all I could do was wait. I heard howling and barking. Then just howling. I ventured out of the garden and checked anxiously up and down the lane. A gang-bashed Pauli lay in the ditch outside our hedge. A gaping wound on his neck as if his fur had been chewed off viciously.

"Oh Pauli, what did they do to you?"

I picked my limp Labrador cross-breed up and carried him into the house. He lay motionless on a blanket under the kitchen table for days, while I nursed him back to health. I also collected large stones and stuffed them into the holes under the fences and walls. Smaller stones served as ammunition. One of the stray dogs dared to run into our garden, only to find itself pelted with missiles.

John Whitaker took pity on me and let me drive his daughter's ancient green Mini Cooper. She had followed her boyfriend to Johannesburg and John thought it best that someone drove the rattletrap around, instead of having it rust away in the garage.

This funny-looking Mr. Bean car gave me sudden freedom of movement. No more walking to Rockhill Primary early in the morning come rain or shine or being growled at by vicious dogs. From now on I drove to work.

It must have looked hilarious. Me in morning traffic, between giant 4x4s with great, big bull-bars mounted to their front and rear - as protection from wild animals.

"Your Mini Cooper needs mouse-bars to compete with those bull-bars," my teacher colleagues joked. *Let them joke,* I thought triumphantly, *I have wheels now!*

It was fantastic, until one day the gearbox gave up its ghost in the parking lot of the Gaborone Sun Hotel. Just like that. I mourned the loss of my new-found independence. Gabby then lent me a wobbly bicycle that she kept in her garage for a friend. It was a whole lot better than walking.

John worked furiously on the Mr. Bean car after hours. It was a good excuse for him not to be in the house that often. For all was not well in my new residence. Khetumile and John didn't get on anymore and often fought violently.

I understood that the major problem was John's frequent philandering, before he'd met beautiful Khetumile.

Hell hath no fury like a woman scorned. Especially a Tswana woman. Suddenly, Khetumile didn't tolerate my presence in the lounge or kitchen anymore. I kept Pauli well out of her way and began to spend more time in my room or out with friends. But that wasn't the worst of it. One of John's past lovers began to stalk him. The frequent phone calls would send Ket into jealous rages.

The same girl kept phoning the house over and over. On

one unlucky occasion, it was me who picked up the phone. A drunken female voice demanded irately to speak to John.

"They are at the Eric Clapton concert and won't be back until late," I said.

"You are lying! They're at home. I saw his car outside in the driveway."

"They went with friends in their car."

Apparently it was not the correct answer and I was subjected to verbal abuse before I could hang up.

Ten minutes later, the first stone crashed through the big lounge window. Then the jilted lover went on to smash every single window in the house. I called the police, but by the time they arrived, the perpetrator had disappeared. John knew the woman and blamed me for involving the police. He was embarrassed and as I learned later, it could have cost him his residence permit. That's why he refused to lay charges and sent Khetumile into a frenzy.

The policemen left confused and I went to my room, which had now extra ventilation.

"You don't love me! I hate you!" I heard Khetumile screech behind closed doors. There was a thump and more yelling.

"You bitch. After all I've done for you!"

It turned out that the ex-lover was underage and the daughter of a government official. Remembering that Manfred Raab's girlfriend Sophie had set his car on fire, I decided that the situation could get way out of hand. Time to look for another place.

This time the house hunt proved more difficult with my African backstreet-special in tow. Eventually, I moved into Andrew Wolpert's house. He was an Australian water prospector from Tasmania and was looking for company.

The new house was farther from the city centre and I had to pedal my way to work along sandy footpaths on Gabby's wobbly bicycle.

Andrew didn't mind my bringing Pauli, as long as he was on a chain in the back garden. My sulking pooch could hardly wait for me to come home and take him for walks every day after work. Tswana pedestrians scattered every time they saw my scary black dog.

The Australian was in his fifties and street-smart and somewhat rough around the edges. He constantly smoked Peter Stuyvesant cigarettes and sat sometimes with a bottle of Scotch on the lounge floor and drank himself into a stupor. Andrew Wolpert called his sullen maid Maddie, although her name was Gaikesitsi. He insisted that he called all maids Maddie, whether he was in Dubai or Venezuela or Botswana. His Australian girlfriend Karen was supposed to join him in a few weeks, but he wanted somebody to talk to in the meantime.

When he was drunk, Andrew would tell me that Karen, his simple-minded bombshell girlfriend of 25, believed that an African chief would marry them as soon as she came to live with him in Botswana. It made him snigger every time. A bit odd, but no concern of mine.

I should have known better.

We were leading our separate lives and just spent some time chatting over daily suppers that Maddie the maid prepared. He told me about his work, prospecting underground water reservoirs in the Kalahari, about his life in Australia, a stint in Dubai and his bitter divorce from the mother of his three children.

After a couple of weeks, it became clear that Andrew's definition of a house mate was rather different to what I had in mind. Then his jealous girlfriend arrived and there were no two ways about it that Karen didn't like Pauli, and she didn't like me.

Karen looked about 40 with her sun-damaged skin and peroxide-blonde hair. And nothing was safe from her temper. Endless arguments between the two lovebirds about African chiefs marrying foreigners or not, escalated from time to time. Karen was not a happy camper. Maddie left after the new madam terrorized her. She was replaced by another, older Maddie.

Between painting her nails and tanning in the unforgiving African sun, Karen found the time for more spite. She accused me of wanting her man badly enough to steal his t-shirt from the washing line and hiding it in my room.

"I didn't take the darn t-shirt," I insisted. "Why on earth should I do that?"

"Of course you did. The one with the drilling platform on it," Karen ranted.

"I've never even seen a t-shirt like that and why would I take it? I have enough clothes of my own."

"What do you think? Something to remember my man by."

"And why would I want that? I have a boyfriend, you know."

Well, not anymore, but for the sake of making a point, Ben was still useful.

"Oh yeah? And where is he? You are after my man. You can forget it, we're getting married, you little minx. So where are you hiding his t-shirt?"

I bit back a remark that would have sent smug Karen hurtling. She searched my wardrobe, my bed and nightstand - and found nothing. How embarrassing! But Andrew Wolpert seemed indifferent to her behaviour. I had become an unwanted house guest, who had overstayed her welcome.

Why was I getting myself into these dicey living arrangements? I bitterly regretted moving out of my old flat in Acacia Court, but it was too late to change that.

Again I had to find the energy to move house. As long as I had my teaching job for stability and things would fall into place somehow. At least that's what I thought.

# CHAPTER 10

As if my life wasn't complicated enough! Before I could even begin to find another home for us in November, Mrs. Mulholland informed me that the school board would not be extending my contract. It had come to their attention that I had no formal teaching diploma. There was nothing the school principal could do. That put paid to my dream of stability. I found myself jobless again and that at the end of the year. Soon I would be homeless too. What to do?

How far I had moved from my plan to find my sister! I couldn't even dream about her anymore. My life was an endless search for a new home or a new job. How was I supposed to just jump off this roller coaster ride?

Summer rains had started late, but with a vengeance. The grade 7 exams were in full swing to the sound of rain hammering down on the tin roof.

Virtually all of Andrew's dianthus and busy-lizzy flowers had been obliterated in a vicious hailstorm and the smell of smashed-up plants still hung in the air. I hated leaving Pauli alone at the house, but what could I do? I was just glad that my housemates went out a lot these days. Perhaps they had married after all. I asked Maddie to look after my mutt while I was at work. The maid promised. She hated Karen with a passion.

When the sunny weather held for a couple of days, hats and sunglasses came out again. I'd met Carol Jenkins at the sports field to watch a friendly cricket game between her husband's company and the staff of TAC Insurance. My bicycle was decidedly inadequate on the muddy footpaths, so she was giving me a lift back home later.

"You see that? Len is batting. That's my husband, that's my man!" Carol shouted. "Six runs. Ah no, only four...four is good. Well done Len!"

We clapped and made the requisite hand movement, like stroking a bedspread. I watched the white figures on the field with rather less enthusiasm while contemplating my circumstances. My colleague Rosemary Bennett was going away on a three-week Christmas holiday with her husband and two young children. She had casually asked me whether I would consider house sitting for her.

"All you have to do is keep the plunge pool clean and feed our cat Napoleon. You can also use our dilapidated VW Golf, if you like."

She needn't ask me twice. Just another month until the Bennetts went on holiday to Cape Town, so I had to stick it out with Andrew and Karen until then.

Gabby had a friend from Munich staying with her and couldn't accommodate me. She would be off to Mauritius for two weeks middle of December. A car made it easier to get to the 'Cinderella' performances at the MOTH Hall in December. Once a day during the week and twice on weekends. Christmas Eve was the last performance followed by a cast party. Sorted!

I had to take care of formalities as well. Once again it was time for a visit to the immigration office. It meant waiting in a queue in a hot, stifling room with people staring at everybody entering or leaving, and having to watch officials eat from oily lunch packets on the files. Not only were petitioners called up at random, which drove the occasional expatriate into a tantrum. One also had to endure the inevitable interrogation regarding one's private life. Here was the place, where patience could be learnt.

I was torn out of my pensive mood, when the cricket game was interrupted for a drinks break.

"Oh, before I forget, Bridget," Carol drawled. "Len spoke to an engineer at his company about accommodation. His colleague's name is William Konenga. His father's a high-ranking judge in Ghana and William's been educated in London. He has a small house with two bedrooms and a very large veranda. William's offered for you to stay there with your dog until Rosemary goes on leave."

I just had to hug the surprised Carol.

"That's wonderful. Are you sure it's alright with him? I mean, I don't know this guy at all and he doesn't know me..."

"No worries. I've invited William to my Christmas party next week so you can meet. Open house for everybody this time. You can also bring a friend if you want."

Since there were a lot more single men around, the more single women came to a party, the better. I ran into Kgomotso Min at the Mall the next day and asked her to come with me to Carol's party.

"Beats a visit to my aunt's house hands down," she grinned. "Emily's not around, but I'll be there. Any excuse to party, right?" Sure, we belonged to the party in-crowd after all.

Carol had gone all out with food and decorations and Christmas songs played in the background.'...Baby it's cold outside...' and '...Frosty the Snowman...' conjured up images that had nothing to do with our African weather.

William Konenga turned out to be the perfect gentleman. Unlike so many other single men about town. He was refined and well-bred and normal and had no problem with sharing his house for a few weeks.

"Oh thank you so much, William, you are a true lifesaver."

"Where do you stay right now? Len Jenkins made it sound as if you were as good as homeless," he frowned.

"Try desperate! My current housemate has a jealous girlfriend."

"I see. That must be difficult for you."

"Unbearable. I promise we won't be any trouble at all. My dog Pauli and I."

Kgomotso was instantly smitten with William. Because he was so intelligent and good-looking, she told me later. A traditional Tswana girl deep down, Kgomotso was shy around men, but somehow she managed to invite William to her get-together on Christmas Eve. Her parents were already on their way to Malaysia to visit family and the deserted town house in Gaborone West was perfect for a party.

Emily spent Christmas at home in Johannesburg and some of our friends were going away. But there would be still at least 12 of us.

"We will have the place to ourselves. We'll cook dinner with turkey, sweet potatoes and trifle and all the trimmings. I've even prepared a vat of bojalwa."

Bojalwa was a fermented beverage with raisins and pineapples, traditionally made in large vats. Some called it gemere and it tasted much like strong punch.

The looming visit to the immigration office was much easier to handle with accommodation taken care of. Perhaps the worst was behind me. All I needed now was an extension of my residence permit and then a job. No matata.

I stood patiently in the queue, trying to remember Kgomotso's words of wisdom: 'You must just chat to them. Be friendly. Say you are engaged to be married and don't lose your temper.'

I was called into a small office with stacks of paper all over the desk and unclean floor. A clerk was slouching over his lunch in front of him. "You are twenty-two?" he chewed. The answer was obviously in my passport that had changed hands moments before.

"Yes," I smiled.

"So you are married?" Again, check my passport! Think

about Kgomotso, I reminded myself, it won't take long now...
"No, not yet."
"You have children?" He wiped his hands.
"No, only after we are married." How easy the lies flowed. Kgomotso would be proud of me.
"How do you like Botswana?"
"I love this country, the people are so nice." This was true.
"You like Tswana men?" I'd heard the question often.
"Tswana men are fine, but I have a boyfriend back home."
I cringed. Enough with the questions already!
"Are you getting married here?"
"Maybe. We haven't decided yet. My fiancé is an engineer in England." This sounded hopefully impressive enough to speed things up. It worked.
"Ehéy," the official cut straight to the chase. "So you don't have a job?"
"No, but I'm going for interviews." At last, we were moving on to actual facts.
"Where?"
"Woodlake Primary, Dubois International, Hedgerow Consultants..."
"Okay, okay. You come back when you have a job. We'll have a look at another work permit, then."
"Thank you, I will certainly do that, sir."
He wrapped his lunch packet. The stamp please! Stamp my passport right there on that page, I pleaded silently - just a short extension of the permit...
As he picked up his stamp, the man was called out of the office and chatted noisily with somebody in the passage. I kept looking at the ticking clock. Would he remember that he wanted to stamp my passport when he came back?
Just before I turned into a nervous wreck, he walked back in. The clerk remembered and I got my stamp. The

others in the queue watched me enviously as I strolled out of the stifling waiting room. I would be safe - for another 30 days.

And then I really did find another job!

Before she went on leave, Emily had asked Wolfgang Klein, her direct boss, to put in a good word for me with the office manager, Mr. Feindlich. After a brief interview and despite his reservations - because of some gossip he'd heard about me - I was hired by Mr. Feindlich as Mr. Klein's personal assistant.

The office manager had noticed the similarity of my surname to that of a previous employee's. I told him that Reinhold was quite a common surname in Berlin. I wrote on the form: Place of Birth: London. Luckily he didn't care to check Claire's file.

If Emily and Kgomotso were right, Mr. Feindlich didn't have much of a choice but to hire me. The company had its headquarters in Hamburg and was in urgent need of German project reports. Liesl had proven to be useless at translating or typing simple letters, which had led to a backlog of important documents.

Wolfgang Klein had managed to negotiate a temporary contract starting in January with a fantastic hourly rate. He needed me on his team. And the job came with accommodation: a room at the smaller company house in Tsholofelo! Sharing with Emily and Kgomotso would be so much better than being trapped in another 'John & Khetumile' or 'Andrew & Karen' living arrangement.

I thanked Wolfgang Klein with a modest Christmas present. A carved sugar bowl from Zimbabwe. Wolfgang joked that he was not supposed to take bribes, but his wife would love the sugar bowl.

The girls took me on a tour of the house right away. It was nowhere near as big as the other company house where Claire had stayed. Only four bedrooms and the interior design leaned toward the essentially bare, but there was a huge front veranda and a large garden. It was heaven to me! The fourth bedroom was occupied by a placid Portuguese draughtsman called Ruí. He usually worked overtime at the office and went to see his wife and children in Johannesburg on weekends. In other words, we had the house mostly to ourselves.

We celebrated with iced tea and rock shandy on the terrace of the President Hotel. I should have been over the moon, had it not been for this dull sadness deep-down. Maybe, just maybe, I could search for Claire now... but I pushed the thought aside. It would be no use anyway.

It was wonderful to see the last of Andrew's house!

William Konenga was a true gentleman and quite the 'coconut', as educated Africans were called. Pauli didn't seem to mind the change as long as I took him on our regular walks. William was mostly at work and I enjoyed the peace and quiet at his small pad. The bathroom lay between the two bedrooms, which gave us a measure of privacy. I unpacked only the most necessary items, because I had promised Rosemary Bennett to move into her house over Christmas.

A punishing heat took hold of Gaborone in December and the ceiling fans were stirring the air day in and day out. The heat felt intensely electrical and it was hard to form a proper thought. Even the birds were too exhausted to warble.

On a particularly hot afternoon I lay in the cool bathtub and relaxed. William would be at work until late. Suddenly, someone knocked outside against the long window under the ceiling. I jumped. Please not another ex-girlfriend, smashing the windows! There was another insistent knock.

"Koko. Koko." It was definitely a woman's voice.

Had I misjudged William Konenga, the gentleman? And how did this woman know I was in the bath? I pretended not to hear. Perhaps it was just a maid looking for a job. Perhaps she would go away.

"Koko, koko!" My sleeping dog, dozing in the lounge, woke up and growled. Silence.

I quickly finished my bath and watched one of William's three videos. There was a knock on the door. Softly at first, then more insistent, followed by wild banging.

Pauli began to bark. What on earth? I opened the door. A young Tswana woman in jeans and t-shirt stood in front of me, panting angrily.

"Why are you staying here? This is my boyfriend's house!" she snapped at me.

Pauli barked and barked. The woman looked intimidated and took a step back. I knew that William didn't have a girlfriend. He had told me so himself and there was no reason why I shouldn't believe him.

"No you are not his girlfriend!" I said. "And neither am I. It's okay Pauli. Alright."

My dog, alarmed by the woman's aggressive manner, planted himself growling in front of me, keeping a watchful eye on her.

"Howe! He didn't tell you?" she asked hot-headed.

"No, there's nothing to tell. He doesn't have a girlfriend and I am just visiting. Not that it's any of your business." I used my best schoolmarm tone of voice.

She looked at me, turned around and walked away without another word. When William came home, I gave him the third degree.

"I'm really sorry about that," he apologised. "It was probably the girl from across the road again. I don't even know her name. She waited for me one morning when I moved in, telling me cheekily that she wanted to go out with me. I asked her to stay away or I'd talk to her parents. Haven't seen her in a while now."

"Perhaps you should speak to her parents now or she could get you into trouble," I said and told him about John's ex-girlfriend, who had taken her anger out on our windows. William was shocked.

"Oh dear! Women in Ghana wouldn't do something like that. Perhaps I should go over there right now."

I saw through the window that he had a short and polite conversation with an elderly man, shook his hand and returned.

"All set. Her grandfather will have a serious talk with her. Apparently I'm not her only 'victim'. He doesn't want any trouble with the police."

"Good to hear. Why did she think I was your girlfriend?" I asked.

"You must remember that in our culture a young woman - as yourself - doesn't visit a young man just like that. She's either his sister or his girlfriend," William said.

"I'm obviously not your sister."

"No, obviously not," he said. "But seeing you here set her off again. But I'm sure she won't be any more trouble."

"You live and learn. I was beginning to think that bad luck is following me every-where I go," I moaned. "By the way, Gabby and I are going to the MOTH Hall sixties party later. Want to come with?"

"No, I'll meet a friend at Giovanni's Pizza later. Have fun, though."

What I didn't know then was that this friend was my friend Kgomotso. Neither of them let on that they were seeing each other, to throw the gossips off their track.

We were supposed to dress in Sixties style for the Moth Hall party, so I put on the most colourful clothes I managed to find. Gabby fetched me, dressed in true flower power style in a maxi dress and headband. She would be leaving for Mauritius after helping me move the day after tomorrow and it was our last chance to party.

Many theatre club members had already left for their Christmas vacations, but there was still quite a crowd. Thankfully, nobody harassed me about my German father and we danced until the wee hours of the morning.

"I'm beat, I need sleep badly," I yawned.

"Come on Bridget. What you need is more stamina for the party season. You still have a bash tomorrow and then you move into Rosemary house, remember?"

"That's exactly why I need some sleep now."

The move was sandwiched between the Hash Harriers' Christmas party at the Oasis Hotel and a dinner at Giovanni's a day later with Herbert and Stoeckl. Then a few private parties and on Christmas Eve it was Kgomotso's place. My roller coaster went round and round.

Reliable as ever, Gabby came to fetch me the morning after the Hash Harrier party at 9 o'clock. My head hurt and I couldn't stop yawning.

"What's the matter?" She asked suspiciously. "Do you have a hangover?"

"I don't know. Yawn. My head hurts." I put on my darkest sunglasses.

"Hey, you don't normally get drunk."

"I know. Tell you about it in a minute. Aspirin should kick in just now."

"Okay, start from the top," Gabby demanded and I told her over a cup of strong coffee telegram-style about the Hash-Harriers Christmas Do the night before.

"After the run, they ushered us into the hall. Didn't have time to change my clothes. Kgomotso was there of course. Susan Lewis from Ridge & Perkmans and Hans Schiffer from the German Movers were also at our table. Yawn. And a quarrelling couple. Yawn. She's from Indonesia and he's American, I think."

"Get to the point, Bridget."

I told Gabby the rest of the story, while we were driving the first load in the back of her little Suzuki across town. She only interrupted me to make sure she had understood properly and to wolf-whistle annoyingly.

The party had been informal. None of us looked particularly attractive after an hour's run through the countryside, but we had fun and danced a lot. The booze was flowing and Hans Schiffer kept our table generously topped up with bottles of red wine. The fact that the food wasn't great didn't matter, and then I met Cliff Bailey.

One of the guys from one of the tables on the other side of the hall demanded one dance after another with me. I vaguely recognised him from the Moth Hall party. He wasn't unfortunate-looking and I felt a little flattered. After a while, I went outside to get some fresh air and cool my feet in the pool.

"Hi," someone said and sat down next to me. It was my eager dance partner.

"Hi." I noticed that he had blond curls and very blue eyes. His ready smile and dimples at the corners of his mouth were interesting.

"Need some time alone? My name is Cliff, by the way, Cliff Bailey." He seemed nice, but he disturbed me somewhat at being alone.

"Yes, I think I'm going to leave soon. Just waiting for my friend Kgomotso to give me a lift home."

"Why don't you come with us to Millicent's flat? Millicent Feather, you may have met her. It's sort of an after-party. She's got caviar and blinis at home. I can drive you home whenever you want."

I had met Millicent Feather briefly at some formal function. She was one of the PAs at the British High Commission and had spent two years in St. Petersburg, before coming to Botswana. Millicent had seemed rather prim and proper.

"Caviar - sounds classy. I don't know, I'm too tired."

"I promise you'll like it. We are all perfectly respectable people. Here, I'll give you a second wind." He made me laugh with his magician's hand movements.

"Okay, I'll come along to Millicent's, but not for long," I said spontaneously.

Cliff Bailey seemed sober enough to drive.

"Perfect. My magic always works. She stays at a

security complex east of the Mall."

"Okay, I must quickly tell my friend first. See you just now," I said.

You will regret this Bridget. If you're tired you should sleep, a weak voice of reason warned me. I ignored it.

Kgomotso didn't feel like going to another party. Most of the Hash Harriers were drunk by now and the party had stopped being fun. She wanted to go home and gave me a funny look as if I was abandoning her.

"Sorry Motso, I'll give you a call during the week," I promised.

"Okay Bridge, til then," she said appeased and hugged me.

Cliff waved from the other side of the parking lot and we left. There were six of us: I, Millicent and Cliff, Brian Jones from Barry in Southern Wales ( no relation to Alfred Jones in Palapye), Harry Mooney and Jennifer Draycott, Millicent's closest friend.

Podgy Harry was from Liverpool, kept calling food 'scran' and spoke Liverpudlian that nobody fully understood. He and Brian worked for one of the many engineering firms in town. That was all I was offered in introductions.

Plain Millicent was the exact opposite to Jennifer, who had long black hair and wore a tight mini-dress. But what she lacked in the looks department, Millicent made up for as a party animal.

Her flat was much like my flat in Acacia Court. An African clay pot with masses of porcupine quills stood in one corner of the lounge and an almost ceiling-high painted giraffe from Zimbabwe in another.

Millicent demonstrated how we had to eat a blini, a tiny Russian pancake. Top it with sour cream and a teaspoon of caviar. "No, the caviar goes on top!" She took the spoon from Harry and gave him a slap. "This is imported caviar from Russia! Do it properly."

The blinis were washed down with champagne and vodka. Then we had slammers, shooters mixed with some lemonade until it foamed. Well, I only had one slammer, but judging by my hangover later, I had one too many.

"I have an idea. Let's have a fun fight in the pool," Millicent suggested.

It turned out to be more of a wet t-shirt contest, with the girls taking turns riding on the guys' shoulders and pulling each other into the pool. I thought it was silly, but joined in nevertheless. The splashing and the raucous laughter could have woken up the dead. Very respectable indeed!

"Won't your neighbours complain, Millicent?" I asked when we changed into the dry clothes Millicent provided.

She giggled at my concerns and just said, "Iss Chrissmass, Bridshid, don't be such a dripp. Mose offem are in the UK, so don't worrrry." Millicent no longer reminded me of a proper Victorian debutante. Unsurprising after all those slammers she'd had by now...

Gabby and I parked on Rosemary's driveway.

"So, then did you leave?" Gabby asked and helped me carry the last of the black bags into the house.

"No. I know I should have," I admitted guiltily.

"You don't say," Gabby said.

Things became even sillier. Jokes were told, no matter how ill-timed and unfunny. We played charades to wild laughter and of course drank the entire time.

"F*** the duck!" Brian Jones yelled. "You're killing me. F***!" Millicent ordered Brian to pay 50 Thebe into a glass jar. There was a 50 Thebe fine for every four-letter-word and Brian used a lot of those. Harry did his charade in increasingly grotesque contortions.

"It's Michael Jackson, Michael Jackson!" Cliff crowed and Harry let himself fall playfully onto the couch.

"Bastards, look what you've done!" Jennifer Draycott screeched as her gin and tonic splashed all over her fashionable dress. When she at last threw up onto the bathroom floor, I knew it was time to go. At about 3 o'clock.

Cliff wasn't exactly sober, but gallantly insisted on driving me. There was practically no traffic in the deserted streets or I would have died of fear. Cliff gave me a last meaningful stare in front of William's house. I thanked him and hurried inside. William wasn't at home. I patted Pauli, who stretched himself sleepily and went straight to bed. End of story!

"Uh oh," Gabby said on our way back to fetch the last load. "Don't do anything I wouldn't do."

"I'm sure I don't know what you mean."

"Oh, Bridget, don't be so naïve. This Cliff guy seems mighty interested in you." Gabby whistled most irritatingly through her teeth.

"Oh rubbish. He was just being nice - I think. And he was drunk," I said.

"Sure. He just wanted to be nice."

"Anyway I don't care, really. He said he's getting a divorce, which means he's still married. So no go. I probably won't see him again until the next Hash Harrier run."

"Hmm, he's married," Gabby said slowly.

"Yes."

"Stay away from him," Gabby gave me an unusual, motherly advice. "He's probably on the rebound."

"Yes I know. I'm not stupid."

"Good. Don't give me grief. I don't want to hear any complaints when I come back from Mauritius."

We were loading the dog blanket, bowls and my loyal canine friend into the back. I said goodbye to William and promised to pay my portion of the phone bill as soon as possible.

"By the way, somebody called Cliff was here just now. He left a note with his phone number for you," William said and handed me a folded piece of paper.

"Thanks Will. Bye then."

"Bye."

"What does it say?" Gabby peeked at the note.

"Let's see." I unfolded the note. "Well, just that he wants to see me again and that I should give him a call," I said unenthusiastically.

"I thought he was married." We hit a pothole. "Wow!"

"He's separated. At least that's what he told me yesterday."

Pauli had pushed his head into my armpit and I scratched the fur behind his ears.

"Really! Why does he tell you something like that on the first day you meet?" Gabby said somewhat upset. "Stay away from that jerk, Bridge. I'm serious. He might just tell you that story to get you into the sack. And then, suddenly his wife shows up from her trip to the UK or so - and the Spanish Inquisition begins."

We were turning into the Bennetts' driveway.

"Absolutely."

"Shoo, what do you have in here? It's so heavy!" Gabby helped me carry the last box, while Pauli sniffed everything thoroughly.

"Books," I said.

I definitely had more stuff now than a year ago, when I'd arrived at the airport with a couple of bags. I also had acquired two wicker chairs for 10 Pula each. And Gabby had given me a slightly tattered wicker table to match them.

I made tea and we sat in the garden on my modest furniture before Gabby left.

"See you in January. And be a good girl while I'm away," she laughed as she drove off.

"Am I not always?" I called and she waved. Gabby would be in Mauritius by evening. I waved until she had disappeared around the corner and wished I could have gone with her.

Rosemary's house was a haven of tranquility and the little plunge pool a blessing in the heat. Rosemary's maid, came to clean once a week and the rest of the time I was alone with Pauli. At last, I could sleep, read, listen to Rosemary's classical music tapes and eat whatever and whenever I felt like it. Life was good. I even planned to write Claire a long, detailed letter.

On the downside, Napoleon the fat white cat, who lived on the washing machine outside the kitchen door, took an immediate dislike to Pauli. Unlike Hinny, our placid cat in Cambridge, Napoleon was an unlikeable scoundrel.

The washing machine was exclusive cat territory and Pauli slept and ate in open garage in the company of the car. But my sociable dog couldn't resist sniffing now and again and had his snout and eye badly scratched in return.

Napoleon's claws dug into Pauli's face at every opportunity and I began to run out of antiseptic cream. Napoleon soon preferred to sit on the tree by the washing line and only jumped onto the washing machine to feed.

"Well, if that's how you feel..." I said to him, while I examined Pauli's blood-shot eye. "I can't help you. Sit on that tree and sulk, then."

Napoleon stared at me accusingly. As if I had driven his family away and taken over his territory with this troublesome canine. Rosemary should have explained the temporary situation to him!

My solitude was only occasionally interrupted by visitors. In the beginning, Stoeckl came twice and helped with the car alarm. I also had some rather unexpected visitors: cockroaches. Large ones! They started their invasion from the kitchen.

I nearly dropped my cup when I detected a large brown insect with chewing mandibles and long trembling feelers on the shelf. Then I saw one in the pot cupboard, two on the toilet floor and another one on my pillow.

I bought insect spray, but the roaches were extremely fast, whizzing across the highly polished lounge floor or quickly disappearing into hidden crannies. I sprayed, I threw shoes and kept books ready for the same purpose. But no amount of insect spray managed to keep their breeding in check. When it was time to vacate the house, I had counted 43 of them in all. Nice.

Kgomotso showed up on a whim one morning and we spent the day doing was girls do. We watched chick flicks with Tom Cruise from Rosemary's movie selection and went to one of the new malls that were springing up around Gabs.

On our way to the 'Kgotla Café', we passed a row of women, sitting on the pavement.

They offered heaps of dried Mopani worms piled high on mats, while gutting fresh supplies into tin bowls. Kgomotso bought a small packet of dried worms and dared me to taste one. I nibbled a tiny piece off the one end. The worm was crunchy and salty as expected, but there was another gamy taste that I didn't like. I handed the Mopani worm back to Kgomotso, who munched on it with gusto.

"How can you eat stuff like that?" I must have had a disgusted look on my face.

"Let's see - don't the French eat slugs and frogs?" She was right of course.

"Yes, they do, but worms? Ugh!" I could still taste the tiny piece I had bitten off and longed for a rock shandy.

"What's the difference? We grew up with that sort of thing and you didn't. I rest my case." She put another Mopani worm in her mouth. "Delicious!"

I liked the Greek salad at the trendy 'Kgotla Café' above the German bakery so much better.

Much later when I already lived at the company house, Kgomotso took me outside one wet evening and showed me thousands of flying termites. The fat, white termites sometimes swarmed after a mild summer rain, but I never had a close look at them before. Kgomotso picked up one from the street. It had a big, rather long white body, wriggled and dropped its wings immediately.

"We eat them," Kgomotso declared. "Pan-fried, they

taste like butter."

"What do you do that for?" I was flabbergasted.

"It's a delicacy like Mopani worms. I guess there wasn't always meat around, so people had to find other food. This here is pure protein and tastes good. Come help me pick up some, I'll show you." Kgomotso was serious.

We collected a number of the wriggling termites and she fried them in a pan. I must say they didn't taste bad at all. My friends in England would have declared me insane, but I liked fried flying termites...

We sat in the 'Kgotla Café' for a while and chatted. "I shouldn't have had so much garlic." Kgomotso smelled her own breath. She confessed that she had a secret date with William Konenga at 8 o'clock. The dates were secret, because she was not supposed to date without her parents' permission. And because William was not Tswana. Even if he were a Tswana, there'd be the awkward part, when a boyfriend had to recite his clan names to ensure that the couple did not share any ancestry.

I was confused.

"Isn't it highly unlikely that you share ancestors? And in any case, what is the problem with foreigners? Your mother is married to a Chinese banker with the family's consent."

"That's different. Martin, my stepfather, is rich. And my mother's beyond child bearing."

"But William is such a special person," I argued. "How could they not like him?" My parents would have been ecstatic, if I introduced a well-mannered engineer.

"I know, I really like him," she blushed. "But it's complicated. Marriage is sort of expected when you date. The forefathers must be consulted. Then there's the question of lobola. I'm just not ready for that sort of thing."

"Your family must be very traditional then."

"In a way."

It didn't make much sense to my western mindset. That with the ancestors and the importance of a dowry.

I never phoned Cliff Bailey after my move to Rosemary's house, but I saw him again at the MOTH Hall. Some of the theatre group members were going to meet at the bar there and I was running late. I had to walk, because Rosemary's dodgy Golf had packed up again. Stoeckl could only come around and look at the carburettor in the morning.

I had no choice but to take a shortcut through the rough terrain. It took much longer than anticipated and I was hopelessly late. They had already left for sure. *Never mind,* I thought, *some kindly soul will give me a lift back home.* What I didn't expect was to see Cliff Bailey waiting for me by the bar! I sat down on the barstool next to him to catch my breath.

"The others went ahead to the Chinese restaurant," Cliff told me. "If you want to, we can still go."

I could have said no, but then there was my transport problem. The alternative was to ask someone else for a ride or walk back in the dark.

"Okay, why not?" I said instead.

As we prepared to leave, a little boy was sent over by his parents to give me a message. "I must tell you that Cliff is a married man and that he shouldn't play around with nice women like you." What was going on?

Cliff made light of it and begged me not to listen. Well, he had waited for me by the bar after all. If he lavished so much attention on a woman he barely knew, he couldn't be such a bad guy...

We went to the Chinese restaurant. We also went for romantic walks by the dam and spent much time in each other's company. When Cliff came over, Pauli sat protectively between us and kept a watchful eye on him.

Two days before New Year's Eve, Cliff needed to leave for Johannesburg on important business and couldn't come to Jane's New Year's Eve party. I went with William Konenga - with Kgomotso's consent. She had to spend the day with her extended family at her aunt's cattle post. There was much dancing as always. At 11 o'clock, Cliff walked in! He ushered me outside onto the terrace and confessed, that he had been to see his wife in Johannesburg.

"We'll give it another chance." It couldn't have been worse if he'd punched me in the face. "I think we'll sort things out after all," he said.

"Oh good for you! And what about me?" I asked to the tune of Slade's 'Far, far away, with my head up in the clouds...'. How fitting! My head had been up in the clouds all along. A concerned William joined us outside. I must have looked pale.

"Are you all right?" he asked.

"We are just talking, William, but perhaps I'll leave early..."

My erstwhile housemate went back inside, but kept watching us.

"Sorry, Bridget, I didn't mean to hurt you..." Cliff was groping for words.

I'd heard enough. "Sorry isn't good enough. You told me you were getting a divorce. Oh, don't bother. You're just a piece of...of... oh whatever."

"Please don't be mad. We can still be friends. What we had was special..."

"Oh was it, really? Friends you can trust," I fumed. "Thank goodness things didn't get serious between us."

"But I'll never forget how..." he stammered.

"Oh please do. Do forget it all, because I'll sure as hell forget you." I turned around and stormed off.

No need for the nonplussed Cliff Bailey to see my tears. And besides, we had an audience. Tomorrow all the gossips would be wagging their tongues. William found me crying on a bench by the pool and took me home. I couldn't believe I had been so stupid - again. Help, I was turning into an emotional lemming! Oh, somebody stop that roller coaster, please...

What a miserable New Year's Eve. Well, maybe when Claire and I had tried to sneak out, when we were just 16, had been even worse. We were supposed to be in bed at home and Dad had caught us crawling through a bedroom window. We were grounded for the first week of the New Year. New Year's resolution: stay away from bad men. Five fat exclamation marks! I felt like a piece of wood and Botswana was the sandpaper that shaped me slowly but surely into somebody else. Mostly not a pleasant feeling.

As I lay sad and sleepless, I sent a silent plea to my sister. There was something inside me that this New Year's Eve had stirred.

'Oh Foompy wherever you are, I'm not giving up on you, I'm just taking a bit of a break. Before I go insane. Sorry I didn't write that letter to you. Stupid idea anyways. I can feel that you are alright and if not, give me some time, before I have to find out... I want to see your pictures again, but I don't know where I packed them...'

Then I dreamt. About Claire sitting by my side with a green and golden bee-eater on her shoulder, that was giving me the eye. I wanted to wake up and speak to her, but I couldn't move.

When I woke up, a praying mantis sat on the bedside table, rocking gently forth and back with its forelegs in Kung Fu posture. I stared at the green insect. Kgomotso had told me once that a green mantis symbolized the blessing of the ancestors. How ironic.

I watched videos in Rosemary's collection. There was this song in the film Cotton Club: 'Oh, ill wind go away, skies are all so grey...', that echoed my bruised feelings.

Pauli comforted me with his sensitive dark puppy eyes and Gabby spared me the 'I-told-you-so' speech. Then I was over Cliff with a little help from my friends and a box of my favourite chocolates.

A letter from Zaheeda arrived with news about Cambridge. As if it had waited for me being myself again:

*18 December 1989*

*"Hi Bridget,*
*Congrats on your new job and all. Don't want to change*

*places with you, moving around so much and all. Must be the pits. How often did you move now? I don't have a good feeling about this guy Cliff you mentioned in your last letter. He seems a bit of a player to me. Stay away, do you hear me?! After all you've been through with this Benjamin guy and all, you don't need any more heartache in your life... By the way, Diane is moving to London, in case she hasn't told you. Apparently she's in love with this guy Felix Eklund... He seems quite decent. Don't you have any decent men in your part of the world? My word, you only write about total pillocks. Get your priorities right, girl. I should personally give you a piece of my mind. Why don't you visit us or just come home now, we all miss you terribly..."*

Zaheeda was always so direct!

She'd be happy to hear that Cliff was already history. And no, Diane hadn't told me that she wanted to move to London. So things were changing back home as well! How long would it take Diane to find out that love wasn't all that it's cracked up to be? Zaheeda didn't ask about Claire. My friends avoided the subject by now. And what should I tell them - apart from my nightmares?

Zaheeda wrote that her father insisted she marry a distant cousin from Pakistan. It didn't seem like something that would lead to romance and happiness. On the other hand, who was I to talk? Happiness was just as distant for me. Instead, one disaster after the other! Did my friends and family in Britain really need me more than I was needed here in Botswana? I missed them, too.

No. I decided, they would be fine without me for a little longer. There was too much that kept me right here. It was complicated - too complicated to explain - but I couldn't leave now. Not yet anyway.

# CHAPTER 11

After the whirl of the festive season, it was back to the grindstone. In January Pauli and I moved into the company house in the suburb of Tsholofelo. The house featured a broad west-facing veranda with space for my outdoor furniture and for Pauli. A shady veranda was a great boon in a sun-drenched country like Botswana and I made good use of it whenever I could. There was also a large bush field across the road, where I could take my dog for long walks.

Things went off to a rocky start - with food poisoning. Not exactly unusual in Africa.

"It has to be the egg salad we made yesterday. Oh shucks!" Emily wailed.

Kgomotso wasn't so bad, but Emily and I lay in bed all day, taking turns with our heads in the toilet bowl.

Monday morning, I still felt nauseous. My first day at the office! A big meeting was scheduled first thing at an office in town. I dragged myself bravely up the first flight of stairs before vomiting out of a staircase window. Nobody had noticed, apart from a few of birds outside perhaps.

The food poisoning passed and a couple of days later, things fell into a pleasant work routine. The team spirit at Packer Engineering was a refreshingly new experience. Ruí, our Portuguese housemate, took me to work in his car every morning, so transport was taken care of for now. I tried not to think too much about Claire and almost succeeded.

The winds of change were also blowing in the neighbouring country of South Africa. In February big news made headlines around the globe. Nelson Mandela was about to be released from prison after twenty seven years.

Optimism was in the air. One news bulletin chased the next, discussing the ins and outs of the political consequences of these changes. A choir in Holland sang Xhosa songs on TV and American school children sent hundreds of post cards to South Africa.

With this hopeful mood around, I couldn't help but become more positive myself.

I once saw Tony by chance at the bookshop in the Mall. But when I looked again, he was gone. I turned around and caught sight of Ben in deep conversation with Jörg Walter and managed to quickly disappear behind a flea market stall. Then - to top it all - Cliff Bailey stood outside Barclays Bank with some girl in tow. All in one day? That was too much.

"Help, I'm being haunted," I complained to Kgomotso, who just watched me shaking her head. I pointed to Cliff and his companion from behind my hideout.

"I know that girl. From boarding school in Harare. Her name is Emma," she said. "Heard that she has a new boyfriend."

"Typically Cliff! But perhaps I should contact Tony again. Haven't spoken to him in ages."

"Who is Tony?" Understandably, Kgomotso didn't exactly follow my ramblings.

"Oh, just somebody I know from Palapye."

"I see."

I still hadn't found the time to tell Kgomotso about my past. And Emily hadn't leaked any information - as promised. I didn't find the right words to explain things in the mall and Kgomotso let it go. Soon we were just chatting about shoes and clothes.

Then we girls decided to decorate the company house.

After listening to our endless complaints about the bare interior, an annoyed Mr. Feindlich reluctantly gave Kgomotso a business credit card with instructions not to go over an amount of 3000 Pula.

Plenty of money to buy curtains and carpets, but we made a show of how we had to scrimp, just to keep our tetchy office manager on his toes.

So we shopped. After some shopping in the Mall on my own, I met Gabby for lunch on the terrace of the President Hotel. I couldn't wait to show her the decorative African baskets I had purchased at the curio shop. I strolled up the broad staircase and - oh no, two of Ben's friends from Kang stood right in front of me, ready to leave.

Stan and Suanne turned around at the same time and glared at me as if I had said something inappropriate. That's all I needed! I barely knew Stan and the red-headed Suanne.

Ben had once introduced us in Kang. We'd spent time around a cosy fire in front of Ben's cottage during a cold and starry desert night, grilling sausages and marshmallows on sticks.

"So, I hear Benjamin's ditched you," Stan pounced on me without further ado.

His thin cheeks seemed to tremble slightly with excitement. I stared at him. Here we go!

"Good day to you too, Stan. And that's old news. We actually ditched each other. Not that it's any of your business. But there you are."

I could have told him that it had been me, who had ditched Ben. But airing one's dirty washing in public was not a good idea.

"Ben told me himself," Stanley blurted out. He actually enjoyed the little squabble! Suanne began to look uncomfortable and tugged impatiently at Stan's sleeve.

"Oh did he now?" I said with as much dignity as I could muster. "Then he told you the wrong thing. And I should know, as I was obviously there."

"I'd rather believe him over you." Stan wouldn't back off.

Oh get a life you two!

"You know what Stan, frankly, I don't give a flying s*** what you think. Or Ben for that matter." I felt like an ice queen, an ever so slightly foul-mouthed one.

"Come Stan, let's go," his girlfriend Suanne begged and pulled harder on his shirt sleeve. She paid the lurking waiter and had to almost drag her smirking boyfriend down the stairs.

"My goodness, what was that all about?" Gabby asked bemused when I finally made it to her table.

"Ben's friends from Kang, trying to harass me. Apparently, the bastard is telling people how he dumped me."

"Twats. You dumped him."

"I know, but that's what he told those buffoons and godknowswho else."

"Good grief, what a snake. Forget about them. Boredom in Kang is probably messing with those country bumpkins. Any excuse for a little scandal. Don't worry, it'll blow over. My word, you're all red in the face. Just breathe, Bridget, breathe," she ordered. I breathed obediently in and out and calmed down.

"I just hope that there were no gossips around. Can one never get rid of obsolete ex-boyfriends?" I asked rolling my eyes.

"Yes, one can. Let's go and have a nice, relaxing swim at my house," Gabby suggested. "I think that'll do you good."

We left the hotel without ordering. On a hot Gaborone afternoon there was nothing better than a cool swimming pool.

A few days later, I was putting finishing touches to the translation of a lengthy letter to a contractor, when an agitated Kgomotso phoned the office. She had been to the bank in the morning and quickly popped into our house.

"Bridget, come home. Right now! Tell Emily. Burglary. Such a mess. Your room. I called the police." She struggled to get the words out while catching her breath.

"Okay, calm down. Got it. Break-in by the house. Sit down and breathe, Motso. We'll be there now-now."

Kgomotso had gone to look for a file she couldn't find at the office and had stumbled on the thieves. They ran away in a hurry, but Kgomotso was still in shock. After all, unlike South Africa Botswana was as good as crime-free.

When Emily and I arrived, two policemen were waiting in the driveway. As we approached, one of them took his index finger out of his nostril. "This is a crime scene. You cannot come inside," he informed us.

"We know, a burglary. We live here," Emily explained in the shortest possible way.

"Ehéy, madam. Sorry. Please check if anything is missing. Can you make a list for us?" the other policeman asked politely. "We wait here."

"We'll do that," I said. "Thank you."

The two of them sat down on the veranda steps and Pauli kept a watchful eye on them. I wondered how the burglars had managed to get past this big dog. Kgomotso met us in the passage and was able to speak properly now.

"The thieves seem to have taken a special interest in your room. Every drawer is pulled out and everything's lying around in utter chaos," she warned me.

"What on earth were they looking for?" Emily asked bewildered, "It's not as if you are Miss Money Bags with expensive jewellery in a safe or something."

I looked through my things that were lying pell-mell on the floor and started folding articles of clothing on the bed. My few valuables were still where I had left them. It didn't make any sense.

"My letters!" I cried suddenly.

"What?" Kgomotso wanted to know, "What letters?"

I stared at the nightstand with my mouth open. "My letters

are gone! From Claire and those from England. And the photos!"

One of Claire's photographs was on my desk at work and two others in the desk drawer, but all the others had been in this night stand, together with my letters.

"You have got to be joking," Emily started to giggle inappropriately. "They broke in, just to steal a few pictures and stupid letters?"

I glared at her and she stopped instantly.

"Sorry, nerves."

It was no joke to me. "They have sentimental value."

"Of course."

"What would anyone want with personal letters and family pictures, unless they have to do with drug dealing or an illicit affair? You're not involved in crime." Kgomotso sat down on my creaking Malawi chair.

"I don't know. I don't know." I was distraught, wiping tears from my eyes. Claire's letters gone!

"Are you going to tell the police?" Emily asked.

I reflected for a moment. Surely, the police would laugh at me as well.

"I don't know. Maybe the thieves were looking for something to do with Claire. We still don't know what happened to her. It should be in the police report."

My head hurt. Why was everything so complicated?

"Claire?" Kgomotso asked.

"Later," said Emily. "Well then. Tell the good officers outside." I went to speak to the policemen while my two friends carried on folding my clothes.

"Ah, that's where my camisole disappeared to," I heard Kgomotso saying as I walked down the passage. "But who is Claire and what has she got to do with this?"

"Bridget will explain the whole thing to you in her own good time. I think she's too upset right now," Emily told her.

As expected, the policemen outside didn't take me very seriously, when I told them about the missing letters and the photographs. Nothing of value was gone. Except a bottle of coke from the fridge. They suppressed a snigger, but told me in a polite manner that I should come to the police station where I would receive a case number. Then they left.

The house was soon restored to order, but my mind was still in turmoil. The more I thought about it, the more questions I had. Why now? And especially who? I was going round in circles - and I needed answers!

What, if it really had something to do with Claire? I felt hope surge back.

Perhaps it was time to consult a sangoma, as Margaret Marducci had suggested.

It was long overdue. Just that it wasn't so easy to find a sangoma. I could hardly ask people in the street 'Excuse me, can you tell me where I can find a sangoma around here?'

Inquiries at the office would have set tongues wagging and Kgomotso mentioned some time ago that she was ignorant when it came to witchdoctors.

There was a chance that Agnes Müller, my former Setswana teacher, knew what to do. I hadn't seen her for months, but that shouldn't stop me from contacting her. She didn't have a phone, but I needed urgent advice.

So on the spur of the moment, decided to visit Agnes. Today still, before I could change my mind. She lived across town on the other side of the Mall in an area I didn't know very well. A roadmap would solve the problem.

I spontaneously took a minitaxi as far as the Mall and then walked. The sun was already dipping low, inflaming orange patches of sky between trees and houses. The cooler air brought relief from the heat of the day, but soon it would be pitch dark. What were you thinking to come here at this time! I reproached myself. But the mall was far now and I couldn't just turn around.

What Kgomotso and Emily were to make of my sudden disappearance didn't even cross my mind.

I arrived at the house just before dark. There you are!

Agnes had a car and would surely give me a lift back home.

But it wasn't Agnes, who opened the door. It was Robert, her fiancé from bonny England. The one she had left her husband in Wuppertal for. I had seen them once together at the Mall.

He looked at me with the expression of a sad hamster and told me that Agnes was still at work, but that I could wait for her inside. She wouldn't be long.

Thinking of the long walk back to the Mall, I accepted thankfully. Alas, I hadn't realised that Robert was stone drunk.

I followed him into the lounge, where he sat down next to me on the couch. We waited for Agnes and the light grew faint. Outside the street lights didn't come on. And Agnes wasn't back yet. As if that wasn't enough, my foot had touched empty bottles under the coffee table. Not a good sign.

"Robert, aren't you going to switch on the light?" I asked and could smell the brandy on his breath now.

"Electricity is off," he said without slurring his words. "Shit, power failure again."

That explained the lack of street lights.

"Oh dear. Where is Agnes, then - shouldn't she be here by now?" I asked.

"Oh, she's coming back soon." Robert was adamant.

Alright then. "Don't you have candles in the house?"

"Must check."

Robert tottered off to the kitchen and came back with one solitary candle in a tin holder and lit it clumsily. The dim light threw shadows against the wall. At least I could see now. I suddenly realized the precarious situation I had landed myself in. Robert was definitely drunk and Agnes wasn't coming home. The prospect of finding out about a sangoma tonight was getting more unlikely by the minute, that much was clear. But where on earth was Agnes?

I should go. I had to get to the Mall somehow. But it was

completely dark outside - new moon obviously - and I wouldn't be able to find my way back. It had been a stupid idea to come her on a whim. Now I was stuck. Great!

Agnes' fiancé sat down on the couch next to me. Too close for comfort. He chatted about this and that, not making much sense. My left arm seemed to be of special interest to him. He ran his fingers up and down my skin and I had to think of the unpleasant experience with Alfred Jones in Palapye. Oh dear, he couldn't be possibly hitting on me!

I jumped up off the couch. "Sis Robert, what are you doing? You're getting married soon. What would Agnes say to that?" I yelled.

"Agnes doesn't love me anymore," he whined. This was getting more bizarre by the minute.

"Why didn't you tell me straight away? Where is Agnes anyway?"

Robert just bawled. I felt panic rising. How did I get out of this bind for goodness' sake? What, if Agnes's lifeless body lay buried in the garden? Get a grip! Agnes was just not coming home for one reason or another.

Without saying a word, Robert moved up closer.

"I'm going to leave now," I announced bravely. Darkness or not, I'd rather walk the dark streets than stay here.

"You can't."

"Why not?" I flew at him. Was this Robert going to stop me from leaving? He must just try!

"It's too dark outside. You'll lose your way."

Darn, Robert was right. I didn't know the area at all. Should I climb into a tree and stay there until morning? No.

"Well, what must I do then?" I asked him harshly.

"You can sleep here," Robert grinned drunkenly and took a swig from some brandy bottle.

"Sure, that'll be the day," I said with determination and walked toward the door.

"I could also drive you, but I must visit my friend Colin at the Oasis Hotel first."

A flicker of hope. Then it faded again.

"You are drunk," I said. The flicker grew bigger. "But then again, perhaps I should drive."

"I can still drive myself," Robert insisted.

What choice did I have? His attention had probably shifted to partying with his friend Colin. Cheers. I knew Colin. He was an engineer at Robert's company. He wasn't a bad guy. At least I wouldn't be alone with Robert anymore. I had to take the risk.

"Alright... let's go to the hotel then," I sighed.

It took Robert about ten minutes to find his keys. Then he fumbled around with the lock of his bakkie in the dark driveway. I already regretted my decision. How was this man going to drive in a straight line?

He made a little joke at my expense by letting the bakkie roll down the driveway without me and thought it hilarious. I climbed onto the passenger seat and said nothing. The truck's headlights were the only light as Robert slowly picked his way to the main road. At least he wasn't speeding. My relief was short-lived. The bakkie was zigzagging between the white lines in the middle of the road, once narrowly missing a drunkard, stumbling about in dark clothes.

I sweated blood.

Just before the main road, the street lights began to flicker overhead and came on. Fortunately, only two other drivers came our way. They had the presence of mind to swerve out of the way.

I virtually fled from the bakkie as soon as it came to a shaky halt in the hotel parking lot. The hotel was miles from the town centre and the mall. Too far to walk back to Tsholofelo from here. A few people came down the stairs and looked reasonably sober, but they suspiciously refused to give me a lift. Bugger!

I barely knew Colin Dalglish, but he was now my only hope of getting home. It wasn't difficult to catch up with

Robert, who staggered toward a row of motel rooms.

Colin looked a lot like Asterix, just that he had less hair and spoke with a thick Aberdeen-Scottish accent. The normally rational Scotsman had also been drinking heavily. Was this nightmare never going to end?

Nevertheless, I told him what had happened. He understood enough. I waited patiently for him to sober up with cups of strong coffee. Robert had passed out on the smudgy couch, snoring loudly. At last, I learned that Agnes was far from lying six feet under in a shallow grave. Literally. She had left Robert a week ago to return to her husband. Which meant, she was in Germany?

Colin appeared less drunk by the minute. He was a solid family man, whose wife and children were waiting in Scotland to join him in Botswana. And he was just lonely and Robert was company. After I had suffered through a few Scottish drinking songs and looked at family pictures, Colin agreed to drive me home at last. It was 2 o'clock in the morning.

"So you like Robert, then?" he asked on the way into town.

"What - are you out of your mind?"

"He told me two days ago and now you are here."

"He did now - didn't he?"

I was beyond caring what stories Robert was concocting. All I kept thinking was: home, bed.

"Why were you at his house in the middle of the night?"

"I told you! I wanted to visit Agnes, if you must know. There was a power failure and it was pitch dark outside. So I was stuck with him at the house. I had no idea that she'd left Robert."

"I see." I had just about enough of this!

"No, you don't see. I'm not interested in that greasy friend of yours!" I said tetchily.

"Alright." Hold your tongue, Bridget, we are getting closer to Tsholofelo! When Colin turned into our road, I couldn't wait to get out of the car and leave this weird night behind. Pauli whined and greeted me enthusiastically.

"Thanks so much Colin. You saved my life," I said and was genuinely grateful.

"You owe me one." Colin was joking - or was he?

I was in no mood for jokes. "Bye then and thanks again," I said and hurried into the house.

My first attempt at finding a sangoma had failed spectacularly. Could it be a sign that seeing a witchdoctor was a bad idea? Emily was still up, watching a movie on TV.

"Why did you go there in the first place? So late! All sorts of things could have happened."

"I wanted to ask Agnes Müller, if she could get me in touch with a witchdoctor. How was I supposed to know what was going to happen there?"

"Right. A witchdoctor." Emily looked at me with big eyes. She tried to understand.

"Yes, I wanted to find out what's going on with the burglary. And with Claire."

"And you thought a witchdoctor could help you with that - right now?"

"Yes, just that now I'm not so sure anymore after that experience," I said.

"You want to try everything possible - right. I wish I could help you somehow, but shamans are not my area of expertise. But please don't be so careless in future. This town is full of horny men."

"Perhaps I should get myself a car."

"Now there's an idea. Then you're independent. And if you decide to roam the town again in the middle of the night, you can come home anytime. By the way, you could have just borrowed Motso's car..."

"I didn't think about that. Was in a rush to get to Agnes and took the next minitaxi to the Mall."

"At least write us a note when you do something like that

again! Then we'll know where to look for your body."

"Haha, funny."

Not long after that, Stoeckl told me that one of his friends wanted to sell his 1974 VW beetle. I went to look at the beetle. Stoeckl had already told me that it was in good condition, apart from the exhaust and the brakes, which could be fixed cheaply.

I knew as much about the inner life of cars as an elephant knows about flying an airplane, but the light blue VW took my fancy.

Apparently it was a gift for two thousand Pula. I bought the beetle on the spot and had the papers two days later.

Stoeckl kept his promise and doctored the exhaust and the brakes so I could drive to work. It turned out that none of the auto garages in Gabs had brake pads, so Stoeckl offered to buy the spare parts on his next trip to South Africa.

In the meantime I had to cope without. This meant, I had to bring the beetle to a drawn-out halt by shifting into second gear. It became ridiculous when I had to stop at an army roadblock every five minutes. Sometimes I was even forced to stop on the gravel next to the tar road. Nervous young soldiers, loaded machine guns and faulty brakes. Not a great mixture!

My only saving grace was the fact that I was a female driver - and that grabbed by a bout of creativity - I had painted goldfish, seaweed and air bubbles on the light-blue beetle.

This prompted more mirth than fear. It seemed unlikely that a terrorist would drive around Gaborone in a ridiculous goldfish bowl. How naïve of me!

Rumours made the rounds that a young Brit had unknowingly turned into the road where the president had his sprawling villa. When he saw soldiers with machine guns, he tried to turn his car around. Just that it was too late.

He died in a hail of bullets, before he could drive off. Killed for taking the wrong turn! The story sent cold shivers down my spine. That wasn't something to gamble with.

After that, Stoeckl helped me very quickly to fit the brake pads and I felt a lot safer for it.

At the end of February, my boss, Wolfgang Klein, invited the design team out to a movie evening. As a thank-you for our hard work on the project. 'Rainman' with Tom Cruise and Dustin Hoffmann had just hit the circuit. We were all looking forward to such a spanking new film.

As we waited in the queue outside the cinema's glass façade, I detected Benjamin sitting on a low wall surrounded by female volunteers. We hadn't spoken since the cancelled Namibia trip. Don't see me, don't see me, don't... He had seen me. Ben languidly peeled away from the wall and strolled over.

"Hi Bridget," he said with a charming smile.

"Hi." What did he expect me to say: nice to see you?

"How are you?" He probably feigned interest in front of the ladies. Showing off what a swell guy he was, being so civilized with an ex-girlfriend. Of course, they knew who I was.

"Okay and you?"

"Just going to watch 'Rainman' with some friends."

"Yes, we too. We are here with the whole team." I turned around to introduce my colleagues. Benjamin's face grew longer and longer when he realized that I wasn't alone, yearning for him. He seemed intimidated at the strapping guys, who were gathering around me. Ben's confidence crumbled.

"Oh, I got to go. Enjoy the movie." He turned abruptly and went back to his own group.

"You too," I called after him. It felt good. Almost as if I had played a prank on him.

"Who was that yob?" asked my boss. "Was the jerk bothering you?"

"Just an ex-boyfriend. A bit awkward, that's all. Thanks for moving in."

"No problem," he grinned.

*That's what it must feel like to have older brothers*, I thought. A whole bunch of them. Unfortunately the gossipmongers never slept.

After a long day at work, Theunis Grobelaar, a Dutch-Indonesian friend of Gabby's, asked me to go out for drinks. I had nothing better to do and agreed. As soon as we sat down at the hotel bar, he pleaded with me not to ruin the marriage of Richard Fourie. I nearly dropped my glass.

Richard, an engineer who had joined our team temporarily from the Windhoek office, was happily married. He had been seen helping me out of his car at the movies. I had become my colleague's mistress overnight. Theunis himself had been through a recent acrimonious divorce and allegedly understood the situation.

What?!

"Listen here Theunis, you are barking up the wrong tree! Richard is my colleague. That's all. The whole design team was there. Better get your facts right, before you accuse anyone of adultery."

"Well, you are single and tongues are wagging. Jennifer said… oh never mind. Are you sure there's nothing between the two of you?" Theunis probed.

I should have known. Jennifer Harland had advanced to queen of gossip in Gaborone. As if I didn't have enough on my plate already!

"Damn sure. If you will excuse me now. I suddenly feel nauseous."

When I came home, Kgomotso and Emily were lounging in front of the TV, watching some documentary.

"Hi guys." I threw the keys onto the new chest of drawers by the door.

"Hi there. Is Wolfgang being a disgusting slave driver again?"

"Yep, urgent deadline. And then I went for drinks with Theunis."

"Did you have a nice time?"

"Yes, he basically accused me of having an affair with Richard and I nearly throttled him."

"Oh, that's good." Emily was distracted by the TV.

Kgomotso giggled. "Such a prick. Did you give him a piece of your mind?"

"You bet I did. What's so interesting on TV?" I asked a little irritated.

"Come here Bridge, watch this," Kgomotso said.

I plunked myself into the sofa cushions. Ah, just to fall asleep now. "It's about African initiation rituals. These guys are Xhosas."

What was so interesting about that? I forced myself to look up at the glimmering TV screen. The music score just took on a dramatic quality. *Typical National Geographic*, I thought. A group of about ten young Xhosa men, wrapped in blankets, stumbled barefoot up a rocky mountain pass.

"Why are they all painted white?" Emily wanted to know.

"Because of the ancestors, I think," Kgomotso answered.

'...their bodies are painted white to honour the forefathers...' the narrator's voice droned on cue.

"Why, are the ancestors white?" Emily asked naïvely.

"No, don't be daft! That's just how it is."

Emily handed me a plastic bowl with potato crisps. The green packet was still lying on the coffee table. I stretched my legs out under the low table then found it more comfortable to put my feet on top of it.

"Hey, Bridget, take your shoes off," Kgomotso scolded.

I obeyed and listened to the narrator's monotonous voice with my eyes closed.

'... no food or drink are allowed. The makwetha must sleep on the bare floor, no matter how cold it is...' I put another handful of chips in my mouth.

"Ooh, that's horrible." Kgomotso was appalled.

"Mhmm."

"Why do they do that?" asked Emily.

"As far as I know, they learn to be men," said Kgomotso.

I was still upset about Theunis and just wanted to relax.

"Right, I'm going to take a shower and shave my legs," I announced.

"About time!" Emily joked. So, that she had heard!

I came back, rubbing my hair with a towel. Some silly sitcom had replaced the documentary. Emily stood by the window and stared out into the street. It was almost dark and a few sunbeams mingled with the light of the street lamps.

"What's so fascinating out there, Emily?" I asked.

She jumped. "Oh nothing. Don't sneak up on me like that."

"Sorry."

"Let's make supper. Chicken or curry?"

She quickly moved away from the window and over to the fridge. I had the distinct feeling that she was trying to distract me.

"Chicken!" Kgomotso and I said in unison.

"Where did you buy that fantastic lettuce and those cherry tomatoes, Motso?"

"At this new organic market, they sell flowers too," Kgomotso answered a little too eagerly. Were they gesturing behind my back?

I went to the window and scanned the street - and caught a glimpse of Ben, walking hand in hand with a blonde giggly girl on the other side of the road!

What was he doing here? We had also walked hand in hand like that. Just that I hadn't giggled all the time. The girl showed off her midriff in a tight boob tube. As they stood directly under a light pole, he gripped her waist and bent her backward, playfully kissing her on the throat.

My towel fell on the floor.

"Sorry, Bridge. I didn't want you to see that. Ben's such a jerk," Emily said and took the chicken out of the fridge. "Come away from that window or he'll see you."

She walked to the table carrying the naked chicken.

"I couldn't care less," I said stubbornly. Emily picked up

the towel and wrapped it around my shoulders.

"You could have fooled me," Kgomotso said bluntly. "Do you think he did it on purpose, strutting around like that in front of our house? I mean, what is he doing in our street at this time?"

"Who knows. Ben's just a jerk with a capital J." Emily switched on the oven. "Come help me with supper."

I got out the spices and covered the pink chicken in smoked paprika and salt with trembling hands.

"I'm pretty sure she's Jörg's daughter. I heard she's visiting him with Jörg's girlfriend," Kgomotso said.

"Well, I never! Maybe she's the postman's daughter, looking like that."

"Doesn't old Jörg have his flat around here somewhere?"

"Yes, on the main road," I answered mechanically.

"That explains why they strut around our neighbourhood at this time of night."

"Ah, whatever, let's forget about it." I really didn't want to think about them anymore.

"Ben wraps women around his little finger. Didn't you see him yesterday at the cinema?" Kgomotso asked.

"Yes, I did. She'll probably find out soon enough what he's like," I said with bitterness.

"Exactly!" Emily cheered me on. "You go girl."

The dressed-up chicken was ready to go into the oven.

"It hurts a little, but I'll get over it." That was the understatement of the year.

"Why the long face then?" Kgomotso was suspicious.

"I don't know. I feel restless. First the stupid gossip from Theunis - now that. Perhaps we could go out later."

"Actually..." Kgomotso looked at the kitchen clock. The clock was always 15 minutes fast, but everybody was used to that. "There's an Amapondo concert at Maitisong tonight. If we hurry, we still make it for 8 o'clock." 'Amapondo' was a traditional group from the South African south coast.

"Sounds good to me. I could do with some distraction.

What are we doing for supper then?"

"We can have the chicken tomorrow and Chinese after the show," Emily suggested. It was the fridge again for the bird.

We went to the concert and had Chinese after the show. And Ben and his new girlfriend were no longer on my mind. It was so good to have friends and time heals all wounds, doesn't it?

Soon news came from England.

Diane got engaged to Felix and I hadn't even met him. She wrote that he was an exchange student from Denmark and that they were getting married as soon as he graduated as an architect. I looked at the two photographs she'd sent.

Brunette Diane and blond Felix proudly showing off their engagement rings in 'Jesus Green'. And on the other photo, Diane grinning from ear to ear, sitting on Felix's lap in our favourite pub.

Well, good for her. Why shouldn't at least Diane be happy in love?

I also learned that my friend Liz was now translating travel brochures in London and Zaheeda still had to fight off eligible bachelors her father kept introducing her to. I felt a pang of home sickness. Botswana was so far away and none of my friends had money to come and visit.

My parents were planning a trip to the Italian Amalfi Coast in April. Italy had been their dream for a long time. With tears in my eyes, I looked at the Christmas pictures of aunts and uncles and cousins. How I wished I could just hug them again.

As arranged, my mother phoned me at Gabby's house a week later. Mom's phone bill must be astronomical by now, but she insisted on at least one phone call a month. We had a phone at the office, but it wasn't very private. You never knew who might be eaves dropping.

Mom gave me a breathless account of how the local press had gotten wind of Claire's disappearance. A reporter had shown up on my parents' doorstep in Tenison Avenue a few days ago.

'I was alone in the house and could barely get rid of that man.'

My mother was still upset about the whole episode.

'Did you tell him anything?' I inquired.

'Good Lord, Bridget, no!' she cried. 'I threw him out. There is no telling what he might have quoted me on. Or worse, made up some story altogether. And news travel so fast, even to Africa, I'm sure.'

She was right. I was still incognito here. That sounded terribly like James Bond. Reporters and the media...no thanks! At the same time I felt terribly guilty. Poor mom. And what exactly had I done for Claire lately?

'We didn't answer the phone for a while and there was just this short article in the newspaper. Luckily without pictures. Then the whole thing blew over. I don't think they knew much of anything or got wind of your 'mission'.'

Mom couldn't help a little sarcasm. She had stopped a long time ago trying to persuade me to come back to Cambridge. I wished I could look into her eyes now, instead of speaking into a clumsy telephone receiver.

,I really want to know who tipped that reporter off in the first place. I thought the matter was handled as top secret. David perhaps...' I stopped myself.

Gabby walked past me and into the kitchen, no doubt checking on dinner. I heard voices, then Beauty the maid was pottering around with the dishes.

'How's Dad doing?' I asked in a low voice.

'He gets grumpy at times. Keeping himself busy with consultancy work at the college and with his stamp collection.'

I could see my father at his desk with bifocals on his nose - reading lamp turned to the side - delicately handling the stamps with tweezers, while checking his collectors' catalogue.

'Italy will do both of you good. Give him my love, Mom.'

'I will, he loves you very much, you know.'

'I know Mom, I know…'

'Oh, before I forget it child, your grandfather has booked a flight to Gaborone.'

'What? Why? When is he coming?' I stammered, swallowing a tear or two.

'Next week Thursday. The 22nd of February.'

'Already?!!!' That completely took me by surprise.

'Wait, I've got the details right here.' Mom gave me the flight number and time of arrival. A bit of a warning would have been nice. A letter or a postcard!

'He says best not to bother meeting him at the airport, everything is organised. Grandpa will phone you at the office later. He'll be staying at - wait - the Gaborone Sun Hotel room 113. That's it.' She cleverly skirted the issue why Grandpa was coming to Botswana just now and I was too stunned to push for an answer.

'Thanks for the heads-up, Mom. That's some - surprise - can't wait to see him.'

'I'll tell him that. Got to rush now, love. Take care of yourself. I'll phone you again on Friday, same time?'

I couldn't believe it. My grandpa was on his way to Gaborone!

Somebody from back home was coming to visit.

# CHAPTER 12

Grandpa arrived on Thursday in Gaborone without much fuss. He'd taken a taxi to the hotel.

"Give me a day, Bridget, just to acclimatize. I'm no spring chicken, you know. The long flight was rather tiring," he told me on the phone.

"Sure Grandpa, I understand... how do you like the weather here?"

"It's hot for February and the sun's still too bright for me. It was cold and grey back in the UK. But apart from that - not bad. Right now, the swimming pool is calling me. See you tomorrow, love." I knew he'd acclimatise by tomorrow.

We agreed that I should wait for him at 4 o'clock by the swimming pool. I felt excited and a bit nervous to see him. It was an interesting wait. Children splashed merrily in the shallow end and I saw my first g-string bikini on a lady, whose plump behind was not ideal for this fancy, new swimwear.

A red-haired tourist, sprawled on one of the deck chairs close by, kept winking at me.

Perhaps he thought that I was one of the easy girls, who picked up rich tourists at the hotel. Apparently he didn't know yet that they were pretty Tswana ladies. Like many overseas visitors he seemed also oblivious to the dangers lurking in the harsh African sun. His freckly skin had already turned a fiery red, peeling deeply on his arms and shoulders.

The tourist sat up, just as Grandpa appeared in the door of his ground floor room. Grandpa waved and saved me from a cheesy pick-up line.

Still handsome with piercing blue eyes, he didn't look 72 at all. The red-haired man on the deck chair was getting the wrong idea and turned around with a sullen grunt.

"Hi Grandpa!" I walked across the grass and gave him a bear hug. He planted a kiss on my forehead as he always did.

"There my darling. How are you?"

"I'm fine. Did you recover from the long flight?"

"Oh love, I'm getting too old for these long-haul flights. It took 12 whole hours…"

He complained about the discomforts of sitting next to an uncouth passenger with a sharp elbow the whole time. "It's first class for me again next time 'round!"

As far as I could remember, Grandpa had always come to visit us after a trip abroad with little presents in his bag. He bounced Claire and me on his knee and taught us little songs. Eventually we got too big for such games, of course.

'Good Lord, you are growing heavy!' He would cry, feigning horror. 'Sarah, what are you feeding these girls?' We'd giggle and flex our arm muscles. 'You are both are growing into giants.' We'd climbed back onto his lap for another round of songs and rolling off his leg.

'Girls, leave Grandpa in peace awhile. He's just back from a long trip. Come and help Dad cook supper.'

We'd run into the kitchen to watch Dad cook his famous Spaghetti Bolognese or the best sauerkraut ever (which was worlds apart from the 'Sweetkraut' an Austrian chef produced in Gaborone). We'd fetch flour or a tin of tomatoes or washed vegetables, allowing Mom to have a quiet chat with her father.

I was glad that it was Grandpa, who had come to Botswana. As much as I loved my parents, I felt that Grandpa would understand my situation better. He'd spent some time in Africa and could surely relate. We sat down at the bar next to the pool.

"Gin and tonic. Single," Grandpa ordered. "… and…?" he prompted me.

"Same please." I moved the barstool closer to the counter. "Two gin and tonics then... and the menu please."

"Coming up sir." The barman deposited with smooth movements two oversized menus in front of us.

"So how are things back home?" I was the first one to break the awkward silence.

"Your parents. They want you to come home, Bridget." Just as I had expected. Mom hadn't said anything, but Grandpa didn't beat around the bush.

"I know Grandpa, but I can't. Not yet. I have to first find Claire."

"Really. Love, we all miss Claire, but there are limits to what we can do. I spoke to the MI 5 detective agent this morning. They haven't found any more clues. Apart from the stolen car. Everything points to an accident - and vehicle theft. There's little hope of finding Claire now, after such a long time." Grandpa quickly wiped his eyes.

So, he had wanted a first-hand account of the situation.

"I'm not surprised - the way they work," I said. "Don't you see, if anyone can find her it's me and I know she's still alive. I can feel it. How can you all give up so quickly?"

I said those things to convince Grandpa, but was Claire even still part of me?

"Quickly? Bridget, it's been almost two years. I just want you to face reality. Staying here is not going to bring her back and you have your own life to live..."

I didn't want to argue with him. How was he supposed to understand? "I know you mean well Grandpa - but we are twins, you know. I can't just leave her here by herself. I know it doesn't make much sense, but I can't really explain it."

"Alright then, but are you sure that's the only reason why you are still in the country? Do you have a boyfriend, Bridget?"

I was surprised. Grandpa didn't normally blurt out things like that. Then again, there was nothing normal about the situation.

"No - at least not anymore. There...was somebody...for a while," I stammered.

I was rubbish at this. But I couldn't just tell Grandpa what was really cooking. That I was close to losing my connection with Claire. How everything was going down the drain. My search was not exactly exhaustive. A pang of guilt gnawed at me and it must have shown on my face.

"I see."

"He was more of a distraction and anyway... he didn't want to commit."

"Sorry about that."

"Don't be Grandpa. It wouldn't have worked. I came to find my sister, I didn't come for romance, but —"

"I know child, I know. We are all human. I'm not here to be pushy or to judge you. I'll do my best to help you while I'm here. Maybe even rekindle the police's interest in the case. We will see."

The bartender put the gin glasses on the counter and poured tonic from small yellow tins. Grandpa thanked him and asked for a few more minutes before ordering food.

"We were just getting the impression that you're burning the candle at both ends. Perhaps you should take it a bit easy. And that would be best at home in England."

"Family decision?"

"Not really, just common sense."

"Well, I'm doing just fine."

"Are you really? This whole thing is so unlike you. Perhaps a bit of a break from all this would do you good? Just to find your focus again."

There was an awkward silence, while I mulled over this.

"I think I could do with some moral support. But England? I can't go away for too long."

"You don't have to decide right now on the spot. Of course your parents would like you to come home, but if you are not ready - I'll stay for two weeks, perhaps even three.

Take your time, love."

We were quiet for a while and I studied the menu. The silence didn't feel tense anymore and the roller coaster that was my life now, slowed down ever so slightly.

Colin MacDougal and his wife, who had just arrived from Scotland, entered the restaurant and waved through the open door. The incident with his odious friend Robert was water under the bridge. I waved back and we ordered snacks.

"You are so much like your Grandma, you know —"

Really? I barely remembered my grandmother. She had been soft and gentle and always smelled good. And she would sing us to sleep, me and Claire. The few memories I had, were linked to the photographs in the lounge at home. A beautiful, smiling face with dimples, framed by silky brown hair and a string of pearls around the slender neck. Grandma had died of cancer a long time ago.

"Why would you say that?"

"Hannah was graceful like you. And there's this quiet determination. Taking on anything that's thrown your way, not knowing if it will lead anywhere."

"I don't remember her much," I confessed.

"It's been a long time." Grandpa's gaze drifted over to the teeming crowd in the swimming pool.

"What would Grandma have done in my place?"

"Good question. Probably the same, I guess. You are not going to change your mind, are you?"

"I'm sorry. I just need more time here."

"Your mother will be disappointed."

"Yes - sorry. There are some things I must still do. Like speaking to a witchdoctor, for example."

"A witchdoctor? You are becoming more African by the day, darling," he laughed.

"I'm serious, Grandpa. I have to try at least."

"Who are you and what have you done with our shy little Bridget?"

"I think she stayed behind in England," I sighed. "Please

try to understand —"

"Can't say I do. Just be careful, no matter what it is you must do," Grandpa said.

"Sure I will. Can you please speak to Mom and Dad for me? To explain? It's so difficult over the phone." Grandpa would surely convince them to be patient a little longer.

"Then you will have to explain things to me first, child."

And so I recounted the burglary and Margaret Marducci. And how I tried to speak to Agnes Müller about meeting a sangoma and how I had failed spectacularly. I left out, how I'd persistently ignored the scolding, little voice inside.

Our snacks arrived.

More people filed into the outdoor bar to have a few drinks after work. I poked around my Greek salad, not really hungry.

Two of my former grade 7 students, dressed to the nines and in full war paint, sat on the red sofa in the open passage. They looked nothing like 14 and were probably waiting for their much older boyfriends. I tried to ignore them. After all, I wasn't their French teacher anymore.

Grandpa chewed on his barbecued chicken wings while I told him about Tony, about Benjamin and the Kalahari Desert, about Ronnie Immelman and my accommodation odyssey.

"Sounds like you've had a rough time, child. No wonder you are so caught up in your life here," he said and I felt relieved.

In the end, he pushed away the plate with the gnawed chicken bones and wiped his fingers on a white serviette. "Thank you for being so open with me."

"Oh by the way Grandpa, I have actually read one of your books. 'El Jadida'."

"Now, either you're not feeling well," Grandpa said and his eyes twinkled, "...or it's going to snow tomorrow."

"Ha, unlikely!" I laughed, then I was serious again. "Can I ask you something?"

"Sure, out with it."

"Do you believe in life after death?" He looked up with an astonished expression.

"Well, you know - us going to another dimension or something like that. African people believe in the 'Land of the Forefathers'. That's where you go when you die. Do you think there's something to it?"

Grandpa didn't say anything for a few minutes and played with his gin and tonic glass. I tried not to stare at him too keenly and watched a gaggle of children with orange swim aids jump over and over into the pool.

"You know, Bridget," said Grandpa eventually and looked right past me. "When your grandmother died, I just couldn't believe it. She was the centre of my universe. She made me so happy. Hannah could be so mischievous sometimes..." He smiled and I knew he could see mischievous Grandma before his inner eye.

"When I lived in Afghanistan, I came across this idea of reincarnation. I thought of it as complete rubbish at first and dismissed it out of hand. But then - I missed my wonderful Hannah so much that I could hardly bear it - it gave me a sense of comfort to think that maybe, just maybe, there was a part of her still alive. That she might be in some sort of waiting room in heaven. That one day we'd meet again."

It wasn't easy for me to say something after that.

"Sometimes... I feel so close to Claire that... I just cannot believe that she is not standing right next to me. Maybe she is also in a waiting room... waiting for me..."

"Now, now. No morbid thoughts allowed today. I want to know what you thought of 'El Jadida'. Since you've read the book. Wasn't it a bit too..."

We spent the rest of the afternoon discussing 'El Jadida' and sangomas and then my parents. It conjured up images of our house and the summery back garden, the smell of our kitchen and of the pub where I'd meet with friends. I missed Mom's soft embrace and Dad's quiet strength and was sorry that they felt sad for my sake. And Claire's.

I even thought about David for a moment, although I didn't miss him at all.

Grandpa told me about his latest book project. A novel set in Egypt. He planned a stopover in Cairo on his way back. We talked much over the next two weeks. More than ever before. As promised, he soon paid the police headquarters a visit. Alas, without much success, but at least he'd tried.

We went to the Gaborone Dam and on a mini safari to a private game reserve just outside Gaborone. Emily had told me about the place. Although there were no predators to gawk at, it was exciting to discover giraffes, kudu and zebra camouflaged between the thorn trees.

Gabby drove us in her 4x4 to the famous pottery in Tamaga. The Suzuki scaled the rocky track, carried us over streamlets and past an unassuming Livingstone memorial. Grandpa wrote incessantly in his notebook. He also met my friends, had a meeting with a bunch of author colleagues from South Africa at the President Hotel and celebrated my birthday with me.

I'd already given up tennis, but tried my best in a match with Gabby and my fit grandfather at the Gaborone Club. Pauli immediately took to Grandpa and the two of them often played fetch in the open field in front of our house in Tsholofelo.

A letter arrived from Italy. The photos on the beach and on a steep curving road in Positano spoke for themselves. Dad smiling and Mom with wind-tousled hair, laughing happily. I had been back in the lap of my family for a fortnight and hated to see Grandpa leave, when I drove him in my fishbowl to the airport. His presence had made me feel safe and grounded. Now I was alone again.

Back at the office, I overheard two of the engineers, Desmond and Werner chat in the small copy room. I waited in the kitchen next-door, lost in thought, for the kettle to boil.

"Wonder if the new materials order is going through," Werner said.

*Just some work talk*, I thought and watched Kgomotso through the kitchen window, chatting outside to some relation of hers.

"I hope so," Desmond whispered or he thought he did. "Claire figured out the cheap stuff on the list in Feindlich's office, remember. We have to be careful."

I stood rooted to the spot. It was the first time I had heard anyone mention Claire's name at the office. What did Claire have to do with some stupid materials list? Didn't that give me the right to eavesdrop?

"Yes, I know. She shouldn't have made such a fuss about it. The building department could have gotten wind of the whole thing. I mean we could have lost our jobs. Just as well she disappeared." Just as well? I gasped for air.

"I mean what's the big deal? She was only a draughtsperson anyway. Perhaps she told her sister Bridget about it and now she'll snoop around just like Claire did."

How did they know about me and Claire?

"I don't think so. Come on, Feindlich's watched her like a hawk ever since I told him who she is."

I had to hold onto the stove. How long had they known and - who had told them?

"Oh hi Liesl, pretty dress you're wearing today," Werner flattered Desmond's dim girlfriend.

Liesl gave off some mind-numbing nonsense about the new dress she'd bought at Berger's just last week and the price was so incredible and so on. Go away Liesl, I wanted to shout. I needed to hear what it was that Claire had discovered. Liesl sashayed past the kitchen door in a garish yellow and green dress.

"Okay, last lot of copies." That was Desmond, who had said that I might start snooping around just like my sister Claire had done. A long time ago.

"Yeah. The official materials list fits in nicely with the

tender amount. Liesl doesn't know what she's writing and it's best if nobody else knows, either. Especially not Bridget." Werner's voice was so low by now that I had to guess the last few words.

I didn't know much about book keeping, but it was clear that some sort of fraud was being committed at Packer Engineering. Did my boss know who I was? And what if that list had something to do with Claire's disappearance?

My mind raced. I had to speak to Kgomotso and Emily as soon as possible.

The opportunity presented itself at home that night. Ruí was still at the office, as usual. First I had to tell Kgomotso why I was in Botswana and so I began to talk.

"Sorry, Motso. Please don't take it personal. The whole thing was just too ...close to the bone."

"How should I take it? I understand that you didn't want people to know in the beginning. But you've known me for a while now, and you could never find a minute to let me know the truth?"

"I guess, I didn't want to think about it myself anymore. I hurt too much. When I couldn't get anywhere with the police, I just went into denial. It had nothing to do with not trusting you." Kgomotso thought for a while.

"Okay, I can't say I understand completely where you're coming from, but then I have never been in your shoes either. You're on parole. I want to be in the loop from now on. If people are already breaking in because of the whole thing with your sister, then I think I deserve that much."

"Thanks, "I hugged my friend. "I will discuss everything with you guys from now on."

"Yessee, Bridget. That's heavy!" Kgomotso whispered in a rasping voice, "You think you know somebody and then something like that happens —"

"Yes, that's something," Emily echoed her words. "And you told only Gabby about Claire?"

"Well, I also told Rita Winckler, but she left the country

some time ago. She wouldn't have told anyone."

"What about Benjamin?"

"He doesn't know a thing. Don't know why I never told him."

"Can't say I blame you. Then who is the culprit who told those twats? You can be sure it wasn't me. What about Gabby then?" Emily asked in an undertone. Could my helpful friend have blabbed?

"And the police, of course."

"Kgomotso's right. Anybody there has access to the information."

"Oh, that's just great."

The whole thing with the materials list was easier to discuss.

"Okay, that being out of the way…do you think there's a connection between our two planks at the office and the break-in - or worse: did it have something to do with your sister's disappearance?"

"I hope not!"

"They cannot use cheap, inferior materials on one hand and then draw up official tender documents according to building regulations. What if the buildings leak or crumble? It's going to come out anyway."

"They'll be long gone when that happens," Kgomotso said. "I don't deal with those lists and I'm sure that Wolfgang Klein doesn't have a clue. Feindlich and Desmond do all the ordering. Feindlich just gives me the figures and keeps the receipts in his office."

"In other words, Feindlich and Desmond and Werner…"

"…cream off for themselves," Emily said shaking her head. "Who knew that old Feindlich could be so corrupt? He's mean, yes… but corrupt?"

"Oh, please, isn't that sort of thing common? One hand washes the other?" Kgomotso didn't seem too surprised.

"Hey, if everybody did this…" I threw in.

"Welcome to the real world, Bridget. It's a high-stakes business."

"When did you become so jaded, Motso?" Emily punched her lightly in the shoulder.

"Do you think this could have anything to do with Claire's disappearance then?"

I was anxious to make a connection.

"I don't buy into it. There's a big difference between low-scale corruption and kid-napping or even murder. Oh sorry." Kgomotso realized what she had said. "That was stupid of me. Of course Claire is still alive," she corrected herself.

"If Desmond and Werner know about Claire being your sister, then... we should tell Wolfgang about it!"

"Great, they think that I'm here spying on them, because of these lists."

"Try to stay out of their way for a while." Emily looked serious.

"That's difficult if I have to work with them all day long."

"I know, but you can't give it away that you overheard their little chat."

"Perhaps they were just testing me. What if they knew I was in the kitchen?"

"Nah, they're way too dumb for that," Emily said.

"Just act normally around them. We'll try to find out something." Easier said than done.

Kgomotso spoke to a relative, who worked in the ministry and had cautioned her against blowing the whistle. They would investigate in the meantime.

I stayed out of Desmond and Werner's way. After a while I discarded the connection to Claire's disappearance. It was too far-fetched and we didn't turn up any evidence to support it. At least their dealings were eventually found out, after I'd already left the company.

I became clear that I had to face my real mission in Botswana again. Grandpa's visit had jolted me back into real time. I had to think about Claire more often now. It was painful, but I forced myself to think about her and became restless like a tiger trapped in a cage. There must be something I could do. Just what?

Emily suggested a change of scenery. She had to work, but her parents in Johannesburg would surely be more than happy to have me over for the weekend. It was better than waiting for an inspiration. So Emily arranged for me to stay at the family's residence in a suburb called Parkhurst. Our colleague Thomas Taylor agreed to take me with him to Johannesburg.

Emily and Kgomotso promised to look after Pauli and to feed him punctually every afternoon.

"Make sure he has enough water in his bowl and that he doesn't run into the street," I told my eye-rolling friends.

"Relax, we will look after him as if he were our own baby," Emily said. "You go and have a great weekend. Things will fall into place, you'll see."

"It takes about 5 hours from Gabs to Joburg," Kgomotso said. "So part of the trip you'll be driving through the night. Don't look so worried, there won't be any cows lying in the streets."

That's how I ended up travelling to Johannesburg with Thomas Taylor.

He looked every part the wild Scotsman, Claire had described in her letters: burly, with a flaming red beard and booming voice. His caring nature stood in stark contrast to his appearance, but Thomas Taylor unfailingly instilled respect in those who made his acquaintance. Thomas went home almost every weekend to see his family in Benoni, east of Joburg.

We left early in the afternoon. Rows of large maize silos, the mountains, endless vegetable fields and mining towns flitted past. I looked at everything in amazement. Who knew that all this existed so close to Botswana!

Thomas was a proud family man. He told me in detail, how he had come from the town of Bath, with his wife

Janice and two toddlers, to South Africa years ago. All due to a lucrative job offer in the mining industry.

They had now four children and a big house with swimming pool. I also learned how he had specialized in computer programming and was now a sought-after expert. His wife was a nurse and had started working nights shifts when their youngest daughter Gillian was three.

His fifteen-year-old son Sam was a snake fanatic and shared his room with two corn snakes and a python. Yew! Hopefully the guest room was far from the terrariums.

While Thomas talked, I began to reshuffle my own thoughts. I never really had the time to stop and think. The memories of my breakup with Ben and the unpleasant episode with Kurt Köhler rolled past my inner eye and then faded away between the green hills. Aaaah! It was easier now to think about Claire - and who was Cliff Bailey again?

After 3 hours, Thomas felt rather less talkative and played music tapes by the group America. 'A Horse with No Name' and 'Ventura Highway' still followed me around for days.

I must have dozed off somewhere in Krugersdorp, on a broad, well-lit road. The car suddenly stopped in front of a large gate. Thomas Taylor's house in Benoni.

It was 10 o'clock and I couldn't see much in the dark. Milo, a little spaniel was ecstatic to see Thomas, who had to carefully navigate to the garage around the jumping mutt. Janice was far less happy. She needed to start her shift and had been waiting for her husband to drive her to the hospital. We were half an hour behind schedule.

"Tom, I'm late for work," she scolded at once, ignoring me completely.

Given the fact that she had four children, Janice was amazingly slim and looked attractive with her high cheekbones and short black haircut. Thomas didn't have a good excuse other than that it had taken the guards at the

## SINGING LIZARDS

Zeerust border post longer than usual to rifle through the contents of his car boot.

This wasn't quite what I had imagined, after listening to the glowing accounts of happy family life during the long drive. Only much later did I learn that Thomas apparently did have an affair sometime in the past and that his wife was still suspicious when it came to other women.

A contrite Thomas showed me the guest room, put a plate with dinner leftovers on the kitchen table for me and drove his wife to work.

"You can phone Emily's family tomorrow morning," he told me on his way out. "It's too late for that now."

No matata.

I sat in a massive kitchen. Just like the farm kitchen I had envisaged with Claire sitting at the table, drinking hot chocolate. Telling me on the phone, 'I must tell you all about it, Foompy. You won't believe what happened to me.'

I was practically alone in the house. With four sleeping kids, a curious dog and three snakes. I traipsed to the back door and looked out into the garden. The moonlight shone brightly on a big swimming pool and... cows and sheep.

In the morning I phoned and Emily's mother sounded very friendly. Buses were unreliable and Thomas Taylor was taking me to Parkhurst.

While I tackled a large portion of fried eggs and bacon, Sam, Justine, Heather and Gillian gave me the third degree. After all I had the privilege of their father's company during the week, when he was far away in mysterious Botswana. Janice was still asleep, of course, having finished her shift only at 6 o'clock.

"Why don't you have children?" seven-year-old Heather demanded to know. Although I had some experience with children by now, I was taken aback by the direct question.

"Well, you know... because I'm not married yet."

Heather pondered this for a moment. It seemed to make

sense to her.

"So why don't you get married then?" the older Justine chimed in.

"You see..."

"Enough with the questions, guys. Leave Bridget to eat her breakfast. We must leave soon," put Thomas an end to the interrogation.

"Are we going shopping later, Dad?" Sam asked. He took after his mother; so tall and dark. His voice had already broken.

"Yes, of course. Anybody want to come with me to Joburg?"

The question caused pandemonium. Naturally, all four children wanted to come with us for a ride in the car. They hadn't seen their father for a week, after all.

"Shhht, Mom is still sleeping." The children fell silent. "I'll take Heather and Gillian," Thomas decreed. "Sam and Justine, you still need to do your homework for Monday. We can't all go. Mom will wake up and wonder where everyone's disappeared to. Now out with you!"

The children reluctantly left the kitchen to play ball outside. It wasn't half as interesting as interrogating a stranger, who worked with their Dad, but soon they made quite a racket.

Thomas's morning had already been pretty busy. One of the sheep had foolishly fallen into the swimming pool, while trying to drink the water. Thomas took it in his stride, but he needed to change his sopping wet clothes afterwards. "Oh, things like that happen all the time," he said. "The beauty of living with animals."

So, I hadn't dreamt it last night. They really had sheep and dwarf cows in the back garden! I also saw a pony, ducks and chickens under the Bluegum trees. Who knew that my colleague Thomas Taylor, the computer genius, led such a rural existence?

Benoni was farther from Johannesburg than I had realized. We even passed the airport at some stage. After my quiet life in Botswana, the sheer number of cars racing up and down the city highways was mind-boggling. Could it be called a culture shock in reverse?

We left the highway and drove along the curvy Jan Smuts Avenue. This Jan Smuts must have been quite important, to have both the airport and a street named after him.

Thomas took a detour through leafy, old suburbs called Parktown and Westcliff for my benefit.

Even the children oohed and aahed at the sight of so many ducks and the fountain in the middle of Zoo Lake. South Africa was not at all what I had imagined and Johannesburg was so much more cosmopolitan than Gaborone.

As soon as Thomas had taken off with his children, I was slotted into the van Heerden family's plans for the weekend.

There was an awkward moment when I discussed mad Ronnie Immelman with Emily's parents, Charmaine and Hendrik.

They kept apologizing for having saddled me with their friends' son. Thankfully, we didn't linger on the subject.

Emily's Dad seemed most comfortable in khaki-coloured shorts and shirts. At least I never saw him wearing anything else. He was a kindly man, who didn't say much. He liked to crack jokes peppered with Afrikaans expressions, I never quite seemed to understand. I laughed at them regardless.

Hendrik van Heerden's hair was neatly combed and he had a short moustache. He worked for some big insurance company in Pretoria and there was something ever so correct about him.

His bubbly, blonde wife was quite the opposite. She loved to chat, and with her colourful kaftans and quirky Twiggy hair, wouldn't have been at all out of place in the hippie era. Somehow she reminded me of Rita Winckler.

Charmaine ushered me into the spare bedroom that I shared with an obsolete home trainer and a sewing machine. The elaborate patchwork quilt on the wall looked impressive.

"Charmaine, that's just beautiful!" I admired the quilt.

I had dabbled in sewing projects at school, but this was true fabric art.

"I'd love to show you how to make one darling, but, I'm afraid there's not enough time this weekend."

"You made it? Yes, of course," I stammered.

"Tell you what. I'll give you a couple of quilting magazines to read. If you feel like patchwork the next time you come to visit, we can tackle it for a couple of hours."

"Sounds good to me," I said still in awe.

I put my bag down and handed over a letter and small packet from Emily.

"Thank you. Make yourself at home, Bridget. We'll be off to town in half an hour."

Did she just say town?

"Hi Mom." A sleepy face appeared in the door frame. It had to be Emily's younger sister Leanne. She was a paler, blonder version of Emily.

"Morning, Leanne. Meet Emily's friend Bridget. She's down here from Gaborone for the weekend."

"I see. Hi Bridget," the girl croaked.

"Hi, Leanne."

"Leanne was out last night. Only seventeen and already a night crawler," Charmaine said drily.

"Yeah, yeah, Mom."

"How was the concert last night?"

"It was fine."

That had to be the teenage answer for all parental questions: 'How was school?' 'Fine.' 'How are you feeling?' 'Fine.' 'How was the concert?' 'Fine.' Claire and I hadn't been any different.

"I'll go to Rosebank later - with Debs and Elaine."

"Sure."

"Can I have some money for the bus?"

"I gave you some money for the weekend yesterday."

"Yeah, but I also had a hairdresser appointment and..."

"I can't give you any more this week, ask your Dad," Charmaine said cheerfully and added with a mischievous grin, "or you could walk —"

"Nice meeting you," Leanne grumbled and disappeared down the hall. Almost instantly, a song by 'Supertramp' rang out from her room.

"Isn't it dangerous to go into town?" I just came out with it. The question had been bugging me, since Charmaine had mentioned us going into town. "I've heard so much about bombs going off and violent demonstrations and things like that."

"Well, it should be quite safe where we go. Last week there was a blast at a night club on the other side of town. Somebody apparently didn't get the message that Nelson Mandela has been released."

"Only last week? So it could happen again?"

"Security guards go through handbags and search with metal detectors, before people are allowed into shops. Dustbins in the city centre, where bombs could be planted, have been removed. But we can't live in fear all the time, so we do the best we can. Put it down to pioneer spirit."

"Gaborone is so peaceful in comparison. Are you sure we should go?"

"There won't be any demonstrations today," she assured me. "I've got errands to run, but if you'd rather stay here..."

I mustered my courage. After all, I hadn't come to Johannesburg to sit around all weekend. "No it's fine, I'll come with you."

After all, Emily's spunky mother had to deal with this every day of her life.

"Good, I'm glad you're coming," she said simply. I heard patio furniture being moved around at the back of the house. "Oh that's Gladys by the way. Let me introduce you to her."

She took me out to the terrace at the back and I made the acquaintance of Gladys, resident maid in the van Heerden household for the past 17 years and a valued member of the family. She was dressed in a crisp light-blue maid's outfit with white lace trimming on her apron and a matching headscarf.

"Good morning madam," She beamed. I was used to being addressed as madam by now and didn't mind anymore.

"Good morning Gladys, how are you?" I greeted her back.

"Fine madam, thank you," she said brightly.

"Gladys is Tswana and comes from Bophuthatswana. That's not far from the border. She has family in Lobatse and Rustenburg," Charmaine said.

Lobatse was on the Botswana side and I had a vague idea that we had come through a town called Rustenburg yesterday.

"Dumela Gladys, le kai?" I switched to simple Setswana.

"Re teng, re teng, wena o tsogile kai?" she beamed even more.

"I'm fine, Gladys. Ke utlwa gologonje Setswana." I understand a little Setswana.

"Ehéy sorry. No matata, madam." Gladys let me off the hook.

She smiled and returned to cleaning the patio furniture, humming a church hymn to herself. I went back to the spare room to unpack. Then I page through a couple of magazines that were lying around.

"Are you ready?" Charmaine called from the kitchen after a few minutes.

"Yes, I'm coming!" I got off the bed.

"Good let's go."

Charmaine drove a red beetle that sounded worse than two motor bikes. We went down Jan Smuts Avenue, over the highway, past Wits University, through Braamfontein and over a railway bridge into town.

The quiet, leafy suburbs made way for a bustling city center with high concrete buildings, a surge of colourful people and hooting minibuses that were called minitaxis. Women of every creed and colour were fashionably dressed in gaudy frocks with big shoulder pads. There was much pushing and shoving. Long queues lined up at bus stops in central Eloff Street and piled into red double-decker buses everywhere. London sprang to mind.

Charmaine parked her Beetle in a guarded parking lot and we walked past department stores with names like OK Bazaar, Foschini's and Edgars.

Not a single dustbin in sight. I relaxed.

"In South Africa Minitaxis are only used by African people," Charmaine said. "Passengers wave them down with hand signs that indicate to the drivers in which direction they wish to go." She showed me different hand signs. "The drivers then either stop abruptly on the side of the road, annoying drivers behind them, or they simply ignore the hand sign and drive past."

"In Gaborone everybody takes cheap minitaxis to get around town. They always stop in the same places and the drivers also behave fairly civilized.

"It's still different here. Buses are also still segregated," Charmaine revealed as we turned into a side road. "There are white and black bus stops. So you have to be careful where you wait for a bus or the driver might not stop for you."

"Still? That's really odd." I was surprised. Johannesburg seemed like any other city with lots of people pushing impatiently past each other.

"Yes, it is. Things happen rather slowly in Africa. There are also black and white toilets and park benches to this day. But most people ignore them. Let's go in here."

We were searched before we could enter and came out

of the department store, loaded with plastic bags.

"Hold onto your handbag, Bridget. There are pickpockets around," Charmaine warned me as we walked along Diagonal Street. I immediately clutched my purse and plastic bags tighter.

"I've only heard of one incident of a bag being stolen in Gaborone. It nearly made the headline of the Gazette newspaper."

"Yes, Emily keeps telling me how safe Gaborone is."

We walked past a big glass building that looked a lot like a cut diamond. I greeted an elderly black lady, who passed us and was taken aback by the icy stares I received. In Gaborone, it was considered good manners to greet people in the street, but obviously not around here.

"People are not as friendly as they are in Botswana," Charmaine said with a sigh.

"Because of apartheid?" I was confused.

"No, I think it's just a big city and people are more suspicious of each other. It's still different in the rural areas. Ag nee man!" Charmaine steered around an unexpected pile of dog pooh. And I had assumed that customs were the same everywhere in Africa!

"Last stop," Charmaine said.

We entered a peculiar looking store. It was dark inside and narrow and there was an unpleasant smell. When my eyes adjusted to the dim light, I saw dried animal parts hanging from the ceiling. Small reptiles, ostrich heads and feet and various other unidentifiable, dark shapes lay in boxes on the dirty counter. Next to an assortment of rolled-up hides, horns, beads and seeds. I was disgusted and fascinated at the same time. This had to be a muti-shop!

"Emily told me that you are interested in witchdoctors. Well, this is where witch-doctors come to shop."

An old woman behind the counter was busy crushing dried herbs and seeds in a wooden mortar. Her long hair hung in long thin braids adorned with white beads over her shoulders. Behind the old woman were shelves with colourful powders, seashells and small bones in glass jars, small bottles and decorated gourds. Strings of beads, little figurines and amulets hung from hooks on the wall.

An Indian shopkeeper in a yellow sari asked us what we were looking for.

"I wanted to show this young lady from Botswana what a muti shop looks like," Charmaine enlightened her. I stared speechlessly at the creepy confusion around me.

"We sell everything witchdoctors need to do their job," The Indian lady said.

"Do they put dead animals into muti?" I asked and pointed to the ceiling.

Muti was a very broad term, describing anything from herbal medicines to magical potions, spells and curses.

"Sometimes. I'm not a witchdoctor myself, but I hear that they are necessary in some spells." Sickening. No muti for me, thank you!

"The Chinese also use animals in medicine. Just that they usually pickle them. Like snakes for example," Charmaine said, winking at me. She searched through a wooden box full of pendants.

I felt nauseous. The smell was overwhelming and the thought of pickled snakes was not exactly appealing. We bought a couple of lucky amulets and a few strings of glass beads for Gladys. I didn't want to insult anyone, but I couldn't wait to get out of this muti shop.

"Here, that's for you." Charmaine put a string and carved pendant over my head. "For your protection."

"Thank you. I might need it, should I ever have anything to do with witchdoctors."

"Better safe than sorry." Charmaine finished her errands and we drove back to Parkhurst in the rattling VW Beetle.

The van Heerdens were warm and hospitable and I had a great time that weekend. What I didn't know back then was that for two years, Emily and Charmaine had been organizing secret messages between South Africa and Botswana.

Hopefully nothing to do with violence or bomb attacks. Just letters and notes between relatives, who were separated in Botswana and South Africa because of politics. That's how they had met the Immelmans and their son Ronnie.

Thomas Taylor arrived just before 7 o'clock on Monday morning to pick me up. He stared at the plastic bag, bursting at the seams with magazines, letters and a care packet for Emily, but then stowed everything away in the boot of his car without comment. No matata.

Two cans of coke and the morning paper were draped on top. The guards at the border post wouldn't be searching the boot too closely, then.

In broad daylight, the hills looked like wart-covered backs of giant reptiles. In fact, I wouldn't have surprised to see a couple of dinosaurs scamper down the slopes towards us.

We arrived at the office just before lunchtime. Mr. Feindlich had the flu and didn't make his usual snide remarks. I handed Emily the letters and her care packet and went straight to work. A pile of urgent documents for the head office in Hamburg and a project report from Mozambique were waiting.

Soon, everybody went to lunch, except for Richard and Thomas. I searched for some Fisherman's Friend peppermints and bent down to look for them in my handbag. When came up, I stared through the large window behind my computer monitor at a strange face. A young Tswana man in a striped shirt pressed his nose and lips against the glass. I got such a fright that I dropped the peppermints and screamed.

"What's the matter, Bridget?" Richard hurried into the open-plan office.

"Some guy...out there..." I stammered and pointed to the window. Richard and Thomas ran outside and chased the intruder as far as the gate. The rascal leapt around two cars, parked in the street, and was gone in a flash.

"Simply no security around here," Richard grumbled, breathing heavily when he came back from the chase. "A chancer probably. Thought everybody was out and tried to find something that's not nailed down."

"I don't think he'll come back in a hurry," Thomas said in his deep voice and nervously twisted a curl of his red beard. "But I'll have a serious talk to Feindlich about security around here."

I felt something around my neck. It was the amulet Charmaine had given me in the muti shop. *Perhaps it really has the power to protect me,* I thought and for the first time, had a closer look at the wooden pendant.

It was carved in the shape of a lizard.

## CHAPTER 13

Of course, Mr. Feindlich claimed that a low budget kept him from beefing up security at the office. Gaborone was a safe place after all. We were anxious for a few days, but soon everything was back to normal.

I couldn't help but wonder if there was a connection between the young man at the office and the burglary in Tsholofelo.

I should be proved right. And that was only the beginning.

After the double-dose of family life in Johannesburg, I was more determined than ever not to give up on Claire. I had broken through some invisible wall between us and needed to try again now. And if I had to use the services of a witchdoctor, so be it.

And suddenly things started to happen, as if to prod me into action. I went on a lunch date with Gabby at the Parks Restaurant. We'd never spoken about the thing with Desmond and Werner and how they knew that Claire was my sister. Had Gabby told them? Perhaps I was afraid she'd feel insulted, if I asked her directly. Gabby had just come back from home leave in Bavaria and we hadn't seen each other for weeks. So I didn't bring it up.

She told me over marinated black mushrooms - the chef's specialty - how she had gone wind surfing in Czechoslovakia with friends near the small town of Karlsbad. They had camped by a lake and visited the famous spa. Gabby had brought me a tin of sweets. Karlsbader Obladen.

"It was fantastic," Gabby gushed while I listened enviously. "You must take a trip there sometime. Prague is so worth a visit. Want some cow juice?" I nodded and she poured milk into my coffee.

"Well perhaps, when I get a chance," I muttered.

"Oh, it's so good to be back here. I can't stand all that drizzle in Europe."

"I know what you mean —"

"And I'll be deployed to Germany soon!" she lamented. "Love your new necklace by the way —"

I looked down at my lizard charm. "Yes, it's a..."

"Du liebe Güte - is it that late already? Got a tennis match at the club. Pity you stopped playing. Ich muss gehen." She skipped in and out of German and rustled with the things in her bag.

"Give me news, give me news..." I had to laugh. Gabby was always in a rush.

"I'll pay, don't worry. Drink up in your own good time. We still have the auditors at the office, so I must beetle. I'll see you at the party tonight," she said and her brown eyes twinkled.

"Mwa, mwa." Gabby breathed two kisses over my cheeks and was gone in a flash. So I sat alone in front of my rock shandy for a while and looked around. All the tables at the popular eatery were occupied by groups of young employees on lunch squeezing into the red vinyl benches.

That's when I saw her.

I saw Claire! My brain shot to attention. Three tables down on the other side of the aisle, there she was!

Her hair was the same from behind: a blonde, tousled bob. She even wore the t-shirt I remembered her packing. Pink and green stripes. How was that possible? I rubbed my eyes and blinked. She was still there. I had tears in my eyes and felt hot, then cold, then hot again.

Who were those laughing, talking strangers she shared a

table with? They had to be her new friends. I didn't care.

Before I knew it I stood behind Claire, touching her shoulder, laughing and crying at the same time. But the surprised woman, who turned around was not my sister. She looked puzzled. I'd never seen her before. My heart skipped a beat. Oh Claire, don't play cruel games with me!

"I'm sorry, I'm so sorry," I stuttered. "I thought you were somebody else."

"Oh, that's ohraight, lurv. No harm done." The woman, at least ten years older than Claire, spoke with a broad accent. She saw my tears and had pity in her dark brown eyes. I wished the ground would open and swallow me up.

"Again, I'm really sorry. I really thought... you look just like her. How silly of me." I dragged myself back to my table.

The blonde woman's friends kept looking in my direction, giggling and whispering. What a nutcase, they were probably saying to each other. She thought you were somebody else! How hilarious.

Deflated, I took a few nervous sips from my glass and walked out, still trembling.

My old friend, the light blue beetle with the painted aquarium on its wings, greeted me cheerfully. Don't worry, it seemed to say, I'm still here. The sight was strangely comforting.

What if it was a sign? *I have to get hold of a sangoma*, I thought fiercely, *no matter how! Straight away.*

But first there was still Gabby's garden party.

I was planning my party wardrobe for the evening, when a fresh gust of wind grabbed the acacia trees outside the window with sudden vehemence. It wasn't the usual rustle, more like a painful creaking.

Big raindrops splattered against the windows. The rain came down harder and faster by the second, pounding the house. Plink plonk bang. It started hailing. Pauli was outside!

I let him into the lounge and he huddled under the table as the first lightening stroke sliced through the grey sky. I huddled on the floor next to the table. The thunder was deafening. Hailstones as big as golf balls bounced off cars and roofs.

After a hot day, an African rainstorm could be fierce. What if a window burst or the roof lifted off? *Please don't let me die!* I thought in desperation. The thunder crashed and rolled, but the windows didn't burst and the roof stayed where it was.

When the storm had finally blown itself out, trees and bushes stood tousled and tender flowers lay crushed on the ground. The temperature dropped. I looked outside. A tiny bird lay dead on a heap of hailstones. It must have fallen out of its nest.

Gabby's garden party was postponed to the following Saturday. But it was too late now to look for a sangoma.

'You won't believe what this place looks like...' I wrote to Liz that night. 'As if the streets were covered in snow - but only for a few minutes! And the smell of all those mashed leaves and flowers..."

My friend probably wouldn't believe a word of it. Hailstones as big as golf balls? Storms just weren't that brutal in England. But reality could be stranger than fiction sometimes.

Then something else happened, just to keep me on my toes. I was home alone one day, when I spotted a familiar face through the kitchen window.

That was surely the same man on the veranda, who had stared at me at the office! He was wearing a red shirt now, but it was definitely the same man. What on earth...

I jumped up. The plate on my lap fell to the floor and broke. The noise startled the intruder. He leapt down the veranda stairs. He was running away again! Pauli, who had been asleep in the sunny backyard, barked and bolted after him.

I caught up with them three houses down on the corner.

Pauli stood growling in front of the man in the red t-shirt and an old woman, who must have waited for him in the street. They held unto each other. Afraid. Those two were supposed to be robbers?

"Okay, Pauli, okay... What do you want from me?" I flew at them, arms akimbo. "I want you to stop harassing me, do you hear?"

Pauli barked in support and the two of them shrunk against the garden wall behind them. My anger vanished when I saw their fear.

"What do you want from me?" I repeated calmer.

"Ga ké utlwé," the man said and pointed to his ears. "Ga ké utlwé!" I don't understand.

The woman looked at me chin up, challenging without giving me an answer. What was going on here?

"Arré, tsamaye," the matron said at last. Come on, let's go

They daringly ignored my dog and me, turned and walked toward the main road.

It took the wind out of my sails. I held a straining Pauli back by his collar and watched them disappear around the corner. Should I follow the pair or just go home?

What was the point of aggravating the Tswanas waiting for their minitaxi at the main road? I couldn't communicate what had happened. It also seemed that the two intruders weren't able to tell me what they wanted, either. So I turned around and went back to the house. Pauli trotted next to me, looking even more confused.

I didn't report the incident police this time. Nothing had been stolen and they had done no harm.

My instinct told me that those two weren't really thieves. But if not, why did they stalk me then?

Kgomotso found me an hour later on the veranda. Brooding about the whole thing, sitting on the Hollywood swing and my dog sprawled out next to me. She pulled up a chair and I told her the whole story.

"That sounds weird," she crinkled her forehead. "An old woman and a young man stalking you? For what reason? It doesn't make sense!"

I sighed. "I'll say! I have no clue, who the woman is, but the man is the one from the Packer office. I think I saw him even in the Mall, staring at me. And now again."

"Weird," Kgomotso repeated. "Why would they come here like that? Maybe they didn't find what they were searching for in your room."

"If it was them at all. But just to stare at me like that —"

"Not exactly pros when it comes to house breaking. Maybe they are crazed fans."

"Ha funny - do you think they are dangerous or just curious?"

"Hmm, hard to say. My guess is that they want something from you for some reason," she said. "What are you wearing around your neck?"

The amulet had slipped out.

"Oh just a talisman from Emily's mom. Supposed to protect me," I said.

"Hmm, let's see - a lizard. That gives me an idea. We better check that they didn't leave any muti outside."

Of course, I hadn't thought of that! Muti was not to be taken lightly.

When Emily came home, she helped us check the veranda and by the kitchen window. Nothing. Then next to the hedge in front of the house. Pauli also tried to help and sniffed around the garden.

"I've got something!" Kgomotso suddenly yelled.

Emily and I were turning over leaves in the former flowerbed by the driveway. We looked up and Kgomotso held up a small piece of tattered fur.

"See, I told you," she said triumphantly as we walked over to the tattered hedge. It hadn't been pruned in ages, but the Storm had stripped off enough leaves to expose the - thing. It turned out to be a small symbolic doll, made of sticks and wrapped in a piece of rotting hide with white and black hairs.

"That's goat's hide," Kgomotso said knowingly.

Attached to the doll was a tiny purse made from the same hide. Something square was inside the purse, but we didn't bother to find out what it was.

I felt the hairs at the nape of my neck stand up. "I've seen something like that before. By the GVO office, also outside in the hedge."

"This is supposed to be muti?" Emily inspected the small pouch. "Ooh, it smells bad. Yerré!" She wrinkled her nose.

"What is this muti doing on our hedge?" I asked. "Do you think the man and the old woman put it there?" I couldn't think of any good reason why these people should have deposited muti for my sake.

"Don't think so. At least not recently. It's been here for a while by the looks of it," Kgomotso said.

"So it might not have anything to do with me? That doesn't explain then what those two want and why they are following me around." I eyed the object suspiciously.

"Some kind of spell. Typical sangoma stuff. As far as I know it has to do with a person and there's often fur involved. But why goat's fur?" Kgomotso wondered." But then – what do *I* know about stuff like that…"

"Claire hit a goat with her car. Maybe somebody wants compensation for the goat. In case the thing has something to do with us. But how do they know about me?"

"Could be that they used a sangoma to find you," Kgomotso said. "Sangomas sometimes use such things as photos or personal items."

"Oh dear!" Emily was alarmed. "You mean like voodoo?"

"I'm not sure. Sangomas cost money and a goat isn't that valuable. All this effort just for a goat? But then this muti shouldn't be here," Kgomotso concluded her theory.

She held the crude doll far from her. Pauli tried to sniff the muti and we all shouted at the same time, "No Pauli, yuck, stop it!"

Tail between legs, he slunk away and rather watched us from a safe distance.

"Let's burn the thing or dig a hole somewhere and bury it," Emily suggested.

"You can't burn it," Kgomotso said and we didn't ask why.

Eventually, we threw doll and pouch into the big rubbish bin outside, where they made the acquaintance of rotting vegetable peelings, stale pizza and soggy teabags. The muti would end up on some dump, where it hopefully did no harm.

My mother sounded alarmed, when I told her about the possible voodoo spell. Stupid of me. She had such a vivid imagination these days. Mom had recently told me about an alleged UFO crash in the Kalahari and an ensuing cover-up by the American government. According to some documentary on television. Good heavens!

Anything Mom could find on Botswana interested her and the Britannica Atlas seemed to be her constant companion. She marked all the different places where I had been. It was the closest thing to travelling to the country that had abducted her two babies.

Dad took the phone from Mom. I jubilated soundlessly.

'Hallo Kleine, whatever it is you're doing, keep doing it,' he said. 'Things will be alright. You've got a job, you have friends. Just come home once in a while, will you?' He didn't seem worried by a spot of voodoo.

I knew that Dad was somehow proud of the daughter he thought would never fly the nest. I was becoming an independent young woman, even if it was in darkest Africa. And so far so good, knock on wood.

Early the next morning I felt something bothering me. Like an ache that wouldn't go away. I had to get out and into the cool, grey morning. Alone.

## SINGING LIZARDS

I drove my aquarium into town. The Mall was still deserted and the first shops would not open before 9 o'clock and I sat down on a bench not far from Corner's Supermarket between a yesterday-today-tomorrow bush and an exuberantly flowering bougainvillea. No walkman, just birdsong and silence. I missed the silence of the Kalahari, where I could just be myself. My thoughts wandered here and there. Nothing specific. The bright blue roller birds were pecking at crumbs and I had no idea, how long I sat like that.

It was Saturday and a flea market set up right in front of me. I watched the craftspeople lay out their jewellery and African curios under shady gazebos. Earrings, the size of small pizzas and pot holders in African prints. Someone tugged at my sleeve and disturbed the flow of my thoughts.

"No, I have nothing for you today," I said to two street children, who had come early to ply their begging-trade. . I had given them money before, which had turned me into a soft target. These kids never seemed to forget a face.

"Pleeese madam, pleeese..." They gave me pitiful looks. "Re batlá mádi!"

"No not today," I repeated. "Tsamaya, móna. Ga ke ná mádi!" Go child, I don't have money.

The two boys eventually gave up and ran after a lonely tourist with a big camera hanging over his shoulder. After another hour or so, the sun began to tickle the back of my head. The Mall was buzzing with people by now. Shops and flea market stalls were receiving noisy attention.

It was time to leave. And I had come to a conclusion.

Getting in touch with Tony again would be the first step. I would pluck up my courage and write him a letter. Or better still, phone the Botsalo Hotel or just drive to Palapye. Neo probably knew of a suitable sangoma in the area. There was no other way: I had to speak to a witchdoctor. The genuine kind. It was time for me to know the truth. Maybe discovering the muti doll had something to do with it. And the day I thought I saw Claire at the Parks Restaurant. Or maybe Botswana had just realized that it was time to let go of me. I wanted no distractions. Not anymore.

Instead of going to lunch with my friends, I went for a long walk in the stretch of wilderness opposite our house. Pauli somehow understood me with his canine instinct. He pulled me up and down the stony path with abandon. When he took the time to stop for a couple of minutes, he looked at me as if to say, 'Hey you can count on me'.

Gabby, Emily and Kgomotso demanded an explanation for my sudden withdrawal. I asked them to be patient with me. Explained that it had to do with Claire.

In April, I handed in my notice at Packer Engineering. My savings would tide me over for a few months. I was now free to make my own decisions and Claire became my priority again. At least I would give it my best shot.

I went back to the immigration office to get my temporary residence permit extended and was given another month on top of the two remaining weeks. That gave me the whole of six weeks to get results.

Next I moved in with Gabby. I had also to write a letter to Tony. Would he join me in my quest? I had to find out. I was brimming with determination and suddenly things began to fall into place.

Beate Belseck, the German volunteer I had befriended during my days at the GVO, came to visit. She carried her 3-month-old baby girl - and a letter from Tony!

Beate produced the letter well into her second cup of tea and another slice of carrot cake. Could this still be coincidence? The letter had been biding its time in a cubby hole at the GVO office for two weeks, before Beate had spotted my name on it. She'd decided that I needed to get my post straight away. Hence her surprise visit.

I could have hugged her. Actually I did, careful not to wake the baby in her arms.

Tony didn't know that I had changed jobs and moved a lot in the past year. So the letter went to the old address. After Beate had left, I opened the envelope impatiently and could hardly believe my eyes:

'Hi Bridget,                              (no date!)
*Long time no hear. I was up to my eyeballs in midyear exam preparations. You know what it's like. Don't get a fright, but I have news for you regarding Claire...*'

I sat down. News about Claire!

'*A young man by the name of Thabang came to the house yesterday. I didn't understand a word he was saying, so I went over to fetch Neo. Thabang turned out to be from a village in the Tuli Block. He told us that the Inyanga, a kind of chief witchdoctor, had sent him to find you. He had been here before when you were still in Palapye and spoke to you...*'

Really? It had to be the young man in the white polo shirt and sunglasses, who had waited on the stairs by Tony's house. He had run away when I called Tsanana's name. I faintly remembered the encounter.

'*...His brother and grandmother in Gaborone had been sent to do the same thing, but it was difficult to find you. It took them quite a while to catch up with you. First somebody chased his brother away and then you were so riled that you set the dog on them. You thought they were thieves and they couldn't communicate properly with you.*'

The young man at the office and then at the house!

'*Thabang says they didn't want to scare you again. He asks if you could please come to Palapye. Neo can translate. They know how to find Claire and need your help. Will*

*explain everything later. Please come as quickly as you can.
Best, Tony'*

The news were breathtaking. In the true sense of the word. I took a deep breath. I needed to re-read the letter a few times to make sure that I had understood everything.

There was no doubt about it: Tony clearly wrote that this chief witchdoctor person knew where Claire was!

Blood was rushing in my ears.

The young man, who called himself Thabang, had wanted to tell me this long ago and I couldn't understand him. But why did they need me of all people to find her? Why didn't they just go and get her? Why did they need to speak to me directly when I spoke so little Setswana? It didn't make sense. Tony said he would explain later. Alright then.

I didn't have to think twice. I had to go to Palapye right now!

Packing a few things into the beetle and put Pauli on the backseat took no time at all. Then I drove past the office.

"I must go to Palapye today. My brother- in-law wrote that something to do with Claire came up. Please tell Gabby. I couldn't get hold of her. I'll take Pauli with me."

I explained to Kgomotso and Emily as simply as possible what the letter had said. They were both surprised, of course, but promised to help me out where they could. My two friends had tears in their eyes when we said goodbye.

"Good luck, Bridget. I hope that you find out something at last."

"Take care of yourself. Don't do anything I wouldn't do," Kgomotso cried and hugged me again.

"I can't promise that, but I'll see you soon. Something will come out of it," I said.

And then - just like that - I left Gaborone for good.

# CHAPTER 14

My aquarium-car attracted a lot of attention along the Francistown Road. People laughed and waved and pointed at my car. I waved back, but my mind was elsewhere. *Claire - it went round and round in my head - Palapye, Shaka Zulu, Tuli Block - sangomas can help, they know where she is - Benjamin...* No!

I shook my head vehemently. No, I didn't want to think about Benjamin! I had to pull myself together and keep concentrating on the potholes. But I had little control over my thoughts. *Kalahari, magic starry sky - Claire, ohmygod, Claire, Claire!*

Before I knew how, the tyres of my car were ploughing through the fine deep sand, when I took the shortcut in Palapye. Tony was not at home, but Gina was. The puppy had grown into a beautiful young dog lady with silky black fur and a white patch on the chest. Just like her dad's. Pauli whimpered on the back seat and couldn't wait for me to open the car door.

The two dogs greeted each other enthusiastically in dog-fashion, while I stretched out in a wicker chair on the familiar veranda. Here I sat and waited.

Much had changed around me: Mrs. Poppelmeyer was no longer scanning the surroundings from behind her lace curtains. I had heard that she'd left a while ago and gone back to her habitual life in Cobblestead. But the houses across the road looked all inhabited. A green motsetsi hedge now guarded Tony's house and a proper lawn carpeted the sandy ground. In the wakah, made from car tyres, fronds of lettuce and herbs spilled over the edges. The acacia tree was spreading its spindly branches in all directions and sturdy succulents studded the rock garden.

Just the view of the hills over the tree tops hadn't changed at all. A light breeze caressed the plants. I sat on the veranda and dreamily watched the misty hilltops turn into shades of orange in the sinking sun. At last my entangled thoughts slowed to a virtual standstill.

It didn't take long for Tony to find out that he had a visitor. Somebody had told him that a strange-looking car was parked in his driveway. He knew it was me and Neo also came with him. It had been a long time and we hugged each other. I noticed that Tony had lost weight and Neo looked somewhat chunkier.

"I'm sorry it took so long," I said. "I'm no longer with the GVO. A friend brought the letter around only this morning and I left immediately."

"Ah, it's alright, Bridget," Neo said. "That's how it is with African time." We all knew, of course, how it was with African time in Botswana.

"As long as you are here now," Tony said.

I couldn't wait to start.

"So what is it that I need to do? When are we going?"

"In a minute. We have to talk first. Would you like some tea or juice?" Tony asked and pulled up two more chairs.

"Some juice would be nice, thanks."

Although it was almost winter, the days were still hot and I noticed only now, how thirsty I was. Pauli was lapping up water from Gina's bowl then sniffed around the outdoor scullery. I filled the bowl again and Pauli thanked me by licking my toes.

I sat down next to Neo and Tony pottered around in the kitchen. Neo leaned forward. "How much did Tony write in his letter?"

"Not much. Only that some chief sangoma knows where to find Claire and that I am supposed to help somehow.

People were apparently looking for me in Gaborone. That led to some misunderstandings."

Spoken out loud, it didn't sound terribly logical anymore, but Tony would tell me what was going on any moment now! I started to wriggle around in my chair and tapped my foot on the waxed veranda floor.

"Yes, the Inyanga, the chief sangoma, is trying to put things right," Neo said.

"Put what right?"

"Okay, that's not exactly straightforward, Bridget. You must try and keep an open mind," Neo warned me.

"What do you mean by that? It sounds terribly mysterious," I said. "I've been in Africa long enough. What could possibly still rattle me?"

Except perhaps... I felt a knot in my throat and immediately pushed the dark thoughts away. Pauli lay down on top of my feet now and Gina cuddled up to him. They were like two living hot water bottles.

"What is it Neo? Come on, dish it already!"

The screen door snapped closed. Tony carried juice glasses and a bowl of crisps on a tablet and set it down on the table. The dogs sniffed the air and plunked their heads down again.

"It would be better if Tony told you," Neo said.

Tony sat down and silently poured us some juice. "Oh will you two start with it, already! When can I see Claire?" I said impatiently.

"Well, here's the thing..." Tony began and told me the whole story from the top. How this sangoma from Neo's village had contacted him in an important matter. Neo first thought that somebody in the family had died, but it was nothing of the kind. It had to do with Claire!

"The sangoma summoned both of us and then she explained —" In a nutshell, a less respectable witchdoctor in the Tuli Block area was at the centre of it all.

"That night, after Claire had the run-in with a goat near

the village, this witchdoctor ended up treating Claire's head injuries. The sangoma left Claire to sleep in her hut. So far so good. But apparently, Claire woke up in the wee hours of the morning, couldn't remember anything and ran away."

I drew in a sharp breath.

"So the entire village went out to look for her. Some boys found Claire, cowering in the shrubs." I struggled to follow Tony and stared at him open-mouthed.

"So where is Claire now? They didn't..."

"No. Wait, I'll get to that just now," Tony said. "The next day, Claire had disappeared again! This time nobody could find her. She couldn't have made it very far and the witchdoctor knew that she wouldn't survive in the wilderness, all alone and injured. And that it could mean only one thing —"

"What, Tony, what did it mean? Oh talk already!"

"There is a place by the hills that cannot be accessed easily. A type of opening. Only sangomas know how to get through there. Claire must have somehow found her way in," Neo said instead.

"What?!" I laughed. "You two are pulling my leg!" Pauli stirred under the table.

"What? No, we're not," Neo said in all seriousness and I stopped laughing.

"What's that supposed to mean? Some kind of opening —"

"It's the place where the ancestors are."

"The ancestors?"

"Yes."

I was too shocked to speak.

"The access to the 'Land of the Forefathers' must not be revealed to strangers. So this witchdoctor had the brilliant idea to just leave things the way they were. She tried to cover up the accident with the goat, gave orders to dig a hole under a tree and bury Claire's things. Young men from the village had to drive Claire's car to Mochudi as a distraction to lead anybody looking for her off track. Problem solved."

"Ha!"

"She also intimidated the local police and anybody who knew about the whole thing. Unfortunately that's not unusual. Nobody here dares go against a sangoma's wishes."

Right. So by now I understood that it was the fault of this nameless witchdoctor from the Tuli Block that I didn't get anywhere with my search. She had been blocking things in her own fashion.

"Why did she do such a thing?"

"She had a good reason from a sangoma's point of view. Just how she did it was not acceptable."

"Damn her! I was hoodwinked by that lousy witchdoctor!" I fumed.

"Have a sip of your juice, Bridget. That's not even almost the end of it," Tony said and offered me chips, but I was too angry to eat or drink.

"Some people in the village didn't approve of what she had done and the village elders disobeyed quietly..." Neo said. "They sent someone to summon you."

"The young man, probably" I began.

"What?"

"Never mind."

"We were told that she also tried to break up all relationships Claire had. How do I put this... with some kind of... spell." Tony struggled to find the right words.

"She did? How?"

"With muti. It backfired and things got out of hand. But I'm getting ahead of myself."

Neo took over. "It worked for a while. But then the Inyanga, the chief sangoma, found out. It's not allowed and nothing goes unnoticed in the spirit realm. The ancestors were angered. What the witchdoctor was supposed to do was help Claire find her way back. Now things were out of balance."

"What? What balance?" I asked.

"Wait. That's when the Inyanga tried to resolve things from a distance. He usually lives somewhere in the Kalahari. The wishes of the forefathers must be respected. The elders then sent Thabang again to ask you to come and help in the matter, but you'd already left Palapye."

"Excuse me? Are you talking about forefathers as in... deceased relatives? I mean as in dead?"

"Well yes, of course." Tony spoke so glibly about these things. When I left Palapye, he couldn't even say Claire's name, now he was telling me about realms and the wishes of deceased relatives' spirits.

"Who is this Thabang again?" I asked.

"My cousin," Neo said.

"Okay." I took a deep breath. "That sounds all rather confusing, but let's assume that these witchdoctors can speak to - dead people. Then I still don't understand. Where was Claire this whole time and what does she have to do with all of that?" My ability to understand the African way of thinking was being taxed to the extreme.

"Well, I'm not quite finished yet. I'm trying my best here and I'm not so sure myself." Tony coughed a little.

"Okay, the sangoma from Neo's village told us... that this other sangoma still thought her magic was powerful enough to keep everything under control and to keep troublesome Lekgoas from tracing Claire back to her village. That's why it went on for so long. She went against the elders and against the ancestors and that made things worse."

"I still don't understand."

Tony scratched his head. "What's there not to understand?!"

"Excuse me for living - but I've never heard such a thing before." I laughed uneasily.

"She cast a spell to break up relationships, remember?" Neo continued. "You were already in Gaborone by then.

The spell was actually too powerful for her to control. It got out of hand and possibly affected a lot more than just a separation from Claire. She didn't know that you were twins, after all."

"The spell was meant to separate Claire from all relationships. And I guess it also badly affected my connection with the two of you," Tony added, "and your relationships as well."

My mind raced. Affected my relationships? My relationship with Benjamin? Kurt Köhler and Ronnie Immelman? Was there a perfectly good explanation for all my personal mishaps in Gaborone over the past couple of years?

Neo saw my confusion. "We even found out that this defiant witchdoctor used muti to keep you well away from here and occupied with other things. But she struggled to keep up with your movements in Gaborone."

"I'm not surprised; I could hardly keep up with them myself."

Maybe that's why there had been a doll in the hedge. Actually two of them! The other one by the GVO office. But I didn't want to interrupt Neo.

"The forefathers sensed this, of course, and were infuriated by her lack of obedience. That's when the Inyanga became involved again and finally came all the way to my village to take care of business himself. The Inyanga needed to throw the bones for Tony to see what needed to be done. And that's all there is to it."

I needed a couple of minutes to digest this information.

"Why did he come to your village, then, and didn't go straight to the other village in the Tuli Block?"

"Because the ancestors told him to. The ancestors also want Claire to leave their realm as soon as possible. By now the strong bond to a blood-relative is necessary to pull Claire back," Neo said, "and that's why we need you."

"That doesn't make sense. Pull her back from where?"

"It does make sense, Bridget. Just hear me out," Neo

pleaded.

"Okay then, carry on," I said.

Tony seemed to find some bee-eaters on the motsetsi hedge incredibly fascinating. Although he tried hard, he must also be struggling to get his head around all this stuff. I took a sip of strawberry juice and padded Pauli's back. A breeze carried up smoky scents from the village.

"The Inyanga then gave instructions that all the muti be removed at once - to weaken the spell. I couldn't leave work, so Thabang's brother and his grandmother in Gaborone were asked to help —"

Oh no! If I hadn't over-reacted, this whole thing could have been sorted out long ago. *Hang in there Claire,* I thought, *we're nearly there. It won't take long now!*

"The two of them found lots of muti, but they couldn't communicate, why they needed to see you. They had Tony's letter with them. But you thought that they were thieves. That's why Tony had to mail you another letter."

"They didn't just want to drop off the letter, because the big black dog could have eaten it," Tony said. He chuckled a little and pointed to Pauli.

"Sorry. We had a break-in at the house where I was staying. Only my photographs and letters were stolen. That's why I thought they had something to do with it, when they kept showing up. And yes, Pauli would probably have eaten the letter."

"Oh dear, I don't blame you for not trusting them. Maybe that was the doing of that awful sangoma woman. She possibly needed something to make the separation-muti stronger. Can you believe it?!" Neo shook his head. "Defiant to the end."

"But what about Claire? Where is she now?" That horrible thought crossed my mind again. "Is she dead? Was she... killed for...muti?" I could barely get the words out. Body parts were being used for magic purposes and that meant a horrible death. Princess, the Wincklers' maid, had told me that some people used the services of such bad witchdoctors. I felt faint.

"No, nothing like that - calm down."

"Then tell me what's going on!" Why didn't Neo get to the point already?

"Claire is alive, but not - here," Tony sighed.

Relief washed over me and tears stung my eyes. Claire was alive! That's all I heard. She was probably hidden in some cave or hut, too hurt to leave or she was in a coma and had to be cared for by the locals... What else could it possibly be?

"So, can we go and get her now? I'm here - the blood-relative the Inyanga wanted. What are we waiting for?"

"It's a little bit more complicated than that. You must understand..."

"Oh stop faffing around! I do understand that this is not that easy. My stars... what is it that I have to do?" I wiped the tears that had been streaming down my face. But Tony and Neo just looked at me with this strange expression.

"There is no easy way to tell you that —" Tony said at last. "Okay - Claire is in the 'Land of the Forefathers'."

"What do you mean, Claire is in the 'Land of the Forefathers'?" I sniffled.

"Claire is in a different sort of - realm. In the 'Land of the Forefathers'; they call it the 'Abzu'. She crossed over somehow without being - dead." Without being dead?!

"What?! That's impossible...that just doesn't...exist!" I stammered. How could Tony with his rational mind believe in such rubbish? Absurd!

"I can't explain it any better," Neo said slowly. "She is there now and cannot come back on her own. That's what the Inyanga explained and you need to fetch your sister from the Abzu; pull her out of there."

"You can't be serious!"

"I'm afraid I am." There was not even a trace of a smirk on Neo's face. It didn't occur to me to ask what or where exactly this Abzu was. Obviously, Claire was there and the 'opening' was somewhere on a hill in the Tuli Block by Bobonong. So I listened reluctantly what else the two of them had to say. I mean, what choice did I have?

"Nobody knows how she ended up on that cliff and in that secret place. But she must have tripped and fallen. She must have fallen... into the Abzu," Neo continued. "The last time this happened was when a shepherd tripped in the same place about 80 years ago. He returned a week later with a spirit guide. People around here haven been very careful on the hill ever since."

"Are you telling me that Claire fell into some sort of... portal that you call an opening and into some sort kind of realm of the dead?" Maybe it would sink in when I said it myself.

"I wouldn't call it that. It's more like a... oh, I don't know what to call it," Tony flared up.

"Hmm, if that is true - and I still have my doubts about that - then why didn't she come back the same way, just like that shepherd before her?"

"It's possible that Claire can't remember what happened. After all, she had an accident," Tony said.

"Yes, of course." I felt discouraged. She couldn't remember where she belonged.

"Of course, the Inyanga sent a spirit guide in, but Claire refused to go. Your sister doesn't understand why she shouldn't be in the Abzu. Nobody can be forced to leave that place." I was perplexed. They'd sent in a spirit guide?

"And what am I supposed to do?"

"You must help her remember who she is. You go there with the spirit guide. You speak to Claire. The two of you return," Neo said telegram-style.

"Oh no. No, no, no! I can't go to a realm of the dead or some Abzu or whatever you call that place," I balked at the idea.

"Okay, I think it's time for a bit of a break," Tony said.

"When I heard about this the first time, I wanted to run for the hills, it sounded so crazy to me!"

I nodded silently and took a sip of juice. Yes, a break was a good idea. My head was spinning from all this mad talk about muti and shepherds and realms and what not. And I felt guilty. How could I have allowed this ghastly witchdoctor to fool me with her magic all this time?

*Listen to that*, I rebelled inside, *you do believe in magic, don't you?* But it was a lot to take in. I took Pauli and Gina for a short walk down the road. It helped me think, while Tony prepared hotdogs for dinner. The light was fading and we sat and ate in silence. Candles were flickering in glass jars on the table and at last I could rest my brain for a bit. It became too chilly on the veranda and we went inside.

"So, what is it that I have to do?" I asked resignedly and leaned back into the cushions on the couch.

I saw a glimmer of hope in Tony's eyes. Hope was the only thing that had kept us going all this time, even him.

"I'll send word to the Inyanga. He holds the key to the Abzu - so to speak. He'll come and help us," Neo explained and warmed his hands on a cup of tea. "The sooner you get Claire to remember the better for everyone."

There was absolutely no logic to it. But if Claire was really in this - Abzu - then I had to go there and bring her back. That's all there was to it. I pulled myself together and threw logic to the wind.

In the morning, Tony and Neo went to the training centre and I prepared for our imminent trip to Bobonong. The lizard-talisman was still around my neck and perhaps it would help with my fear of the unknown. The two of them were back in no time. They had asked for special leave, because of an urgent 'family matter' and the leave had been granted forthwith. But Neo hadn't heard from the Inyanga yet, so we had to wait another day!

"We've waited for the whole of two years," Tony said. "What's another day?" He put dishes in the sink and began to clean up when a young Tswana walked into the house. He resembled someone I had met before. The white polo shirt with the sunglasses tucked into the neck... Neo greeted him cordially.

"This is Thabang from Bobonong, the chief's son. A cousin of mine," he introduced the young man.

"Hello, I am Thabang," Thabang said. He pronounced every syllable slowly.

"Hello Thabang, I am Bridget."

"Yes, I know," he said and I instantly knew where I had seen him before.

"You have learnt English then?"

"Yes, I learn. I speak English."

"Why did you run away the last time we met, Thabang?" I asked him. It had nothing to do with our mission, but I needed to know nevertheless. Neo had to translate my question.

"He says he saw one of the helpers, sent by the sangoma from his village, lurking behind an empty house across the road."

"Really - here?"

"He says he didn't want the man to recognise him. The risk was too great that the sangoma would do something dangerous."

Thabang said in Setswana that he had a message from the Inyanga, that we were to all go to Thabang's village in the Tuli Block and meet him there early the next day. Thabang would come with us. He indicated the low position of the rising sun with his out-stretched arm. It was very common among Tswanas to express the time of day in that way. Thabang repeated the same story twice before he left.

The morning promised to turn into a cool, fine day when we set out at the crack of dawn. We'd packed some food and our tooth brushes - just in case. Alfred Jones and Tsanana thought that we were on our way to a funeral and promised to feed the dogs. Then we picked up Thabang in the village.

I clutched the talisman and tried not to think too much about what might happen when we arrived at our destination. Instead, I wanted to imagine Claire as I remembered her: blonde, with adventurous blue-green eyes, smiling at me mischievously. 'Hi Bridget, there you are...'

The idea that I might see my sister again was electrifying.

When we drove into the village, the Inyanga had not arrived yet and unfortunately, we ran straight into the witchdoctor, who had caused all this trouble for us! And understandably, she didn't seem too pleased to see us, either. The woman wore the same beaded braids and furry clothes as the other sangoma, I had seen at a funeral two years ago. However, 'our' witchdoctor was a coarse woman with an angry manner and the villagers seemed to be treading on eggshells around her.

I couldn't help but glare back at the woman. Why was she still around? Neo had said that she was no longer allowed to practice, so what was she still doing here in the village?

Thabang wanted to go and talk to his father, so he disappeared into one of the larger huts. The witchdoctor motioned roughly for us to follow her. We could hardly refuse. Perhaps the Inyanga had instructed that we were to wait in her hut for him.

But I didn't let her out of my sight and Neo seemed to be thinking the same. The rondavel she led us to was made of woven grass and twigs and fitted with all sorts of sangoma equipment. A big mortar and pestle, drums and clay pots on the floor, and there were dried herbs and animal parts hanging from the walls right next to calabashes and ladles. How cosy.

Red charcoals were smouldering inside a circle of rocks. We sat around the fire place and stretched our hands forward to warm them. Tony and Neo sat protectively on either side of me. The fire gave off a comforting warmth, but I still shivered. The witchdoctor sat down opposite us.

"Your sister has caused me too much trouble," the woman said harshly and carried on speaking Setswana. Neo translated almost in disgust. "She wasn't allowed to go to the secret place. Godknows who told her about that. It's meant to be left alone by nosy Lekgoas." She was hissing words under her breath; many more than Neo was willing to translate.

"The Inyanga asked us to come," I said curtly. The woman stared right past me and took out a dirty pouch. She let small bones, the odd coin, short sticks and seed pods fall into her hand and threw them on a grass mat. Just as the phony sangomas had done for the tourists in Victoria Falls. The witchdoctor read the 'bones' and pushed the objects on the mat furiously this way and that.

"I see that you won't be stopped!" She rocked back and forth, whipping her beaded braids around. Then she fell into a chilling singsong that sent my heart beating in my throat. The woman was obviously quite mad!

"Where is the Inyanga?" I asked nervously.

Thabang appeared at the entrance. The witchdoctor gave a screeching speech and he answered her respectfully.

"We should go," Neo decided and stood up. "She wants 50 Pula for her services."

"What services? We aren't here for some soothsaying." Tony sounded irritated. Neo translated and the witchdoctor stared at us with utter hatred before storming out of the rondavel.

"I don't think she was supposed to meet with us at all. We can wait for the Inyanga somewhere else."

We waited in Thabang's hut, a furnished rondavel that was much bigger on the inside than it appeared from outside. The smell of the thatched roof reminded me of the Kalahari. We made ourselves comfortable and were just drinking tea when a motorcade arrived.

It was the Inyanga, accompanied by clan elders and the sangoma woman of Neo's village. They had been held up by a defective starter motor. The chief sangoma was a tall, imposing man of about fifty, a little like Shaka Zulu in the TV series, but very modest and sane and dressed in a suit. I knew we could trust him.

After a short greeting, we lost no time and entered the witchdoctor's rondavel. To my relief, the crazy woman was nowhere to be seen. We settled on the earthen floor and waited in expectation. The Inyanga pulled his trouser legs up just a little and squatted on his haunches. The stone circle was still filled with red-hot embers. The female sangoma from Neo's clan took some herbs from her pouch and ladled water into a cooking vessel, then placed it in the hot coals. Then some sort of ceremony began.

*

The Inyanga took ash from a calabash on his belt and poured it into his hand. Then he began to clap his hollow hands together. The ash clouded the air. He motioned for his assistant to do the same and they both began to call out in Setswana.

"They are calling for the help of the ancestors," Neo whispered. The chanting grew faster. The Inyanga leapt to his feet and began to wave around a long whisk, made from black animal hairs, and stomped his feet to some silent rhythm.

"It attracts the spirits," Neo whispered again.

The two sangomas clapped all the while, making a hollow sound. The sound sent shivers up and down my spine.

"They summon the spirit guide now," Neo whispered. The Inyanga spoke to him briefly. "He wants you to think as hard as you can about your sister and how much you want her back with you."

I concentrated so hard that my head ached.

The assistant filled a wooden ladle with hot liquid from the pot and gave it to me, motioning for me to blow on it and to drink. I blew on the tea and took a few sips. It was hot and bitter but I had to drink up.

Then the long black whisk swished through the air again. The sangomas walked around me in circles, chanting relentlessly as I held my breath, fully expecting a bang or flash of light that would bring the spirit guide straight into the hut.

Nothing happened. Nothing I would have understood anyway. I felt as if a cold finger moved down my spine and I shivered. Tony, who suddenly sat behind me, put his hand on my shoulder. "Are you okay?"

"I will be, as long as we'll find Claire now."

The spirit-calling took its time and I felt myself grow drowsy. The Inyanga and his helper sang, waved around the whisk and stomped their feet. Then they suddenly stopped.

The assistant melted into the background and I was told to stand up. At last! After swearing on the bible that we would not tell a soul about this - just imagine - the Inyanga gave me a signal.

"He wants you to take off the talisman and to follow him. The spirit guide is here. We must stay in the hut and wait for you," Neo said and looked at me with an intent stare.

I nodded silently, handed the lizard talisman to the assistant and followed the Inyanga outside. I felt so light.

"See you soon. Good luck!" Tony called after me. His voice sounded strangely deep!

I squeezed my eyes shut against the bright sunlight. Not one of the villagers was in sight. The Inyanga led the way up a slope not far from the village, waving for me to follow him. I felt like dreaming. Suddenly we were right at the top of the hill.

"Listen." The witchdoctor held up his index finger. He spoke intelligible English. "You must speak to the wind, when you are ready to come back from the other side." I nodded and listened to the wind. It didn't seem strange at all.

## SINGING LIZARDS

A light breeze skimmed the slope but to me it sounded like humming. Then I had to repeat something in Setswana. I was not to forget those words. I repeated the four words over and over. I must have pronounced them properly, because the Inyanga gave a satisfied nod, which made the jewellery around his neck clink. He waved for me to step forward.

A shape huddled under a low thorn tree. It seemed to be waiting and lifted its head. The shape unfolded and stood up in one fluid movement. It was an old woman, her rough features framed with fluffy white hair. Her face had a blank expression and her black eyes seemed to see deep inside me. A necklace with a large ornament hung around her neck. The stone in the middle looked so shiny.

"Skuá haaf!" Everything's all right! The Inyanga patted the air soothingly in front of me. "She is friend...spirit guide."

This was the spirit guide, who had been summoned? The humming grew louder. I looked around for the Inyanga to ask him, but he was no longer there. Just me and the spirit guide on the top of the slope. It was alright. I listened to the humming in the cooling wind.

The soft contours of the landscape and the woman were surrounded by strangely hazy sunlight. Was the woman herself a ghost? She took my hand. Her hand felt solid enough and even a bit rough and calloused. No ghost then?

She led me to the edge of the cliff. Everything was still. Nature held its breath. I was standing next to the peculiar old woman with the fluffy white hair, facing the valley below. Just rocks, sand and thirsty plants. She watched the plain with a thousand yard stare.

I couldn't see anything out of the ordinary in the distance. A gold and green bee-eater chirped in the tall agave to our left. I turned my head to look at the bird and looked down into the valley again. I was just standing there quietly, listening to the wind.

"Jump!" The woman said.
"Off the cliff?" I stared at the stony ground below and pulled back a little.
"Jump!" The spirit guide closed her eyes and nodded once. Then she pulled at my hand and we both jumped off the cliff.
It was the strangest sensation, like being caught in mid-air in a supple glove, closing softly around me. We arrived below and the glove released me. I opened my eyes just a little, just enough to see the outline of a landscape that was different than before.
We were standing at the bottom of the hill. The spirit guide still held my hand and took a step forward. I felt her firm grip and soft, dewy grass that touched the soles of my feet, not sharp stones as expected. The misty air felt fresh. I took a deep breath and turned around.
The hill behind me was still there, it just looked greener somehow, covered in tropical plants instead of tough grass and agaves. I heard muted birdsong. Sunshine reached us through a thin veil of mist and a lake glinted in the distance, underneath a rose-coloured sunset. There was a luminous quality to everything. Was this the Abzu?
The spirit guide loosened her grip. I looked at her and she began to fade away. Her outline grew paler and paler but it didn't bother me; I just stood there and let the warm breeze caress my hair.
"Musungu! Musungu!" *Oh no, leave me be*, I suddenly thought, *I just want to stand here and dream!*
But there were the calls again. "Musungu! Musungu!" Loud calling did not belong here in this gentle place and it made me feel uncomfortable. Why had the spirit guide left me alone? Alarmed, I tried to crawl under a white-flowering bush to hide from the noise. I was wondering if it was the ancestor of a modern bush. It wasn't a very good hiding place and they soon spotted me. A group of dark-skinned men formed a half-circle around the bush and I

kept hearing words like 'Musungu' - and - 'O mang?' Had somebody asked my name?

How did one speak to forefathers? Would they understand me? I had to say something. "I'm Bridget, Bridget. Ke mang Bridget," I heard myself repeating my name.

"Brishd," an old man with a grey beard said.

"Ehey," I praised him and he touched my arm.

"Arré." Come.

Together we walked to a kraal. There was a motsetsi hedge and behind it many huts. The huts looked very neat. We went to one of the huts and perhaps it was just a dream after all, because I must have fallen asleep in this hut. Don't ask me how I knew. I just knew, when it was time to wake up. I opened my eyes and sat up straight.

A young woman with blonde hair, wearing a long dress, knelt down next to me. I rubbed my eyes and saw that a small parrot sat on her shoulder and looked at me sideways. The parrot was honey-yellow and green. Perhaps it was the ancestor of a parrot.

"Is your name Bridget?" she pronounced the words in a foreign sort of way. My heart leapt. This was no dream! Her hair was longer now and she wore this white tunic, but it was definitely - Claire.

I didn't care if this was a farm kitchen or a hut in some strange place I didn't understand. I didn't care about the odd accent because she was real enough for me. It was Claire! I felt like laughing and crying at the same time.

"Claire!" Tears blinded me. I just wanted to hug her. "Oh Claire it is you. I found you, I found you at last!"

But Claire moved away from me. She didn't want to be hugged. There was no recognition. It had slipped my mind for a long, happy moment that she might not remember me. And sure enough, I was a stranger to her.

"I don't know you," my twin sister said indifferently. There was no malice in her voice, Claire just didn't recognise me. *Think, Bridget, think!*

"But you do know my name," I said.

"Yes, the people tell me that's what you call yourself. I don't know why, but it seems familiar. You speak a strange language only I can understand."

I cleared my throat to cover my confusion and wiped the tears from my eyes so I could see properly. The parrot danced up and down Claire's shoulder and nibbled on strands of her blonde hair.

"Who are you?" She asked in wonder and studied my face.

"I'm your sister," I said with urgency, forgetting my plan to be subtle. "Your twin sister. Oh Foompy, I've missed you so much!"

She crinkled her forehead. "I don't have a sister and you look nothing like me."

I felt desperate. "Yes I do. Our eyes look the same. Look at me." Claire looked intently into my eyes.

"You are from my tribe then?"

I racked my brain. What was the best thing to say?

"Yes, I'm from the same tribe. Do you remember Cambridge, Foompy? And Mom and Dad, our house in Tension Avenue? Botswana? Tony Stratton - your husband?" I lingered on the word husband. Oh how should I get through to her?

"What's a Foompy?"

I had to laugh. "Wait, Claire." I felt the photographs in my pocket. The ones I still had. "See, here - this is you." I pointed to one of the pictures. "And here are the two of us. We are twin sisters. And on this one you can see Mom and Dad." I held up the photo from Italy.

That's when her expression changed. I don't know if it was the photographs or seeing me again that did the trick. I don't remember anything clearly from that point onwards. Time didn't seem to flow the same here in the Abzu.

Claire was summoned to a group of dignified-looking older people and I sat next to her. They looked at the photos and spoke to her gently. There was a familiar sound in the background. It was a humming sound, but different to the humming of the wind.

"Singing lizards," Claire said and I hadn't even asked the question. My thoughts flew back to the cool Kalahari morning, when Benjamin had showed me the singing lizards in Kang, bouncing on thin branches in the bush.

It must have been a long time ago in another life time. Then somehow we stood together at the bottom of the hill and the next thing I remember were the words the Inyanga had made me memorise, the words I had to speak when I was ready to return. So I spoke those four words over and over.

I spoke to the warm breeze and something before us shifted. A shape walked toward us. It was an old woman with fluffy white hair. She looked more solid with each step.

We didn't even have to jump, we just floated together onto the rocky cliff in the bush, holding each other's hands and were suddenly standing on top of the hill.

At least that's how I remember it.

\*

I saw the Inyanga again... as he knelt by the fire in the sangoma hut, throwing herbs into the flames. There was a monotonous drummed rhythm. *How did I get here?* I thought. *I don't remember walking back to the village.*

The smoke of the herbs made me cough. Then I saw Claire. She just sat there next to me, all dazed. I reached out and touched her. She felt warm and firm and real. It wasn't just my imagination, I was sure of it. My heart jumped for joy. My sister was really here in this wretched hut; here with me.

I think I fell asleep in the back seat of Tony's car, while the Corolla bounced over bumpy roads all the way back to Palapye. Claire's head rested on my shoulder. The sky was turning to violet and to a dark navy blue, when my eyelids felt just too heavy to stay open.

I woke up in Tony's guest bedroom, filled with the

lingering remnants of a strange dream. The sun shone brightly through the drawn curtain and the smell of delicious coffee wafted through the house. Coffee. I sat up with a jolt. I remember seeing Claire next to me in a hut and then in Tony's car and then... nothing.

I nearly fainted when I jumped out of bed and held onto the back of a chair that squeaked lamentably. My empty stomach wanted to turn. Was I sick? Was I here in Tony's house in Palapye, because I was sick?

I looked straight at an Africa poster on the wall. Six colourful birds. A golden-green parrot looked straight at me with its head tilted. My stomach settled down and the rushing in my ears subsided. A good thing because I heard something that made my heart leap for joy.

"Are you awake Foompy?" A familiar voice asked outside the door. That was Claire's voice! Oh please let it be Claire! She peeped into the room and I broke into tears. Again.

"Oh Bridge, don't cry again! I'm here. We're okay."

I began to remember what had happened yesterday: the sangomas and jumping off a cliff with an old woman holding my hand and the strange sensations in what they called the 'Abzu'. Then I had returned to the top of the hill with Claire by my side.

"Claire, you're back," I bawled regardless and let go of the chair to hang onto my twin's neck. "You're really back!" It was just too much. Despair made way for overwhelming happiness.

"Yes I am - silly," Claire said, as if I never had a reason to doubt this fact. "Come freshen up a bit and - oh my stars - brush your teeth!" That was typically Claire.

Tears rolled down her cheeks now as well. She laughed and waved away some imaginary smell. At least I hoped it was imaginary.

"Tony made us some coffee and a late breakfast. Scrambled eggs and bacon..." She squeezed me tightly. We were back together and Claire knew who I was!

"What about your injuries?" I suddenly remembered and looked her in the face.

"You mean this?" Claire touched a pale scar on her forehead. "It's not sore anymore. They took good care of me."

"Who did?"

Claire looked puzzled. "You know..." No I didn't know. Perhaps she wasn't so sure herself. I changed the subject.

"You know what? I could really do with some coffee. That tea yesterday... I can't wait to get the bitter taste out of my mouth..." I cried, "... and you are here with me, Claire!" It would take me a while to behave normally again.

"Yes I am, Foompy, yes I am. I got you to travel with me again, didn't I?"

"You sure did. All this time I thought you were stuck in some cave or something. Probably in a coma... and that the locals kept you hidden and were too scared to say anything," I gushed.

"Oh, but that's a ridiculous idea. I was there with people all the time, in this gentle place... and I wanted to be there." For two whole years?

"You think it's ridiculous? What else was I supposed to think? That you were in some sort of parallel universe?"

She looked at me as if I had fallen off my rocker. "I missed you so," she said quickly and hugged me. "Let's talk about the whole thing over breakfast."

And that's what we did.

I cautiously asked her burning questions. The few things she did remember still didn't make any sense, but I guess it's okay not to have it all figured out all the time.

It was impossible to keep the whole thing secret any longer. Too many people had gotten wind of what had happened to us. In the coming weeks, Claire made great progress and our story made headlines.

A young British woman, thought to have died in the African bush two years earlier, had been found by her twin sister in the obscure country of Botswana. Claire was supposed to have fallen into a coma after her accident. A local people in a remote, inaccessible area had kept her alive. When she woke up from her coma, I was called. Happy End. Curiously, the two young women were the granddaughters of a famous novelist. Details to follow.

But the details didn't follow and after a while the public lost interest - as always. Nobody mentioned witchdoctors or anything more than what seemed logical. And it was for the best. At least we didn't look like freaks in a circus.

We went back to England for a few months afterwards. Claire spent a week in hospital under observation. But just as Dr. Ritter in Mochudi who had examined Claire, none of the British doctors were able to diagnose anything out of the ordinary.

It was wonderful to see my friends and family again, but after a while, I realized that I had changed. So much so that I simply didn't fit back into my old life. Of course, Claire was already restless after only a few days in Cambridge.

Mom and Dad fussed over us and threw a Welcome Back Party. Everyone had a good cry and Grandpa was there, too. He treated the whole family to a week's holiday at Lake Windermere, where the press didn't find us. We stayed for Diane's wedding in London and then made travel plans again.

Claire took up a post in New Delhi and Pauli and I moved to Johannesburg, where we shared a garden flat with Emily for a year. Then she got married to Craig and I met my future husband at the wedding. He was a friend of the bridegroom's and not just a pretty face. Finally, I was happy in love - to this day.

Most of my friends got married and one is already divorced. Emily and I still live in South Africa and we see each other often. Her two girls are about the same age as my two rascals. Oh and I did learn from her mother how to make quilts!

By the way, my friend Zaheeda also got married a year

after I did. To an Irish artist who dyed his hair!

Gabby left Botswana and after a few weeks in Germany, she was re-deployed to Thailand. I went to see her while honeymooning in Phuket.

She was still her old, cheerful self and played tennis with her usual passion. Gabby spent a couple of years in Canberra, then went on to live in Buenos Aires. She wrote to me recently that she got engaged to a German businessman from Munich and I'm seriously thinking of going to Argentina for the wedding in August.

Kgomotso married William Konenga at last and landed a well-paid job in the IT industry. They moved to New York and had a son. Kgomotso sometimes sends me e-mails and pictures. I've sadly lost touch with virtually all other friends from my time in Botswana, but that's the way it goes. I have only words to describe my life in Botswana and the other thing that I never really understood: the 'Land of the Forefathers'.

Once in a while, a rather important and wise sangoma from Soweto comes to visit. He knows that what happened to me was real and we talk about things I can't tell any of my friends here in Johannesburg or in England. They would probably declare me insane.

Claire still travels a lot. She worked for a charity in Indonesia for a while, until the tsunami happened. We are more alike now than ever before. Although sometimes she travels for months on end and I don't hear from her, it's no longer a problem. As long as I can still feel that she's all right. I have a suspicion that she went back to Abzu a few times, but I can't be sure. She has never admitted to it.

Claire is no longer married to Tony but I understand that they have remained good friends and I'm glad. Tony has been living in Australia with his Japanese wife for a while now and he seems to be doing well.

Things are also changing around us. Europe is catching up fast with Botswana in the heat wave stakes and the Botswana

I used to know and love, has changed as well.

The Trans-Kalahari Highway now cuts right through the desert where I used to whizz along the old sand roads and Gaborone is almost unrecognisable. No longer a small town, it now boasts new suburbs - and hotels and tarred roads.

Even as I sit here looking out into my wild Johannesburg garden, I can still feel and smell the wilderness of Botswana. And although there are plenty of wide open spaces on our South African side of the border, I saw my first lions and leopards only last year, during a visit to the Kruger Park.

But the bush is familiar to me. I have lived in the Kalahari after all and I listened to the lizards sing. And not many of us Lekgoas get to do that.

The light outside had faded and I saw that yellowish clouds were announcing more summer rains for tonight. Had I fallen asleep in the armchair by the window? The divorce decree stared at me from the computer screen on my desk.

Oh dear! Peter would be home soon with the kids.

I got up and stretched myself. Then I placed the beeping receiver back on the phone and took my tea cup to the kitchen.

After a few minutes the phone began to shrill - and this time I answered.

**The End**

# SINGING LIZARDS

## ABOUT THE AUTHOR

Evadeen Brickwood grew up with two sisters in Germany and studied cultural sciences and languages. As a young woman, she travelled extensively and many of her books are inspired by her experiences abroad. Feeling adventurous, the newly qualified translator moved to Africa in 1988 and worked for two years as a secretary and language teacher in Botswana.

The author eventually settled in South Africa, where she got married and raised two daughters. In Johannesburg, Evadeen Brickwood studied computers and management of training and worked as a corporate software trainer, professional translator and lecturer at WITS University.

In 2003, she began her writing career with youth novels in the 'Remember the Future' series, about adventures in prehistory. Book 1, the award-winning 'Children of the Moon', has been published twice in South Africa and translated into German. The author now self-publishes and other books in the time travel series are released on a regular basis. Her works include the novels 'The Rhino Whisperer' and 'A Half Moon Adventure', which are now also available in German and the 'Charlie Proudfoot Murder Mysteries'.

## About Writing This Book

When I started writing my journal in Africa in 1988, I was a young translator from Berlin on her way to join a German fiancé in a very remote village in Botswana. The relationship was rocky from the start to say the least, and he seemed a different person now. I'd learned that he was having affairs and flaunted them. I went anyway to find my own luck. Regrettably, he became abusive before I moved to Gaborone, the capital of the country. Here I found incredible support and also judgement from people, who didn't even know me.

Eventually, I ended up in Johannesburg, forging my own way in this part of the world. All this made me a stronger person and things started to turn around for the better. I chose the sister-theme, because my sister Barbara, who is just one year older than me, had missed me all these years and was thrilled to learn the details of my journey, which I painstakingly recorded. I guess writing down what I experienced made it easier to deal with all the challenges that were thrown my way.

Little did I know that this particular journal would one day be used to write 'Singing Lizards'. It became an important source for place names and stories that had actually taken place. The singing lizards are also real. To my knowledge, they belong to the Kalahari skink family. A large part of the novel is pure fiction, but I couldn't resist working my own experiences into the mix. Africa was a wonderfully innocent place when I first arrived, and at the same time bewildering. I chose to live in South Africa, which has become my second home and where I still draw inspiration for some of my novels.

*Evadeen Brickwood*

This book is available online and from all good bookstores.

The e-book can be purchased at major online stores, such as Smashwords, Amazon, Takealot, Loot, Kobo, Tolino, Kindle, Apple i-Store, Neobooks etc.

The author's websites:

http://www.evadeen.wixsite.com/novels
http://www.evadeen.wixsite.com/youngbooks
http://www.evadeen.wixsite.com/charlieproudfoot

She is also on social media, incl. Facebook, Twitter, Instagram, Pinterest, YouTube, google+ and Goodreads.

# SINGING LIZARDS

Another mystery novel set in modern South Africa. This time, the murders of a ranger and a rare black rhino in the idyllic Shangari Safari Park rattle the local community of Rutgersdrift. Sofia Helenius from Finland lives at the lodge with her boyfriend Tom Rutgers, the owner of Shangari. Sofia is tormented by a secret she yearns to share with Tom, but the cruel events grab the limelight and put everything else in the shade. One of the native Khoi-San families is known to communicate with wild animals, but what if the criminals get wind of this gift?

When another murder happens in the city of Johannesburg, smouldering secrets begin to unravel. How are the murders connected and will it be possible to halt a relentless crime-syndicate in order to save an African paradise?

As if growing up in the seventies wasn't difficult enough, teenager Isabell Bertrand is also too rebellious for her parents' liking. A novel treatment with hypnosis appears to be the perfect remedy and Dr. Albrecht regresses Isabell to her early childhood and even further back. She experiences previous lifetimes and then one in particular: could this beautiful young woman in a silk sari, who was forced to choose between two men, really once have been her? Years later, Isabell is invited to a wedding in Pakistan and memories of a forgotten love come flooding back - with dangerous consequences.

www.ingramcontent.com/pod-product-compliance
Lightning Source LLC
Chambersburg PA
CBHW010248010526
44119CB00054B/766